STORIES OF CHANGE

STORIES OF CHANGE

Religious Leaders and LGBTIQ Inclusion in East Africa

David Kuria Mbote, Barbara Bompani and
Adriaan van Klinken, with Damaris Parsitau

ZED

LONDON • NEW YORK • OXFORD • NEW DELHI • SYDNEY

Zed
Bloomsbury Publishing Plc
50 Bedford Square, London, WC1B 3DP, UK
1385 Broadway, New York, NY 10018, USA
29 Earlsfort Terrace, Dublin 2, Ireland

BLOOMSBURY, Zed and the Zed logo are trademarks
of Bloomsbury Publishing Plc

First published in Great Britain 2024

Cover design by www.paulsmithdesign.com
Cover image © ClassicStock/Getty Images

Bloomsbury Publishing Plc does not have any control over, or responsibility
for, any third-party websites referred to or in this book. All internet addresses
given in this book were correct at the time of going to press. The author and
publisher regret any inconvenience caused if addresses have changed or sites
have ceased to exist, but can accept no responsibility for any such changes.

A catalogue record for this book is available from the British Library.

A catalog record for this book is available from the Library of Congress.

ISBN: HB: 978-1-3504-1599-7
PB: 978-1-3504-1600-0
ePDF: 978-1-3504-1602-4
eBook: 978-1-3504-1601-7

Typeset by Newgen KnowledgeWorks Pvt. Ltd., Chennai, India

To find out more about our authors and books visit www.bloomsbury.com
and sign up for our newsletters.

CONTENTS

Author biographies viii
Foreword: A testament and source of hope, by Ezra Chitando x
Acknowledgements xiv
Note on text xv
List of abbreviations xvi

INTRODUCTION: RELIGIOUS LEADERS AND LGBTIQ
INCLUSION IN EAST AFRICA 1

Part 1
STORIES OF LGBTIQ RELIGIOUS LEADERS

Story 1
PASTOR CAROLINE: 'GOD IS LIKE A MOTHER WHO HOLDS
YOU WHEN YOU CRY' 27

Story 2
REVEREND JALENDO: 'I HAVE LEARNED FROM MY OWN
WOUNDEDNESS' 35

Story 3
PASTOR TREVOR: 'IF THERE IS ANYTHING THAT HAS
TAUGHT ME ABOUT GOD, IT IS MY SAME-SEX ATTRACTION' 43

Story 4
MAMA ANNETTE: 'MY EXISTENCE AS A TRANS PASTOR IS A
MANIFESTATION OF GOD'S LOVE' 51

Story 5
PASTOR AGGIE: 'I AM LEARNING TO ACCEPT AND LIVE
WITH MY SCARS' 57

Story 6
PASTOR RIA: 'WE NEED TO REMEMBER THAT GOD DOES
NOT MAKE MISTAKES' 63

vi   *Contents*

Story 7
PASTOR DERON: 'THE LORD HAS A REASON WHY I AM A
TRANSWOMAN'   71

Story 8
BISHOP JAMES: 'SOME OF US ARE MARTYRS BY DOING THIS
WORK'   79

Part 2
STORIES OF LGBTIQ-ALLIED RELIGIOUS LEADERS

Story 9
PASTOR SILVANA: 'MY ROLE IS TO BE A TREE THAT BEARS
FRUITS'   89

Story 10
PASTOR NEEMA: 'MY TASK IS TO RESPECT DIVINITY AS
REFLECTED IN EACH OF US'   97

Story 11
EVANGELIST VINCENT: 'MY HOPE IS THAT LGBTIQ PEOPLE
WILL KNOW GOD'   105

Story 12
PASTOR STEPHEN: 'I ARRIVED AT THE POINT OF
REPENTING FOR MY HOMOPHOBIA'   111

Story 13
PASTOR DORCAS: 'I PERSEVERE WITH MY CALLING TO
PREACH LOVE IN THE COMMUNITY'   117

Story 14
EVANGELIST JOSEPHINE: 'AS A MOTHER IN THE
COMMUNITY, I SHOULD HAVE NO BOUNDARIES'   123

Story 15
PASTOR LAURA: 'I FEEL LIKE QUEEN ESTHER, WHO PUT
HER LIFE AT RISK TO SAVE OTHERS'   129

Story 16
BISHOP ROGER: 'WHEN YOU START BEING INCLUSIVE, YOU
ARE BRANDED'   135

Story 17
REVEREND KIMINDU: 'THIS CAN ONLY BE A CALLING, OR
I WOULD HAVE STOPPED LONG AGO'　　141

Story 18
FR. ETTORE MARANGI: 'I DO NOT SUPPORT LGBTIQ
PEOPLE AS AN ACTIVIST, BUT AS A CHRISTIAN'　　149

Story 19
SHEIKH DAWOUD: 'I DO NOT PROMOTE HOMOSEXUALITY,
I JUST PROTECT PEOPLE WHO ARE PART OF OUR
COMMUNITY'　　157

Story 20
SHEIKH ABDALLAH: 'LGBTIQ PEOPLE HAVE GIFTS WHICH
WE NEED FOR THE *UMMA* TO GROW'　　163

Story 21
YOUTH LEADER ABDUL: 'WE HAVE TO STAND WITH THEM
BECAUSE OF THAT BROTHER- AND SISTERHOOD'　　169

Story 22
BISHOP JOSEPH: 'WE WILL COME TO ACCEPT OUR
LGBTIQ CHILDREN AS A BLESSING'　　177

Story 23
PROFESSOR VASHTI: 'MY GRANDMOTHER TAUGHT ME
THAT FAITH AND ACTIVISM GO HAND IN HAND'　　183

Story 24
BISHOP SENYONJO: 'GOD IS STILL CREATING, AND HE
CONTINUES TO REVEAL THINGS'　　195

CONCLUSION　　203

References　　215
Index　　225

AUTHOR BIOGRAPHIES

David Kuria Mbote is an independent consultant and researcher based in Nairobi, Kenya. He is a leading figure in the Kenyan gender and sexual minority rights movement. He has researched religious leaders and LGBTIQ inclusion in Kenya, publishing this work in journals such as *Pastoral Psychology* and *Journal of Sex Research*.

Barbara Bompani is Reader in Africa and International Development at the Centre of African Studies, University of Edinburgh, and Research Associate at the African Centre for Migration and Society, University of the Witwatersrand. Her research broadly focuses on religion, politics and development in Africa. In the past ten years, she has investigated the relationships between sexuality and public religion, in particular conservative Christianity, in East Africa. She has published widely on these topics and was co-editor of the volume *Christian Citizens and the Moral Regeneration of the African State* (2017).

Adriaan van Klinken is Professor of Religion and African Studies at the University of Leeds, and Extraordinary Professor at the Desmond Tutu Centre for Religion and Social Justice, University of the Western Cape. His research intersects religion, sexuality and public life in contemporary Africa. His publications include *Kenyan, Christian, Queer: Religion, LGBT Activism, and Arts of Resistance in Africa* (2019), *Reimagining Christianity and Sexual Diversity in Africa* (2021, with Ezra Chitando) and *Sacred Queer Stories: Ugandan LGBTQ+ Refugee Lives and the Bible* (2021, with Johanna Stiebert, Sebyala Bryan and Fredrick Hudson).

Damaris Parsitau is Director of the Nagel Institute for the Study of World Christianity, Calvin University, and Extraordinary Professor at the University of South Africa and at the Desmond Tutu Centre for Religion and Social Justice, University of the Western Cape. A scholar of religion, gender and sexuality, with a focus on Pentecostalism in Kenya, she has published extensively in this area, with recent articles in *Journal of Law and Religion* and *The Palgrave Handbook of African Social Ethics*.

She currently serves as President of the African Association for the Study of Religions.

Ezra Chitando is Professor of History of Religion and Phenomenology of Religion at the University of Zimbabwe, and Extraordinary Professor at the Desmond Tutu Centre for Religion and Social Justice, University of the Western Cape. He is a social justice activist.

FOREWORD: A TESTAMENT AND SOURCE OF HOPE

by
Ezra Chitando

Stories. Of pain. Of joy. Of hope. Of liberation. In the middle of narratives of acute hatred and exclusion, I have found the stories of love and radical inclusion running through this volume soothing and reassuring. There is hope yet. The human project has not failed. After the final statement of rejection and death comes the declaration of acceptance and life. Like Moses standing before the burning bush,[1] I have had to take off my shoes as I have been standing on ground that is holy. Hearing and processing these stories has been a profoundly cathartic experience for me. Each narrator gives us a doubly rich and captivating account of overcoming stigma, discrimination and violence against LGBTIQ in specific contexts in Kenya and Uganda. Inspired by their faith, they show how the less-emphasized tolerant and liberative dimensions of religion have enabled them to stand for LGBTIQ inclusion. To borrow from the late Zambian LGBTIQ and human rights activist Manasseh Phiri (1958–2019), they have taken the wisdom of the tortoise seriously: in order to move ahead, one must dare stick out one's neck! As the stories in this powerful volume testify, there is very often a very high price to pay for such an act of courage: stigma, ostracism, ridicule and persecution.

The activism and courage demonstrated by the faith actors in this volume need to be put into context. Why has their sacrifice become necessary in the first instance? How do we account for the homophobia by some of the most vocal religious leaders and politicians? These are large questions that require most space to try and process than is available. However, East Africa represents a significant region for understanding LGBTIQ politics, with special reference to the impact of religion. The East African Revival (Ward and Wild-Wood, 2013) looms large, providing the historical context within which contemporary

---

1. Exod. 3.1–17.

outpourings of fidelity to 'Christian values' must be located. British colonialism, with its intolerant laws and the quest to 'civilize' the African, must stay in the picture. The postcolonial African struggle for identity in a world that rubbishes Africa should remain in sight. When one's wealth is plundered, dignity shattered and voice muted, one is bound to dogmatically hold on to what one understands as one's 'culture'. The coalescence of conservative versions of particularly Christianity and Islam in the region needs to be noted, as the role of contemporary conflict entrepreneurs within both faiths must also be acknowledged. An oppressive global economic (dis)order compounds the situation, as do contests for power at the national level. Without condoning homophobia that is driven (others would say instigated) by religion, there is a need to locate it in its proper historical context.

It is within the context outlined above that some religious leaders have joined forces with political actors (many of whom also publicly express their affiliation to particular faith traditions) to deny space (and, in some instances, the right to live) to LGBTIQ people in Kenya and Uganda. The 'combined operations' mantra has been fairly consistent: according to it, sound Christian/Muslim ethical teachings, the Bible/the Quran and African culture have absolutely no space for non-heteronormative sexualities in Africa. While the narratives provided in this timely volume go a long way in debunking all the three premises, it is important to recognize the evocative power of each one of them. The calls to 'defend the African family' and resist the 'recruitment of our innocent children', the refusal to be 'bullied when we are a sovereign people' and the need for 'Africa to stand up for what it believes in' and so on are, at the rhetorical level, powerful tropes. An equally seductive version suggests that, yes, Africa (or those who wield power) would like to attend to LGBTIQ rights at some moment, but it is not the most pressing issue right now. For now, so goes the argument, Africa needs to address the more pressing issues of poverty and underdevelopment. It is not surprising, therefore, that some very progressive (on most other issues) pan-Africanists have come out to denounce the quest for LGBTIQ rights in Africa as part of the Global North's agenda of cultural imperialism. Where indigenous African culture had espoused tolerance and inclusion of diversity, toxicity, exclusion and violence have been actively nurtured by some individuals and groups.

From this strategic resource, it is reassuring to learn that religious leaders who identify as LGBTIQ and those who have chosen to become LGBTIQ allies are presenting the positive side of religion in society. They are demonstrating the social capital that religion possesses.

Drawn from across the religious spectrum, they are a cloud of witnesses testifying to the potential of religion to bring comfort and life in the middle of discomfort and death. Where conflict entrepreneurs have sought to manufacture doom and destruction, they are bringing hope and liberation. Where the agitators are brewing discontent and violence, they are facilitating healing and human flourishing. Freedom is proclaimed and reverberates across the pages of this book. As the narrators refer to liberating passages and characters from the Bible and the Quran, one can only acknowledge the transformative power of the sacred texts. Where some would like to mine the sacred texts to pummel those whom they feel are different from them, the religious actors in this book humbly resort to the same sacred texts to recover life-giving messages.

The stories shared in this volume are truly inspiring. They provide valuable insights into how to grow a critical mass of activists and allies within the religious sector in (East) Africa. Even as there is a need to budget for resistance (most of the stories confirm the existence of extremists), it is clear that there are certain processes that contribute to a better environment for LGBTIQ people in the region. First, it is important for families to nurture the values of inclusion, tolerance and acceptance of diversity. While those who propound the theology of exclusion and condemnation (lubricated by problematic interpretations of the sacred texts) insist on 'protecting family values', it is helpful for families to bring up children who recognize and appreciate diversity as one key feature of human existence. Second, religious leaders who benefit from quality theological education are well placed to embrace LGBTIQ people in their ministries. The stories in this book confirm that both categories of religious leaders (LGBTIQ and LGTIQ-allied) have their awareness of human rights and social justice accentuated by accessing liberating theological education. Their interpretation of human sexuality, theology and the sacred texts is deepened through exposure to diverse voices and strategies. Quality theological education empowers religious leaders to become more self-conscious and deepens their commitment to liberation. In order to win the future, it is critical for theological educators (including those engaging in open, distance and electronic learning) in Africa to become agents of social transformation by delivering transformative education. This will contribute towards the emergence of justice-loving and justice-upholding communities. Musa W. Dube, a devoted promoter of the rights of all of God's people, has consistently called for theological education in Africa to prioritize ensuring that all have life, and have it abundantly (see van Klinken and Chitando 2021, 73–90). Third, exposure through workshops and training is strategic in challenging inherited negative attitudes towards LGBTIQ, including challenging self-stigma. Most of the narrators in this volume indicate that participating in events that introduced LGBTIQ rights had a profound impact on their initial positions. As Paulo Freire (2018) maintains, relevant education is that which liberates. It is, therefore, strategic for the various faith-based and human rights organizations operating in the shrinking democratic/activist spaces to continue to find opportunities to expose as many religious leaders as possible to safe spaces. These constitute horizons of encounter and transformation, enabling more religious leaders to become advocates who accompany those who face multiple and confounding forces of marginalization, exclusion and violence. Finally, it would be naïve for anyone to assume that there shall be a linear trajectory where activists get equipped, depart into larger society and immediately become effective agents of social change. No. The Rev. Gideon Byamugisha, a leading Ugandan HIV and social justice activist, has consistently observed that bringing change is not easy (Byamugisha 2009). As the narratives of pain and hope presented at this Kairos moment confirm, there is no easy walk to freedom. The path is excruciating. It is a test of faith and endurance. But wrestling with the angel is what agents of social change have been called to do. Advocates of justice hearken the message of the Quran and the Bible to love all unconditionally. They draw inspiration from the freedom fighters of Kenya and Uganda who gave all so that all could regain their dignity. This volume serves as a testament and a source of hope: religion can and is surrounding LGBTIQ people in East Africa with love, care, compassion, solidarity and empowerment.

ACKNOWLEDGEMENTS

This book is an output of the Sexuality and Religion Network in East Africa (SERENE), which was funded by the Arts and Humanities Research Council (AHRC) under its research network scheme (grant reference AH/T008490/1). Follow-up funding, which enabled work for this book and its open-access publication, was provided by UK Research and Innovation (UKRI) as a GCRF and Newton Consolidation Account award.

We are grateful to all members of SERENE, especially academics and community-based organizations in Kenya and Uganda, for their participation in and support of project activities. For more information, see https://serene.leeds.ac.uk.

NOTE ON TEXT

Biblical quotations in this book are from the New International Version.
Quranic quotations are from the translation by A. J. Arberry.

ABBREVIATIONS

CAC	Cosmopolitan Affirming Church, an LGBTIQ-inclusive church in Nairobi, Kenya
CU	Christian Union
EHAIA	Ecumenical HIV and AIDS Initiative in Africa
GSM	Gender and Sexual Minorities
INERELA+	International Network of Religious Leaders Living with, or Personally Affected by, HIV and AIDS
LGBTIQ	lesbian, gay, bisexual, transgender, intersex and queer
NGLHRC	National Gay and Lesbian Human Rights Commission, an LGBTIQ legal and human rights organization in Kenya
Nyarwek	Nyanza, Rift Valley and Western Kenya Network, a network of LGBTIQ organizations based in Kisumu, western Kenya
PEMA Kenya	Persons Marginalized and Aggrieved, a gender and sexual minorities rights organization based in Mombasa, eastern Kenya
SERENE	Sexuality and Religion Network in East Africa, a research network
SMUG	Sexual Minorities Uganda, a national umbrella body of LGBTIQ organizations in Uganda
TFAM	The Fellowship of Affirming Africans, a US-based organization promoting an inclusive form of Christianity, which is active in several African countries
UCAA	Universal Coalition of Affirming Africans, a Uganda-based organization of LGBTIQ religious leaders and allies

INTRODUCTION: RELIGIOUS LEADERS AND LGBTIQ INCLUSION IN EAST AFRICA

There seems to exist a single story of religious leaders in relation to issues of sexual and gender diversity in Africa and perhaps globally. It is the story of conservative figures who preach that homosexuality is sinful (if not demonic), who promote hatred towards and exclusion of lesbian, gay, bisexual, transgender, intersex and queer (LGBTIQ) people in society and who lead social and political campaigns against the recognition of LGBTIQ rights while supporting laws that criminalize divergent sexual and gender expressions.[1] It is tempting to mention some names and discuss them as examples here, as there are many of them, and some of them have a high profile and a significant influence. The passing of the Anti-homosexuality Bill (AHB) by the Ugandan Parliament in March 2023, for instance, was the result of a campaign of many years, in which several religious leaders and religious organizations played key roles; when the bill was passed, the news was welcomed by prominent clergy in the country, who urged President Museveni to sign it into law as soon as possible. However, we will not mention these names and examples here, because the aim

---

1. Terminology around sexuality and gender in African contexts is contested. In this book, we use the acronym LGBTIQ to capture a range of diverse gender and sexual expressions, acknowledging that the language of LGBTIQ identities and rights has been widely adopted in the East African region. Yet, we also acknowledge the variations in, and limitations of, this acronym and the existence of other terminology, such as gender and sexual minorities (GSM). In the stories presented in this book, we have standardized the different versions of the LGBTIQ acronym, but we left visible the instances where participants used a different terminology, such as GSM, or where they referred to specific identities under the LGBTIQ umbrella, such as gay, lesbian, trans or intersex.

of this book is not to give more visibility to the religious leaders and institutions who are actively involved in anti-LGBTIQ politics, nor to examine their motivations, strategies and rhetoric or the international alliances they have built. Other studies have already covered and examined this in considerable depth (with a focus on Africa, see Bompani and Valois 2017; Kaoma 2017; van Klinken and Chitando 2016; Ward 2015).

The role of religious leaders in stimulating cultures of 'anti-queer animus' (Thoreson 2014) in various parts of Africa is well documented. Yet, this presents a single story which, in Chimamanda Ngozi Adichie's (2009) words, runs the risk not necessarily of being 'untrue' but of being 'incomplete'. The aim of this book is to complement this single story in order to help develop a more complete and thus richer and nuanced picture of the role of religious leaders in relation to issues of sexual and gender diversity, specifically in East Africa. What is needed, to use the words of another Nigerian writer Chinua Achebe (2000), is 'a balance of stories'. And in order to reach such a balance, this book presents a collection of stories that counterbalance the earlier-mentioned single story. Adichie (2009), in her essay 'The Danger of a Single Story', argues that 'stories matter. Many stories matter.' It is important to note the plural here. A multiplicity of stories is needed to address the danger of the one-sided and thus stereotyping single narrative. This is not just a matter of adding numbers and increasing the quantity of stories available. It is also a matter of carefully assessing which stories are worth featuring and to be added to the archive of stories available. Because, Adichie continues, 'stories have been used to dispossess and to malign. But stories can also be used to empower and to humanize. Stories can break the dignity of a people. But stories can also repair that broken dignity.' These words powerfully resonate with the subject of this book, which is concerned with sexual and gender diversity – a term that refers to a range of sexual and gendered experiences and identities that for long have faced, and continue to face, marginalization and dehumanization. The dominant narrative of religious leaders claiming that same-sex relationships and LGBTIQ identities are 'un-African' and in conflict with African cultural and religious values has perpetuated this ongoing history of marginalization and dehumanization in quite recent times. This narrative illustrates how particular stories of cultural authenticity and religious orthodoxy are used to dispossess and malign people of diverse genders and sexualities. Yet, as Adichie highlights, stories can also empower and humanize people who have been the subject of such ostracism, and can help repair the broken dignity of those people and communities whose humanity is constantly called into question by dominant forces in society, including by religious leaders. The telling and sharing of life stories of LGBTIQ people has become a popular and powerful method through which activists and scholars in recent years have sought to build what Keguro Macharia (2015, 140) describes as 'queer African archives' and make visible 'the names behind the numbers, the faces hidden from view, the stories that so often remain untold'. Through such storytelling, African LGBTIQ subjects reclaim their voice and, in doing so, empower themselves and speak back to the dominant voices in society that deny them belonging and dignity. Examples of the ever-growing archive of African queer stories can be found in collections with telling titles such as *Blessed Body* (Azuah 2016), *Invisible* (Mwachiro 2013), *Stories of Our Lives* (The Nest 2015) and *Sacred Queer Stories* (van Klinken et al. 2021).

The present book makes an original and distinct contribution to this growing archive. Counterbalancing the single story of African religious leaders fuelling anti-queer animus, this book offers stories of religious leaders who, in various ways, support LGBTIQ people pastorally and spiritually and try to foster cultures of acceptance and inclusion in faith communities and society at large. Presenting the stories of twenty-four religious leaders from Kenya and Uganda, mostly from Christian and some from Muslim backgrounds, this book offers a rich and intimate insight into the motivation and inspiration of these individuals who go against the grain of religious cultures of intolerance towards gender and sexual diversity. *Stories of Change* also provides critical insights into the personal, theological and social challenges these religious leaders face in everyday realities dominated by conservative religious interpretations and theologies and into the strategies they develop to respond to these challenges while keeping true to their mission. The religious leaders featured in this book either identify as LGBTIQ themselves or as allies of LGBTIQ communities. By telling their stories, they show us how faith can be a source of empowerment and humanization and contribute to restoring and reclaiming the dignity of people who are marginalized because of their sexuality and gender. As such, this book is a contribution to calls for a reimagining of the engagement between religious actors and LGBTIQ communities on the African continent (West, Van der Walt and Kaoma 2016; van Klinken and Chitando 2021). Introducing these stories and providing context and background to them, this introductory chapter will first outline the context of sexual and gender diversity politics in East Africa. It will then discuss in more detail the role of religious leaders as agents of social change. Subsequently, it will elucidate the methodology employed in this project, which utilizes life stories as narrative texts of social change.

Context: Sexual and gender diversity politics in East Africa

The regional focus of this book is East Africa, specifically Kenya and Uganda. Like other parts of the continent, East Africa over the past twenty to thirty years or so has witnessed an ever-increasing contestation and politicization of issues related to sexual and gender diversity (Currier and Cruz 2013; Nyeck and Epprecht 2013; Tabengwa and Waites 2020). The reasons for this, and the factors driving these dynamics, are multiple and complex and vary from region to region and country to country. Broadly speaking, it is a combination of, first, European colonial and missionary laws and legacies, especially in countries that were part of the former British Empire, such as Kenya and Uganda, where anti-homosexuality laws were introduced during the colonial period (Decker 2021; Epprecht 2009); second, postcolonial African nation-building and the use of sexuality as a site of identity politics and resistance against perceived Western imperialism (Hoad 2007; Ndjio 2013; Rao 2020); third, the globalization of discourses of LGBTIQ identities and rights and the subsequent increasing visibility of LGBTIQ communities and movements in Africa (Ekine and Abbas 2013; Nyoni 2020; Sandfort et al. 2015); fourth, the emergence of new religious (both Christian and Islamic) movements in Africa, often with transnational alliances, which put issues of sexual and gender diversity central in their campaigns for moral reforms, religious orthodoxy and political influence (Chitando and van Klinken 2016; Kaoma 2017; van Klinken and Chitando 2016). As Monica Tabengwa and Matthew Waites (2020, 201) have argued, 'Political conflicts over human rights and sexual and gender diversity in Africa need to be analyzed with a sensitized attention to the complex interplay of local cultural contexts and national political projects, together with colonial histories and contemporary transnational influences.' With that in mind, in what follows we will outline the context of, and dynamics in, Kenya and Uganda respectively, which are two East African countries where sexual and gender diversity politics have become particularly salient. The outline provided here is by no means comprehensive and exhaustive, but will hopefully be useful as background to the stories presented in this book.

Kenya

The shortest but perhaps most apt way of describing the situation regarding LGBTIQ rights in Kenya is with the phrase 'mixed bag'.

Legally speaking, Kenya has retained the colonial anti-sodomy clause in the Penal Code, which prohibits 'unnatural offences' including 'carnal knowledge against the order of nature' (Section 162.a). A report by Human Rights Watch (2015, 17) describes the Penal Code as 'a relic of the colonial era', adding that 'it is unclear whether anyone has ever been convicted for consensual adult same-sex relations in Kenya'. Yet, the same report documents many incidents of violence and harassment against LGBTIQ people, which the victims are unlikely to report to the police because of the existence of these discriminatory laws. The same is also documented in a report by the Kenya Human Rights Commission (2011), which has the telling title, 'The Outlawed amongst Us', to convey the liminal legal and social space in which sexual and gender minorities operate in the country.

A new clause was added to the Penal Code in 2003, prohibiting 'indecent practices between males' (Section 165), which appears to have been formulated to cover a wider range of same-sex practices between men compared to the original clause (there is no similar clause applying to women). The addition of this clause can be seen as part of a broader trend. As scholar Keguro Macharia (2013, 284) observes, from the early 2000s, 'Kenyans have passed a series of laws and policies that wed national belonging to heterosexuality and that pledge to protect the heteronormative family; national heterosexuality has been increasingly protected in law and promoted by policy. Heterosexual marriage and heteronormative families have been so sutured to the nation that an attack on either or both is considered an attack on Kenyan-ness.' Comparing the legal situation with regard to LGBTIQ rights in Kenya to that in other countries on the continent, such as Uganda and Nigeria, Macharia (2013, 285) comments that the Kenyan law 'renders in affirmative, positive terms what other forms of legislation elsewhere in Africa ... have tried to render in negative terms'. Yet, he continues, the effect is the same: it conveys the message that 'the heterosexually reproductive family must be protected against queers, against men who sleep with men and women who sleep with women and against transgender and intersex individuals who disrupt the neat gender binary that anchors the nation' (286).

This script of compulsory heterosexuality is deeply connected to notions of Kenyan identity. Jomo Kenyatta – Kenya's first post-independence president (1964–78), who as an African nationalist played a major role in Kenya's anti-colonial struggle and in the country's transformation from a British colony to an independent republic – famously wrote in his book *Facing Mount Kenya* that 'in the Gikuyu community any form of sexual intercourse other than the natural form, between men and women acting in a normal way, is out of the question. ... Owing to these restrictions, the practice of homosexuality is unknown among the Gikuyu' (1965, 156). The Gikuyu being the largest ethnic group in Kenya, and Kenyatta being the godfather of the modern Kenyan nation, this quote presents an early version of the view that has become popular, and popularized, in contemporary Kenya, which is that homosexuality is 'un-Kenyan'. Kenyatta's son Uhuru Kenyatta, the fourth president of Kenya (2013–22), reiterated this view when, in an interview with CNN, he stated that homosexuality 'is not an issue of human rights, this is an issue of society, of our own base as a culture, as a people' (Amanpour 2018). These quotes, and many similar examples from high-profile politicians and opinion leaders, demonstrate how in postcolonial Kenya, like in other parts of the continent, 'a hegemonic heterosexual identity has come to be constructed or internalized' and how this results in 'the segregation and symbolic "othering" of homosexuals' (Ndjio 2013, 121–2). The latter is evidenced by popular rhetoric claiming that 'we have no room for gays and those others', as reportedly stated by then Deputy President (and current president) William Ruto in 2015 (quoted in NBC News 2015).

In 2010, after a long review process, Kenya adopted a new constitution that was widely seen as including an extensive and relatively progressive Bill of Rights, with potential implications on the existing anti-homosexuality laws (Finerty 2013; Murunga 2014). Indeed, emboldened by this new constitution, LGBTIQ groups in the country went to court, with various successes: in 2014, the High Court ruled to allow changing of names in official certificates in a case filed by transgender activist Audrey Mbugua; in 2018, the Court of Appeal in Mombasa ruled that forced anal examination on people who are accused of same-sex intercourse is unconstitutional; after years of campaigning by intersex activists and various legal battles, intersex people are now recognized as a third gender and have their rights protected by the Children Act 2022.[2] The National NGO Council was forced to allow

---

2. This is illustrative of the relative progress Kenya has made in instituting policy, legal and administrative reforms to advance the rights of intersex

the formal registration of LGBTIQ organizations as NGOs in a 2014 High Court ruling about Transgender Education and Advocacy, and in a 2023 landmark ruling by the Supreme Court about the Kenya National Gay and Lesbian Human Rights Commission. However, the High Court in 2019 ruled negatively about two petitions asking for the repeal of Sections 162 and 165 of the Penal Code, meaning that same-sex practices continue to be criminalized in Kenya; an appeal against this ruling is currently pending. These ongoing legal battles have been widely reported in the Kenyan media (Mwikya 2013) and have generated intense public debate in the country, with politicians, religious leaders and other opinion leaders commonly siding with conservative arguments that same-sex relationships and LGBTIQ rights cannot and should not be recognized in Kenya because they conflict with cultural and religious values. For instance, in response to the just-mentioned Supreme Court ruling in favour of the registration of the Kenya National Gay and Lesbian Human Rights Commission as an NGO, current Kenyan President William Ruto as well as opposition leader Raila Odinga stated that homosexuality is 'unacceptable' in Kenya (Citizen TV Kenya 2023). The First Lady Rachel Ruto called for national prayers against homosexuality. Leaders of various religious bodies, including the Kenya Conference of Catholic Bishops, Archbishop Jackson Ole Sapit of the Anglican Church of Kenya, Bishop Calliston Odede of the prominent Pentecostal church Christ Is the Answer Ministries, the social pressure group Kenya Christian Professional Forum and the Supreme Council of Kenya Muslims, all made public statements protesting the ruling and warning against its consequences on the country's moral character and its threat to the institution of the family. Building on this backlash, and echoing the recently passed anti-gay bill in Uganda, Kenyan MP George Peter Kaluma in April 2023 proposed a new bill titled 'The Family Protection Bill'. The preamble to this draft bill (not yet officially released but circulating online) states that the aim is 'to prohibit homosexuality and same-sex marriage, to prohibit unnatural sexual acts and related activities and to proscribe activities that seek to advance, advocate, promote or fund homosexuality and unnatural sexual acts and for connected purposes' ('The Family Protection Bill' 2023, 4).

persons. For instance, the 2018 national census collected gender-disaggregated data that included intersex as an additional category to the usual M/F categories.

Clearly, the social, political and legal situation regarding LGBTIQ rights in Kenya is a complex and evolving landscape, with progress being made but also with considerable setbacks and challenges ahead. It appears that the recent election of William Ruto – who has strong ties with the Pentecostal Christian community and has a vision of Kenya as a 'God-fearing' nation – as the country's president has strengthened evangelical and Pentecostal-Charismatic groups which are particularly vociferous on LGBTIQ rights and make it the focus of their agenda of sociopolitical and moral reforms (Parsitau 2021; Makena 2022). Yet the country also has a relatively visible LGBTIQ community and a well-established network of LGBTIQ organizations. As Zanele Nyoni (2020, 592) has pointed out, 'The LGBT rights movement in Kenya is constantly reviewing its strategies to incorporate a multifaceted approach to achieve equality and non-discrimination under the law.' The methods and strategies used by LGBTIQ communities and activists are not limited to the legal domain, however. They are diverse and wide-ranging, as they seek to bring about changes in the views and attitudes of society more generally. These include cultural production, such as the music video *Same Love (Remix)*, produced by George Barasa (2016); the films *Rafiki*, directed by Wanuri Kahiu (2018), *I Am Samuel*, directed by Peter Murimi (2020), and *Kenyan, Christian, Queer*, directed by Aiwan Obinyan (2020); life story collections such as *Invisible* (Mwachiro 2013) and *Stories of Our Lives* (The Nest 2015); and literary writing such as Binyavanga Wainaina's (2014) story, 'I Am a Homosexual, Mum'. They also include explicitly religious forms of advocacy and activism, such as represented by Cosmopolitan Affirming Church, which is the first openly LGBTIQ-led church based in Nairobi. How LGBTIQ communities and activists in Kenya will further strategize and navigate a path through the current social, political and legal environment and how effective their strategies and methods will be are yet to be seen.

Uganda

Sexuality has predominantly been a private matter throughout Ugandan history (Sadgrove et al. 2012), but the turn to the twenty-first century marked a clear shift. Indeed, on the back of the heavily internationally funded AIDS prevention campaigns aimed at tackling the spread of the virus through information on sexual behaviours (Vaggione 2005; Wyrod 2016), sexuality decisively entered the Ugandan public domain. According to the public intellectual and academic Sylvia Tamale (2003, 5), 'the HIV-AIDS pandemic has in many ways flung open the doors on sexuality' and made the topic acceptable in public debates in the country. It is against this backdrop that homosexuality also became a highly debated issue in the Ugandan public sphere. In the decade preceding the first (2013) passing of the AHB – a proposed legislation aimed at tightening up the existing law that punishes and sanctions sexual non-normative behaviours – Ugandan President Yoweri Museveni made numerous public statements denouncing homosexuality (Bompani and Valois 2016). The vigorous anti-LGBTIQ debates within the Anglican Communion during and in the aftermath of the 1998 Lambeth Conference took a central place in public debates in the Ugandan public sphere (Vanderbeck et al. 2015; Ward 2015). Bishops in the Anglican Church of Uganda began to formulate theological positions to counterpose steps in Anglican sister churches, especially the US Episcopal Church, towards the recognition of same-sex relationships and the ordination of non-celibate homosexuals as priests and bishops (Rao 2020).

Concurrently, with the first LGBTIQ rights organization officially launched in the country – Sexuality Minorities Uganda (SMUG) – in 2004, queer visibility and spaces were emerging (Nyanzi 2014; Rodriguez 2018). Hostility towards sexual minorities worsened with the tabling and debates around the AHB in parliament in October 2009 by MP David Bahati and supported by a wide range of politicians and religious leaders. Although homosexuality was already considered an offence under the Ugandan Penal Code Act, a legacy of the British colonial era (Jjuuko 2013), the 'Kill the Gays Bill', or simply the 'Bill' as commonly referred in the public (Oliver 2013), further criminalized homosexuality to include 'attempted' homosexuality, the 'promotion' of homosexuality and the failure to disclose knowledge of any offence to relevant authorities within twenty-four hours. It imposed mandatory testing for HIV and death penalty (subsequently dropped in a second version of the reproposed bill) for certain acts classified as 'aggravated homosexuality'. It further allowed the Ugandan state to nullify any international treaty, protocol or declaration to be able to persecute Ugandan citizens while outside the country (Bill No. 18, 2009). In the aftermath of the bill, anti-queer rhetoric and attacks against the LGBTIQ community increased so much that in 2010 the national newspaper *Rolling Stone* (now closed) published a list of the country's 'top 100 homosexuals', with photographs and addresses, accused of 'recruiting one million children by raiding schools' (Akam 2010).

After four years of intense political debate and opposition by Ugandan LGBTIQ and human rights organizations, the AHB was passed by parliament in December 2013 – presented as a 'gift' to the Christian (in particular Pentecostal) community by the then Speaker of the Parliament Rebecca Kadaga (Bompani 2013) – and signed into law by President Museveni on 24 February 2014. In the legislation, the proposal of death penalty was dropped and replaced with life imprisonment as well as mandatory testing for HIV/AIDS, and the crime of 'failure to disclose in twenty-four hours knowledge of homosexuality' was omitted (Nyanzi and Karamagi 2015). The Anti-homosexuality Act, however, had a short lifespan as it was nullified by the Constitutional Court only a few months later, in August 2014, on technicality, as the lack of quorum at the time of passing in December 2013 was identified as a constitutional problem. This period sparked a climax of extreme fear within the LGBTIQ community, so much so that many young people fled the country looking for resettlement and asylum in safer destinations. Indeed, between 2014 and 2015, on the wave of the Anti-homosexuality Act, more than four hundred LGBTIQ refugees reportedly fled to Kenya seeking protection and resettlement through the UNHCR's mandate in their headquarter in Nairobi (Camminga 2020).

Despite the difficulties faced by the LGBTIQ community living in Uganda in the decade after the passing of the bill, human rights and LGBTIQ groups continued to operate with a certain degree of freedom; new pro-LGBTIQ organizations emerged; and social media took a central place in generating creative and open debates around sexual minorities (van Klinken, Bompani and Parsitau 2023). But the advent of 2023 saw an end to this period of tense limbo with a new and energized backsliding on human rights. International development assistance to human rights organizations was placed under scrutiny and received criticism. The Democratic Governance Facility (DGF), an European Commission organization aiming to support good governance and human rights, was forced to close down, and the Ugandan regulatory body for non-governmental organizations – the NGO Bureau – in January 2023 leaked a list of twenty-six organizations that were indicated as involved in the 'promotion of homosexuality' (language used by the bureau). This determined the banning and closing of the first four organizations in the list (including SMUG that already was forced to close in August 2022) while leaving others in fear and uncertainty (although no other organization has been persecuted or forced to close as of now). This led to the release of a new AHB on 3 March 2023. This bill was in some way similar to the 2014 version, but with a view to further criminalize and punish LGBTIQ people, organizations and their allies both in public and in private. With this legislation, Ugandan LGBTIQ people would be precluded from accessing life-saving healthcare services; they would risk eviction, loss of employment and alienation from their own families and kin; and 'repeat offenders' would face life imprisonment or death penalty. Anyone offering health service, housing, jobs or any other kind of support will be persecuted for 'promoting homosexuality'. Anyone who defends the rights of LGBTIQ people could face up to twenty years in prison for 'promoting homosexuality'. Following debate, President Museveni returned the bill to parliament for amendments expressly highlighting the need to align the bill with Uganda's Constitution. Parliamentarians passed it again on 2 May with minor changes, and on 26 May 2023, the president signed the bill into law.

Regardless of the fate of the current legal efforts, in the first half of 2023, LGBTIQ people were already experiencing a massive rise in harassment, blackmailing, and there have been numerous violent attacks on LGBTIQ individuals, acts of incarceration, raids on LGBTIQ-friendly bars and shelters, and protests, such as the one organized by Muslim leaders in March 2023 in the town of Jinja. Since February 2023, human rights organizations have identified 150 acts of violence against LGBTIQ individuals across the country (Byarugaba and Burnett 2023). As Kristof Titeka (2023) stated in his analysis in *African Arguments*, social media, especially TikTok, have played an emerging role in creating an increasing anti-queer climax.

The AHB 2023 has been developed in a slightly different climate from the 2014 attempt as it finds support in a broader network of national and foreign actors. While religious figures have always been behind the proposal and passage of the bill, in 2014 mainly Pentecostal-Charismatic figures were vocal politically in promoting punitive legislation for the irreconcilable 'a-moral LGBTIQ community' (Bompani 2016), for example, through the guidance of the First Lady and Minister of Education Janet Museveni, who is a Pentecostal Christian herself. However, in 2023 the situation was different as high-profile religious leaders from all the main religious groups (including the influential Anglican Church of Uganda and the Muslim minority) were publicly and forcefully supporting the AHB; new funding has been provided by conservative US Christian groups in support of the bill (Whepukulu 2023); a new wave of proposals and appetite for more punitive anti-LGBTIQ legislations across other East African countries has emerged, as in Kenya and Tanzania (see, for example, anti-LGBTIQ positions of President William Ruto in Kenya and of President Samia Suluhu Hassan in Tanzania); and strong anti-Western sentiments have grown from below with citizens more and more detached and dissatisfied with the promises of (Western) development (Bompani and Valois 2016) and losing trust in the political leadership to deliver positive change.

The social, political and legal situation regarding LGBTIQ rights in Uganda remains complex, and the LGBTIQ community is under a lot of pressure with the AHB 2023's passing and being signed into law by President Museveni on 26 May 2023. However, human rights activists in the county and in exile are well organized and prepared for a long-term battle while the Ugandan government may struggle not to take on board foreign donors' human rights conditions considering the high dependency on overseas development assistance (Fisher 2014).

Intervention: Religious leaders as agents of social change

Religion is often seen as a key factor driving the politicization of sexual and gender diversity in contemporary Africa.[3] As Zethu Matebeni (2021, 471) points out, 'There is an intimate connection between anti-homosexuality and religion because the misconception that homosexuality is un-African is similarly applied to homosexuality being un-Christian' (as well as un-Islamic, in Muslim contexts; see Ndzovu 2016). Indeed, across the continent, one can easily find examples of religious leaders supporting anti-LGBTIQ policies and laws, and of religiously inspired arguments fuelling anti-LGBTIQ rhetoric and attitudes in society. The above-discussed case studies of Kenya and Uganda are clear cases in point. However, various scholars have warned against simplistic and reductionist interpretations that reduce religion to an intrinsic homo-/queerphobia, and they have instead called for a recognition of the ambivalent, complex and multifaceted roles of religious actors and beliefs in the politics of sexual and gender diversity in African contexts. The concept of 'public religion' has been deployed as an analytical term to understand the ways in which religious groups in postcolonial African societies have sought to engage and dominate the public sphere in order to exert social and political influence, generating tensions with the also increasingly public manifestation of LGBTIQ communities claiming recognition of their rights (Burchardt 2013; Parsitau 2021; van Klinken and Chitando

---

3. Material in this section is partially derived from an earlier publication (van Klinken, Bompani and Parsitau 2023).

2016). Against this background, it can be argued that anti-LGBTIQ politics are not so much an illustration of the conservative but of the modern nature of religion in contemporary Africa. Thus, as much as we use the word 'conservative' in this book as a shorthand term for traditionalist, sometimes fundamentalist interpretations of religious traditions and the opposition against liberal views regarding sexual and gender diversity, we acknowledge that these dynamics themselves are in fact debates within and about modernity. Similarly, we use the word 'progressive' as a shorthand term for religious views that are open to embracing new interpretations of scripture and tradition, and for a social politics committed to liberal principles of equality, justice, human dignity and rights.

The public clash between religious and sexual politics causes a lot of noise, as it expresses itself in heated public debates, hostile rhetoric and aggressive campaigns on the religious side, which is socially dominant, towards sexual and gender minorities, which are socially marginal. However, this noise cannot hide the fact that within the religious domain, there are different views, for instance, with regard to the desirability of legal prohibitions of same-sex relationships, the recognition and protection of LGBTIQ rights and indeed about the right pastoral and theological approach to questions of sexual and gender diversity (van Klinken and Chitando 2021; Dreier, Long and Winkler 2020). As Joseph Hellweg (2015, 890) puts it aptly, religion is 'neither necessarily a burden nor a boon, but a terrain rich for re-negotiation'. An important point to keep in mind is that LGBTIQ communities themselves actively engage this terrain of renegotiation, considering that many of them identify as religious and given that religious motifs inspire certain forms of LGBTIQ activism and advocacy in African contexts (Mbetbo 2013; Robertson 2021; van Klinken 2019). Thus, there is a strategic and political, as well as intellectual, imperative to engage with religion in its complexity and multiplicity and to explore and capitalize on the potential within religious traditions to contribute to the recognition of the dignity and rights of sexual and gender minorities. As Marc Epprecht (2013, 67) puts it, 'Overemphasizing the homophobia (and sexism) in African religions, and constructing faith unambiguously as an enemy of progress, creates a further danger. It contributes to the impasse between people on the extremes of the debate, and closes down some of the community-building, humanistic potential of those faiths.'

As mentioned earlier, religious leaders (and politicians) are often seen as creating and reinforcing what Patrick Awondo (2016) describes as 'moral sexual panic' around sexuality in contemporary Africa.

A survey of over two hundred Christian and Islamic leaders in Kenya has found that their perspectives towards sexual and gender diversity were predominantly negative: 'Limited acceptance was conditional on sexual minorities not engaging in same-sex practices or seeing such practices as sinful. A substantial minority (37%) endorsed the use of violence for maintaining social values, especially regarding homosexuality and gender nonconformity' (Mbote et al. 2018, 630). In particular, literalist interpretations of sacred scriptures and fundamentalist attitudes where religious groups do not recognize the difference between religious doctrine and civil law were identified as key drivers of such attitudes (Mbote et al. 2021). As much as it is important to study and understand these dynamics, religious leaders are also increasingly recognized as potential agents of progressive social change. For instance, Ezra Chitando and Tapiwa Mapuranga have identified some significant convergences between religious leaders and LGBTIQ activists in various African countries. Pointing out that these encounters have mostly occurred in relation to HIV and public health advocacy, they add that this illustrates 'the potential of extending the scope of engagement between the two groups' (Chitando and Mapuranga 2016, 172). This potential has begun to be explored and realized from various perspectives. For instance, under the leadership and vision of Rev. Gideon Byamugisha – an Anglican priest from Uganda who in 1992 became the first African religious leader to openly declare that he was living with HIV – an international and interfaith network of religious leaders living with or personally affected by HIV has emerged. This network, first known as ANERELA+ and currently as INERELA+, aims to strengthen and enhance the capacity of religious leaders to be agents of change for HIV prevention and treatment, and advocates of human dignity and gender justice (INERELA+ n.d.). As part of its programmes, it has also engaged with sexual and gender minorities, and 'having dealt with the theme of shame and secrecy in the context of facing HIV and AIDS within the faith community, INERELA+'s theology has expanded to become inclusive' with regard to sexual and gender diversity (Chitando and Mapuranga 2016, 178–9). The World Council of Churches, through its Ecumenical HIV and AIDS Initiative in Africa (EHAIA), has facilitated a process where African church leaders and members of LGBTIQ communities meet, grow in mutual understanding and discuss questions of sexual health and human rights and of inclusion in faith communities and society more generally (van Klinken and Chitando 2021, 93–112). The South Africa-based organization Inclusive and Affirming Ministries has also facilitated similar processes of exchange and encounter in South Africa and increasingly in other African countries. In East Africa, several LGBTIQ community-based organizations have developed initiatives to engage with religious leaders as potential allies and advocates at grassroots levels. Some theologians in the region, such as Prof. Esther Mombo at St. Paul's University in Kenya, are making progressive theological interventions in sexuality debates in their churches and society at large (Mombo 2006). In Kenya, PEMA Kenya,[4] based in Mombasa, and Nyarwek,[5] based in Kisumu, started working with religious leaders in 2010 and 2012, respectively. Since then, both organizations have produced training manuals specifically for the outreach among religious leaders, and several of the Kenyan religious leaders who featured in this volume participated in these training programmes. In Uganda, St. Paul's Reconciliation and Equality Centre, founded by Bishop Christopher Senyonjo in 2010, and St. Paul's Voice Centre, founded by Rev. Patrick Leuben Mukajanga[6] in 2013, are examples of faith-based organizations that explicitly aim to promote engagement between, and understanding of, faith leaders and LGBTIQ communities. Indeed, Bishop Senyonjo, a retired bishop in the Anglican Church of Uganda, has become a leading Christian voice for LGBTIQ advocacy in the country and on the continent as a whole (Senyonjo 2016; van Klinken 2020a, 2020b), and we are glad to have his story featured in this book. To date, the two just-mentioned St. Paul's organizations appear to be no longer active, yet their work is continued by SMUG, Uganda's oldest LGBTIQ organization that set up a religious programme in 2018,[7] and by the Universal Coalition of Affirming Africans–Uganda (UCAA-UG), which was established in 2017 as a 'faith-based coalition of religious leaders who came together for the purpose of creating a society that is transformed and all-inclusive, knowledgeable and applies the Biblical norms and principles of love' (UCAA n.d.). The United States-based The Fellowship of Affirming Ministries (TFAM) became active in East Africa in the 2010s, working with local activists to launch initiatives such as Cosmopolitan Affirming Church (in 2013 in Nairobi, Kenya) and TFAM-Uganda (in 2018 in Kampala). Although both initiatives primarily aimed to provide an

---

4. PEMA stands for persons marginalized and aggrieved.

5. Nyarwek stands for Nyanza Rift Valley and Western Kenya Network.

6. Who tragically passed away on 31 July 2020 in a motor vehicle accident.

7. SMUG was shut down by the Ugandan government in August 2022.

inclusive and affirming space to LGBTIQ people of faith, they have also invested in building relationships with other church leaders in the respective countries with a view to building a broader inclusive faith movement (van Klinken and Chitando 2021, 113–26). Most of these organizations operate in a predominantly Christian context, yet PEMA Kenya is based in Mombasa, which has a strong Islamic presence, and their programmes cater to both Muslim and Christian leaders. Their work presents a fascinating example of how the struggle for LGBTIQ inclusion can turn into a space of innovative interreligious dialogue around the contested issues of sexual and gender diversity. UCAA-UG, too, has organized workshops for members of the Inter-religious Council of Uganda, with a view to educate and sensitize them on LGBTIQ issues in the hope that this might help to calm down social, political and religious homophobia in the country.

Although the angles, methods and strategies vary across these various initiatives – with some programmes being run by faith-based organizations, while others are not – the underlying concern is similar: the recognition of religious leaders as gatekeepers of local communities, where they often have authority and influence because of the level of trust and respect invested in them. This insight emerged in development scholarship and practice more generally in the 2000s, where as part of a 'religious turn in development', faith communities and faith leaders were increasingly acknowledged as instrumental in bringing about social change at a grassroots level (Tomalin 2013). Major global bodies, such as the World Health Organization and the United Nations Development Programme, have embraced this insight and actively promoted engagement with religious leaders on matters of public health and socioeconomic development (UNDP 2015; WHO 2021). In African societies, specifically, religious leaders are generally trusted by local communities and known to influence people's views, attitudes and behaviours (Howard 2020). This is particularly the case in countries like Uganda and Kenya where levels of religiosity are very high, with around 95 per cent of the population claiming some religious affiliation (Pew 2022). As such, religious leaders have been engaged to address developmental and societal challenges, such as HIV and AIDS, gender-based violence, sexual and reproductive rights, among other issues relating to gender and sexuality (Gichuru et al. 2018; Le Roux et al. 2016). Thus, engaging religious leaders on issues of LGBTIQ inclusion is only the latest step in a strategy of societal change that has been building over the past few decades.

Asked about the rationale for their programme of engagement
with religious leaders, the executive director of PEMA Kenya, Ishmael
Bahati, insightfully responded:

> Faith plays a big role in terms of decision-making in this country be it
> political, social, economic, or health. We thought that working with
> religious leaders would be a better approach for inclusivity towards
> the LGBTQ community. Discrimination and stigmatization are
> majorly based on faith – some people argue that their faith doesn't
> allow LGBTQ. So, we figured that the best way to deal with such
> a challenge is to involve the faith leaders so that they can educate
> people on the matter of sexuality and gender in relation with faith.[8]

This quotation conveys an important point, being that religious leaders
in countries like Kenya and Uganda are not only influential within a
narrow religious domain but have influence in the community and in
society at large, including in relation to social and political issues. As
another participant explained, 'Religious leaders in Africa hold power,
they are like opinion leaders, what they speak is unquestionable.'[9] On
the one hand, this role of religious leaders as opinion leaders and as
initiators and advocates of new policies and legislation often contributes
to the further exclusion and marginalization of LGBTIQ communities.
However, on the other hand it can, at least potentially, also help to foster
cultures of tolerance and acceptance towards LGBTIQ people in society.
The work of the aforementioned organizations is precisely to explore
that potential. Thus, the rationale for engaging with religious leaders on
LGBTIQ equality and inclusion, as articulated by Bahati, reflects several
of the reasons given by the United Nations Development Programme
for engaging religious leaders in development practice more generally,
including their legitimacy in local communities and their subsequent
roles as gatekeepers and opinion shapers, with the related opportunity
for maximizing community impact, public policy influence and
reinforcing inclusive social values and best practices (UNDP 2015).
Obviously, this does not mean that religious leaders simply are 'a magic

8. Interview with Ishmael Bahati, PEMA Kenya, online, 20 August 2021, by
Keith Embeywa (SERENE project).
9. Interview with Tom Twongyeirwe, United Coalition of Affirming
Africans – Uganda, online, 26 January 2022, by Keith Embeywa (SERENE
project).

bullet of social change' (Østebø and Østebø 2014). They, too, operate in
a complex field of social and institutional power, which frequently limits
their ability to effectively act and intervene, as demonstrated by several
of the stories presented in this volume. Yet, their potential to serve
as catalysts and incubators of change should not be underestimated
either. In a context where religious beliefs and religious actors, by and
large, appear to support cultures of social and political homophobia,
sensitizing and engaging faith leaders can make a critical difference and
initiate a gradual and long-term process of changing attitudes.

Two additional points are worth noting here. First, many LGBTIQ
individuals in East Africa are religious themselves. Even in contexts
of religiously inspired homo-/transphobia, many do not abandon
their faith and often keep attending religious places of worship. Thus,
sensitizing religious leaders, developing their pastoral approach
and theological understanding, is important to create spaces where
LGBTIQ people of faith can negotiate and gradually reconcile their
sexuality and spirituality and find healing from the traumas they
have suffered. Second, LGBTIQ people and religious leaders should
not be conceived of as necessarily separate groups: in fact, several
LGBTIQ-identifying individuals in countries like Uganda and Kenya
are religious leaders themselves, and several religious leaders identify
as part of LGBTIQ communities. This is why, dividing the book into
two parts, we feature both stories of religious leaders who are allies
of LGBTIQ communities, and stories of those who are part of these
communities themselves.

As mentioned earlier, several organizations in Kenya and Uganda
have developed programmes that aim to engage mainstream religious
leaders as potential advocates for and allies of LGBTIQ communities.
The objectives of these various initiatives are diverse, but include the
following:

i. Enhancing religious leaders' understanding of LGBTIQ issues in
    order to correct popular societal misconceptions regarding sexual and
    gender diversity.
ii. Promoting pastoral sensitivity among faith leaders towards LGBTIQ
    persons in their communities so that the latter no longer face
    ostracization and exclusion.
iii. Offering alternative theological readings that depart from dominant
    conservative interpretations of the Bible or the Quran regarding
    sexual and gender diversity, exposing religious leaders to inclusive and
    affirming faith views.

iv. Developing the skills of religious leaders regarding social advocacy and public communication in order to serve as allies to the LGBTIQ communities. (van Klinken, Bompani and Parsitau 2023, 306)

The Kenyan organizations PEMA and Nyarwek worked together – with the support and input from a South African partner, Inclusive and Affirming Ministries – to develop two manuals for use in training programmes for religious leaders. We will discuss these in some more detail, as several of the religious leaders featured in this volume refer to the training they received via these organizations. PEMA's manual titled *Facing Our Fears* was initially developed in 2011. It was produced in collaboration with twelve religious leaders of Christian and Muslim backgrounds, who participated in a three-month-long consultative process. The manual was subsequently deployed in training workshops with other religious leaders. It was reviewed and updated accordingly, with the revised version published in 2018. The title reflects the initial conversations where it occurred that faith leaders themselves 'feared stigmatization and discrimination' for working with LGBTIQ communities.[10] Thus, addressing and facing such fears is a vital step towards overcoming them. According to the manual, the objectives of the training are 'to educate religious leaders on HIV, stigma and discrimination, and gender and sexual diversity, and to discuss their roles in protecting the human rights of all persons' (PEMA Kenya 2018, 2). The training takes place over four days and offers exercises and reflections on issues such as health and HIV; fear, stigma and discrimination; gender and sexual diversity; and protecting human rights. The manual is unique in the ways it draws on both Christian and Islamic traditions, carefully engaging with the Bible and the Quran in order to develop pastorally sensitive attitudes and affirming religious interpretations. Inspired by the positive reception and impact of the PEMA training, Nyarwek also developed its own manual for use in the western region of Kenya. Titled *Safe Spaces*, it has been designed mainly for and in collaboration with Christian leaders of various denominational backgrounds, seeking to equip clergy with tools and resources to fight stigma and stereotypes in their faith communities through learning about sexual and gender minorities and the dynamics of discrimination. Compared to the PEMA manual, the Nyarwek version focuses less on sexual health and is more exclusively Christian in its orientation, explicitly aiming to make a theological intervention.

10. Interview with Ishmael Bahati, 20 August 2021.

Its primary aim is to 'provide a theologically sound basis for tolerance, acceptance and mutual respect for all persons including sexual and gender minorities in society' (Nyarwek 2017, 13).

Research suggests that attitudes among religious leaders tend to be less negative if they personally know and are familiar with LGBTIQ persons. Hence, it has been suggested that 'interventions that promote intergroup contact could be effective in changing religious leaders' mindsets and advancing human rights and health for sexual and gender minorities' (Mbote et al. 2018, 630). Building on this principle of contact theory (Pettigrew and Tropp 2000), the programmes offered by the aforementioned organizations seek to facilitate such interaction, introducing religious leaders to LGBTIQ persons in order to reduce prejudice and allow for human understanding and the building of relationships. For instance, PEMA Kenya facilitates a session 'dedicated to the testimonies of people who have experienced stigma and discrimination' in its training workshops for religious leaders, with the latter being encouraged to 'to listen with love, to consider their fears, and to show empathy and compassion' (PEMA Kenya 2018, 69). A study examining the impact of this training has found that several months later, among the participating religious leaders, 'acceptance of lesbian women and gay men and gender diversity had increased, while attitudes toward gender and sexual minorities became more positive', leading to the conclusion that 'intensive trainings may promote positive changes in their perspective on gender and sexual minorities' (Mbote et al. 2022, 587). Some of the stories presented in this volume, of religious leaders who participated in these programmes, provide further narrative evidence of this.

Several other methods are used to engage religious leaders. For instance, the coordinator of UCAA-UG, Tom Twongyeirwe, speaks about the method of 'peer to peer conversations' that they have deployed in their programme, where affirming religious leaders are trained and facilitated to reach out to fellow religious leaders with more conservative views. He suggests that this is 'a productive means of reaching individuals otherwise unapproachable by LGBTIQ organizations'.[11] Recognizing the lack of affirming religious voices in the media and in public debates, the Uganda-based East Africa Visual Artists (EAVA) in 2021 set up a 'Documenting and Combating Religious Homophobia' programme, through which they 'document faith-related homophobia, and amplify

---

11. Interview with Tom Twongyeirwe, 26 January 2022.

voices of affirming faith leaders who have limited to no access to mainstream media' (EAVA n.d.). In their social media spaces, EAVA artists utilize various creative expressions to help change the narrative of religion and sexual and gender diversity in Uganda, using hashtags such as #SayNoToReligiousHomophobia and #IAmFreeInFaith.[12] Along similar lines, in 2022, UCAA-UG launched its 'This Is My Story' campaign, in which LGBTIQ persons, some being religious leaders themselves, shared their story on camera, with the recordings being published on YouTube and shared on social media.[13] Film is increasingly used to explore the interconnection between religion and sexuality in progressive ways. For example, the documentary *Kenyan, Christian and Queer* (Obinyan 2020) prominently features a community of LGBTIQ Christians in Nairobi and the stories of religious leaders involved in it. The film has been used to initiate conversations with mainstream religious leaders and challenge hegemonic narratives of religion and sexual and gender diversity. These various initiatives utilize the power of storytelling as a method to interrogate and counterbalance hegemonic narratives and help initiative social change.

Methodology: Life stories and social change

As part of the narrative turn (or 'narrative turns', Hyvärinen 2010) in the humanities and social sciences, scholarship in recent decades has increasingly deployed narrative and storytelling methods. This work takes many different forms, yet of particular relevance to our project in this book is the connection between narratives and social change, with narratives having the potential of both reflecting and engendering changes in societal attitudes and structures (Mangone 2022). The stories presented in this volume reflect this two-fold potential. On the one hand, they offer a reflective surface from where we can identify and analyse processes of social change, in this case specifically with regard to sexuality and religion, as these have unfolded and are unfolding in East Africa, and they provide qualitative and critical insights into the impact

12. See Twitter (@eavisualarts) and Facebook (www.facebook.com/Eastafric avisual.artists).

13. Most of these videos were taken offline in February 2023, when homo-/ transphobic speech in Uganda intensified, out of security risks to the people being featured.

this has on individual and communal lives. On the other hand, these stories themselves are also part of, and further stimulate, social change in relation to religion and sexuality, and they do so through the power of narrative critique and imagination. As the anthropologist Michael Jackson puts it in his book *The Politics of Storytelling*, storytelling 'is a modal form of social critique' and it provides us not with a means of changing that which we cannot change but with a way of reimagining it' (2013, 246, 250). Jackson here subtly alludes to the fact that there is not necessarily an immediate connection between storytelling and changing social reality: not everything can be changed, and certainly not overnight, but storytelling as an imaginative practice opens up new ways of thinking about life and society – that is, storytelling is a world-making activity. The aforequoted words from Adichie remind us that storytelling occurs in a field of social power which construes a hierarchy, and indeed often a hegemony, of stories. Yet, even within such a field of social power, constructing new narratives – especially by bringing in stories of hitherto marginalized voices and perspectives as counternarratives – can be the beginning of engendering social change (Hansen 2020). This insight is reflected in the trend in feminist, queer and postcolonial studies of using storytelling, in particular the telling of life stories, as an activist and scholarly method that explicitly embraces the multiplicity of stories in order to interrogate hegemonic narratives and include communities traditionally marginalized in, if not excluded from, society and knowledge production (Stone-Mediatore 2003). As mentioned earlier, this method has been effectively adopted in recent years by LGBTIQ communities across the African continent, resulting in the building of an African queer archive.

As Sarojini Nadar (2012, 274) has pointed out, 'Well before the term narrative theology became popular in the academy, African schools of thought and philosophy embraced and celebrated the power of stories.' She makes this point in a discussion about autobiographical storytelling as a method in African women's theology, and she adequately captures the political and epistemological significance of this method as follows: 'While telling their stories places them [African women theologians] in a position of vulnerability, their stories also become authoritative dialogical texts' (274). Arguably, this insight applies to women's stories as much as to the stories of religious leaders who are part of, or allies of, the LGBTIQ community. The vulnerable position they find themselves in is reflected both in their stories and in the decision of most of them to share their stories anonymously. Having their stories out in public, with their names associated with it, would simply be too risky in the current anti-queer climate. Yet, they share their stories nevertheless, turning vulnerability into strength by offering their stories as dialogical texts, for readers to engage with, reflect on and respond to. As Jackson (2013, 240) puts it, 'Stories make it possible for us to overcome our separateness, to find common ground and common cause.' This is the political potential of storytelling – as a basis for recognition and solidarity – that this book seeks to capitalize on.

Stories of Change presents twenty-four stories of East African religious leaders who are part of, or allies of, the LGBTIQ community. The stories were collected in the last quarter of 2022 and the first quarter of 2023 via biographical interviews undertaken by David Kuria Mbote with the interviewees in person. Informed consent was secured from all participants, following an explanation of the project and its objectives and a conversation about the risks involved. The interviews followed a life history approach, reconstructing the life stories of the participants to narrate how they had become what they are today: religious leaders supporting the quest for inclusion and diversity concerning sexual and gender minorities. The aim was not to offer a comprehensive reconstruction of participants' lives but to explore the key moments in the journey of becoming an LGBTIQ/allied religious leaders, the experiences during this journey and the insights gained. Some interviews included a photo voice element, where the participant was asked to share and reflect on one or two images that figuratively represent their personal journey and/or reflect their dreams for a more inclusive future. Unfortunately, this element could not be included in all interviews, mostly because of time constraints and limited opportunities and resources to prepare and train participants in this method. During the editing process, the voice of the interviewer was removed in order to make the text read as a first-person story. A phrase from each story was selected to use as a title. The edited story and the selected title were shared with the respective participants for feedback and approval. Potential interviewees were identified with the help of community-based organizations in Uganda and Kenya, with whom we had worked under the Sexuality and Religion Network in East Africa (SERENE).[14] All these organizations run programmes where they work

14. The research project 'Sexuality and Religion in East Africa' (SERENE) ran during the period 2020–22, with funding from the Arts and Humanities Research Council (UK). It was a networking project with local community-based organizations in Kenya and Uganda, each of which engages with religious

with religious leaders on issues of LGBTIQ inclusivity (see van Klinken, Bompani and Parsitau 2023). Participants were identified through these networks and invited for an interview. While identifying participants, we aimed at a sample that would reflect diversity in terms of age, gender, socioeconomic position, geographical location, denominational and religious affiliation and across the spectrum of LGBTIQ-identifying persons and allies. We do not claim that the stories presented here are representative for any larger cohort, but we do believe that each of the stories serves as an 'authoritative dialogical text', to use Nadar's just-quoted words, with regard to the insights they provide and the questions they raise. Most of the religious leaders featured here are Christian, ranging from Catholic to Protestant and Pentecostal-Charismatic, which reflect the overwhelmingly Christian religious demographics in Kenya and Uganda. Three of the religious leader allies come from Islamic backgrounds, but we were unable to recruit Muslim leaders who identify as part of the LGBTIQ community. Unfortunately, we were unable to find any religious leader from indigenous/traditional religious backgrounds, as the organizations in our SERENE network did not work with this constituency.

We offer these stories here not to prove the image of homo-/queerphobic African religious leaders wrong but to counterbalance this stereotypical image and establish a more complete and nuanced picture of the lives and experiences of leaders of faith in East Africa.

leaders on issues of LGBTIQ equality and inclusion. Representatives of six of these organizations, as well as academics from the two countries, participated in a workshop, 'Religious Leaders as Agents of Change: Promoting LGBTIQ Equality and Inclusion in East Africa', held at Egerton University, Kenya in February 2022. The aim of the project and workshop was to map these efforts and analyse their strategies to understand the role of religious leaders as crucial actors in achieving social change, promoting equality and building inclusive societies, specifically in relation to sexuality. The interviews presented in this book were conducted under a follow-up project, for which we received funding from UK Research and Innovation under the GCRF and Newton Consolidation Accounts scheme (2022–3).

Part 1

STORIES OF LGBTIQ RELIGIOUS LEADERS

Story 1

PASTOR CAROLINE: 'GOD IS LIKE A MOTHER WHO HOLDS YOU WHEN YOU CRY'

Pastor Caroline is pastor at Cosmopolitan Affirming Church (CAC), an LGBTIQ affirming church in Nairobi, Kenya. They also work as Kenya Country Director of Wawa Aba Institute, a theological institute that uses a womanist framework to centre the experiences of marginalized women in the Bible and, today, in a liberating way. In this story, they narrate the many trials and tribulations that CAC has gone through since its start in 2013 and reflect on their role as a leader providing direction and vision for the future. They are personally inspired by their faith in God, who they see as a mother caring for and comforting her children.[1]

My journey to become a formally recognized religious leader started when I was ordained as a minister in 2015 and then as an associate pastor at the end in 2018. But this story is better told from the beginning. I was born in a very Christian family, although my mum and dad had different religious backgrounds. My mum was from the Anglican Church and my dad was from the Africa Inland Church (AIC).[2] Growing up I attended AIC and I even became a Sunday school teacher there. I however left AIC when I started secondary school, which is then I joined the Anglican Church.

After high school I stayed in the Anglican Church where I became a choir member. However, I was coerced to accept a marriage proposal from a man so that the choir could become more cohesive. The thinking

1. This story is based on an interview with Pastor Caroline on 22 November 2022 in Nairobi, Kenya.

2. Africa Inland Church is an evangelical church in Kenya and neighbouring countries, born out of the Africa Inland Mission.

behind it was that unmarried women were a temptation to both married and unmarried men; therefore they could generate rivalry which would in turn weaken the choir. In addition, since women were allegedly likely to migrate upon marriage, they could not be counted on to hold choir membership numbers constant. As a result of the pressure, I quit and instead joined the Catholic Church. But when I joined the Catholic Church, it was like the Old Testament passage of Sodom and Gomorrah was at the centre of every single preaching. They were speaking about how homosexuals are bad people, cursed people who will bring curses to the land, as if every bad thing that happens is because of them. So, I thought, I do not want to hear these things constantly. I have to find a space where my spiritual needs are ministered to in a calm and discerning way. I therefore stopped going to church and only listened to different Christian songs from my radio and TV for a number of years.

It so happens that in 2012, I joined a lesbian, bisexual and queer women advocacy group, known as Minority Women in Action. This group was part of a larger LGBTIQ rights advocacy umbrella organization, so I got exposed to many other activists. Some of them, who used to watch affirming preaching on YouTube on lazy Sundays, floated the idea of starting a faith group. One of the activists, by the name of George, took this idea very seriously and suggested that we should create a religious space for prayer, worship and bible study, specifically aiming at community members who like to praise God and listen to the word of God. George shared on his social media accounts what he called the gay Bible and that intrigued many of us. We wanted to go and read that gay Bible. As it turned out, it was just an ordinary Bible, but the difference was in the approach we took to reading the Bible, ensuring that we do not take the words literally. Gay Bible meant reading the scriptures in ways that affirmed and empathized with our experiences – the same way Jesus would. So, we began to meet up and share the word of God every Sunday for two hours. Around the same time, a Catholic priest from Uganda, who had taken refuge in Kenya due to what was going on in that country,[3] also learned of the prayer sessions that we were holding every Sunday. He started joining us, and in fact, he was the one who helped us come up with our current name. He told us that if we wanted this to be a church, then we had to have a name for it, and we had to have structures, and we needed to develop a

---

3. It was at the time that the 2013 Anti-homosexuality Bill was debated in Uganda.

programme of how things should be moving. We actually dedicated one of the Sunday meetings to discuss all these things. We finally settled on the name Cosmopolitan Affirming Church (CAC).[4] We defined what 'cosmopolitan' is, and what 'affirming' is. We said: this is a name we can all be comfortable with and that welcomes everyone who wants to join.

It is at this point that my journey to become a pastor started. We needed an usher who would control who was coming in and out, and who was familiar with the church service and sequence of events. I was made the usher. I therefore became in charge of the people and started doing the hands-on administration of church affairs. But just as we were getting started with the formalization of the church programme, the Catholic priest unexpectedly moved back to Uganda. So, we had just launched the new church, but we did not have anyone to preach. His sermons used to be short, but very engaging and accessible. People would leave the service very satisfied. He would not be preaching for an hour like in many of the churches where I went before, but rather just for twenty minutes and the rest of the time, we would sing and dance.

By the time he left, we got in touch with an LGBTIQ affirming pastor from the United States whose preaching we had watched on YouTube. He later became a bishop, Bishop Joseph Tolton.[5] He came to visit us in Kenya, started mentoring us, and once in a while he would preach. One of us, David, was later ordained by Tolton and other bishops from the Fellowship of Affirming Ministries as lead pastor of CAC, and I became his associate.

As you can imagine, being an LGBTIQ affirming church we were facing challenges, such as where to hold our prayer meetings. In fact, if I can use an Old Testament metaphor, the place for us to pitch our tent of prayer, the place where we could witness our version of 'the pillar of cloud' just like in – Exodus has probably been our longest enduring challenge to this day.[6] We are very much a church in exodus, constantly

---

4. See the website of Cosmopolitan Affirming Church, https://cac-kenya. com/ (accessed 7 June 2023). For an ethnographic study of CAC, see van Klinken (2019).

5. Bishop Joseph Tolton is part of The Fellowship of Affirming Ministries (TFAM), a US organization with African American roots aiming to promote a progressive and inclusive form of Christianity (see Lewin 2018; van Klinken 2017). Tolton became in charge of TFAM Global, spearheading TFAM's work in various African countries.

6. In Exod. 33.7–11, the pillar of cloud is a sign of God's presence.

on the move – I think we have been using nine different locations. For instance, one time I requested the director of GALCK+ to give us their office venue so that we could pray from there on Sundays, which she agreed.[7] Then after a while, for safety and security reasons, we had to look for an alternative venue again. Luckily, we secured some funding to rent a space in Nairobi city centre. This venue worked very well logistically, because members found it easy to access due to its central location. But we could only afford to pay for a few hours, and when our time was over the security would come and switch off the lights, leaving us in the dark. It used to be so chaotic that we had to look for a more suitable place.

We were lucky enough to find another place that had an enclosed compound, and a very accommodating landlady too. Yet after several months, the neighbours started frustrating us with unwelcoming actions. Their hope was that we could get tired and leave the place. There was even a time they called the police to arrest us. The police told us that the neighbourhood association did not want us in the area, saying 'you people are making noise'. The real reason, of course, was that the word about 'a church that is harbouring homosexuals' was spreading around and people believed we were a bad omen for the community. The police then said they wanted to arrest the leader. I went to the police station and asked them what crime I had committed. They asked me, 'What people are you having at that place?' We spoke for some time, and I told them that our church welcomes LGBTIQ people. Then they said, do you not know the Bible forbids these people from existing? I asked, which Bible? So, we started having a conversation and while still there at the police station, we received a notice from the landlady to vacate the compound immediately. It was very harsh but at least being evicted was better than being harshly thrown out, which would have exposed our members to physical assault.

Yet, in spite of all these challenges, our members have really stuck with the church and have not gone anywhere. They still follow us to every place we go. In fact, every time we have been evicted and moved to a new space, we got new members. The fact that even with all these exoduses, we have retained our members and grown the church has been very uplifting. People take their time to come every Sunday and our choir, the Affirming Voices, has never stopped singing. It is very uplifting hearing people say that this space belongs to them, and they

7. GALCK is the Gay and Lesbian Coalition of Kenya.

will move anywhere the church goes. If we were to close the church, I know it would be devastating for many people. So yes, this journey has had many ups and downs because sometimes you would find yourself without a space for the community and also because our members face many challenges. Many of them do not work, some still rely on their families, or they have casual jobs. As such when they get a hundred shillings or two it is for food and basic necessities; they really cannot afford to give offerings as is the case with other churches. So, we hardly collect any offerings. The most we can collect is maybe 300 Ksh,[8] which I may end up using to support someone who cannot afford transport to get back home. Most of the time, it is me who buys the snacks that we are having every Sunday after the service. If someone wants to make a contribution, I ask them to bring bread, sugar and coffee so that people can share after the service.

I am really motivated to have, one day, our own church building, a place where every queer person will want to come. I also have a partner who sings so well and from the moment she joined the singing in church has really improved, and this really had a positive influence on how people worship and pray. Someone reached out to me saying, 'I have never gone to a church and want to listen to a song for more than an hour, but in CAC I never want the worship to end.' So, I believe that our Affirming Voices choir is doing a great service. They make people feel comfortable to dance and be themselves. It really makes me proud that people want to come to this space because of the music. And even more can be done!

This is a space where people are free to be who they are. I have seen huge growth, comparing where we are now to the time when we started in 2013. At that time, people would sometimes come drunk to church. I know and empathize with the struggles of our people, and how they end up using alcohol as a coping strategy, but it was very bad at times. Now, with the growth that has taken place over the years, you see that when people come to church, they are presentable. It is amazing to see the effort people make to dress up on a Sunday. And people have reached a point where they point out misbehaving participants, because bad conduct is no longer tolerated in church. This has proved to me that no one wants this place to die or to have CAC doors closed. They want our doors kept open. We are also developing partnerships and collaborations with other groups. It has been a journey but now people

8. An amount that equals roughly £2 or $3.

have started to come on board, and it is amazing how they want to do things with us.

It saddens me to know that some people try to do conversion therapy by themselves, for example, praying God constantly in order to change who they are. This is because they have not come to peace with who they are, there is nothing someone can do to change that. So, some people have gone to Katoloni Prayer Mountain, in Machakos County, to pray God to take the gay away.[9] People normally go there and fast for seven days or even one month and then they say that they have received a message from God. Many LGBTIQ people have gone there saying they seek forgiveness and want to have their sexuality removed, but in my understanding it has never worked. I also know of people who are being excommunicated from their churches or who are forced into conversion therapy. Many people believe so much in the words of a pastor, so if a pastor says that your child needs to be prayed for, then everybody will believe that the child needs to be prayed for. This is because they believe the pastor speaks to God every day and God gives him the message to pass on to us. So, when it comes to someone being gay or lesbian, a pastor may say that this person is an abomination and needs deliverance from an evil spirit, and people will then seek exactly that.

I have personally gone through conversion therapy, and it almost turned into an incident of corrective rape. The pastor in question had told me that I needed to feel the Holy Spirit in a different way so that I can be a full-grown woman who feels the presence of a man. He then told me that if I slept with him in his chambers when he had his vestments on, the Holy Spirit would enter me, and I would start to have feelings for men. Thank God, I managed to get myself out of that situation.

It has been journey, but at CAC we are motivated to keep going and create this space for people to grow. To me, Jesus was someone who wanted people to experience things differently, not in a particular prescribed way. I like it that Jesus chose disciples with many different characters, they were all different and he knew it, yet he wanted to work with all of them. We need people of different characters in the work of God's kingdom, as we all bring different gifts. There is that story about

9. Katoloni Prayer Mountain, also known as Katoloni Fasting and Prayer Centre, is based in Machakos County, about 40 miles (65 km) south-east from Nairobi. Founded in 1995 by a Korean Pentecostal missionary, Pastor Tae Soon, it has become a popular place for Kenyan Christians to visit, fast and pray.

Jesus and the woman who was about to be stoned.[10] Jesus knew very well that she was a sex worker but he did not want anyone to kill her because he recognized that there was something good that could come from her. So, he said to her accusers that the person who has never committed any sin can be the first to throw a stone. He knew that each one of them had done certain things – as humans, we tend to curse others only because our own sin has not yet been exposed by others.

I am also happy to report that CAC has given birth to a new group, Wawa Aba Kenya, who are doing womanist theology especially with lesbian, bisexual and queer women. We try to look at things differently, such as by reading the Bible through our own queer women's eyes, and also looking at God's image differently so that we can relate to God in a different way. In the past, we were used to seeing God as an angry man who punishes people when they sin. But now, we see God as humble and compassionate, someone who can hold your hand. This God behaves like a woman, she is like a mother who always holds you when you cry, wipes your tears away, who forgives and says, 'You are my child, you are created in my image.'

10. The Bible story referenced here is Jo. 8.1–11.

Story 2

REVEREND JALENDO: 'I HAVE LEARNED FROM MY OWN WOUNDEDNESS'

Rev. Jalendo is an ordained priest in Kenya who identifies as gay and has an interest in queer theology. He is affiliated to the Cosmopolitan Affirming Church, an LGBTIQ affirming church in Nairobi. Having come to terms with his own sexuality, he has accepted and reconciled three crucial parts of his identity: being gay, Christian and African. He chose the name Jalendo as a pseudonym, because 'jalendo' is a word that was used to refer to evangelists in the East African Revival Movement;[1] it translates as 'carrier/bearer of good news'. As narrated in this story, his own journey has enabled him to serve as a 'wounded healer' supporting other LGBTIQ people.[2]

There is a photo of me that captures my identity and ministry as a queer priest. At first sight, it is a typical photo of a priest wearing his clerical attire. In my denomination, a priest is expected to dress in a particular way. I was ordained to the priesthood in 2018, which means that I have all the rights to perform priestly functions like baptism, Holy Communion and burial rituals. I have full authority that a priest in my church has. Yet, I also identify as a gay male. So, for me to dress this way describes possibility. The photo shows that it is possible to be a priest, African and gay – because I am. So, it is possible to be a priest who is both African and gay. At second sight, look at what I have on – I have a

1. The East African Revival was a spiritual renewal movement in Protestant churches in the East African region that emerged in the early twentieth century (see Ward and Wild-Wood 2013).

2. This story is based on an interview with Rev. Jalendo (pseudonym) on 10 November 2022 in Nairobi, Kenya.

bracelet, which some people see as inappropriate for a priest. You also see I have a ring – but I am single and not married, an African patriarchal requirement. That ring was given to me by my partner. The ring and the bracelet make the dress code look cool – I am not a typical priest. Thus, in addition to speaking about possibilities, the photo also subverts dominant and exclusive narratives. In fact, in preparation for the photo I intended to dress with a rainbow stole or scarf, but I could not find one. In different liturgical seasons, priests wear different colours: green, purple, white and red. Combining them makes a rainbow. A rainbow stole could be used in any season, but of course is also a symbol of queer clergy. That's me, a cool young priest subverting dominant norms and showing that there is hope for the future. My clerical attire is important to me because it shows that during my ordination, I did not leave any part of me away. I carried all identities on the day of ordination into my priesthood – all of them. I carried my African self, my gay self and my Christian self, there is no self of me that was left out. What was ordained that day was the whole self and not some parts of me. Looking at this photo, I feel affirmed. I feel as a priest who is on the right path. It is a possibility that one can be all these things.

Of course, it has been a journey for me to get where I am now. I grew up in a very conservative Christian environment. Going to church was mandatory and we had family prayers every evening. I went through the normal church rituals like baptism and confirmation. I was the preacher in our family, teaching Sunday school. The village where I was born and raised, in western Kenya, was a traditional cultural environment. In a way, growing up as a gay person there was amazing because living in the village allows you to explore certain things quite easily. Traditionally, boys at a certain age are required to live in their own houses, called *simba*. But then some of us come from very humble backgrounds and our parents cannot afford to build a *simba* for us, so you have to go out there and sleep in a friend's *simba* or sleep in your grandmother's house. That gives you freedom at a very tender age to manage your night affairs. At that time of course I did not know that I was gay, I did not have that term gay then, but I knew that I liked boys. And I discovered that there are other boys in the village who feel the way I feel and do what I do. The fact that we had our own place to sleep meant that we could explore a lot of things. And the good thing is that you are not under the watch of your parents. Once they release you to go sleep in the *simba*, you go and do your things there. The good thing about village life is that *simba* is the best place for hiding because nobody gets to know things you do at night in your small house. But later it became problematic when people noticed that I and a few friends were too close and we did not have girlfriends, so speculations began to grow.

While I was in form 3 (thirteen to fourteen years old), I got saved, as many Christians like to call it, and I gave my life to Christ. It is a decision I have never regretted. It is what I call 'that happy day I fixed my choice in the man I love'. I gave my life to Christ, then I engaged in preaching and evangelism in the village, in town setups. Yet while I was busy with my Christian life, I struggled more and more with my sexuality. There were moments that I wanted to die by suicide because I could not reconcile the fact that I was gay and Christian. Also, there was a lot of bashing out there. At that time, I was outed, and the news went to the wrong person. It went to my stepmother, who is a very lovely woman, but she did not know how to package it. She came and talked to me and said in our mother tongue, 'My son that is not who we are, we are Christians, we are saved, we cannot live in sin.' Actually, she said 'Darkness cannot live with the light.' For the first time in my family, I was called darkness. And that term is religious, she got it from a biblical passage. After being outed, there were times I would walk out of the house and if I noticed anyone looking at me, I thought it was because they knew my story. That outing was my lowest moment in life, and I wanted to kill myself. I was like, 'let it be'. I remember trying to write my own eulogy to give my parents and say, 'If I die this is what I want you to read. Do not fake my story, read the whole thing as it is.'

Yet, that process of struggling and almost killing myself also saved me. It was through a religious leader, a priest in the village who got to know that I was struggling with something. Maybe he had heard my story. He called me and said, 'Please remember, being different is a good thing. Being different makes you stand out, and being different just gives you space to explore a lot of things.' And then he affirmed me and said, 'I have never seen a man like you around the village here. Someone who is brilliant in class, someone who is a very good preacher out there, someone who relates well with people. Look at these women in the village here, they always want their sons to be like you.' And for me that was so affirming, that a priest who might have known my struggle with sexuality told me that I am different in a beautiful way. That was the beginning of my journey of recovery. From there I began to look at the Bible myself, I began to talk about my faith and my journey in very different ways and that has brought me to the place where I am today. That was the turning point. From that moment I stopped looking at religion and faith as things that are used to clobber me. Instead, I deem them as resources that people like me can explore to find answers for themselves, and through which they can respond to claims that they are sinful, they should die, they are worthless. They can respond to such claims by saying, 'I am made in the image of God, God loves me and everything else.'

I kept pursuing my Christian life. I was involved in high school missions and from that a calling for ministry developed and a desire to study for ministry – not to study theology, I did not have that language then, just to study for ministry. And because I was university material at that time, I did not want to go and study in the village, so I told my bishop that because I had a university entry grade, I wanted to go to a proper university. That is when I went to Nairobi and studied for a bachelor's in divinity. I passed well, I got a first class. Yet it was difficult at that time because I was conscious that the Christian narrative in Kenya was anti-homosexuality, so I shifted my theological focus to find out why the church, the Bible and the Christian tradition are against homosexuality while I could see explicit homosexual tendencies in the Bible. After graduating, I got a scholarship and went abroad to study for my master's in theology. At that time, I thought I would be free to explore queer theology, and to find out how it could help the church to overcome that fear of gay people. But the institution where I was studying was difficult, too, because it was a rather conservative university just like the one I had attended in Kenya. So, I ended up writing my thesis on something else – about Christology from the margins, using the story of Jesus and the bleeding woman to explore how in the Gospel, people who are ostracized in society are affirmed and given new life.

My favourite character in the Bible is Jesus, because of the way Jesus engages with diversity, with what through the cultural lens would be defined 'different', what society has excluded. How Jesus deals with that is for me the biggest highlight in the Bible. Jesus is concerned with the marginalized, he has a 'preferential option for the poor'[3] – poor as those in the margins. Jesus always has a preferential treatment for them. There is also the way in which he challenges power. He comes to a world steeped with laws and rules and norms and things to be done, and he challenges that. He says that is not the right thing. And then of course he says, 'I did not come to abolish the law but to fulfil it.'[4] So, all these requirements do not really matter. So, the way Jesus

3. Jalendo uses a phrase here that originates from Latin American liberation theology (see Gutierrez 1973).

4. Matt. 5.17: 'Do not think that I have come to abolish the Law or the Prophets; I have not come to abolish them but to fulfill them' (NIV).

speaks to power inspires me. For those of us involved in queer activism and ministry, Jesus is a good role model in terms of speaking truth to power and embracing those at the margins. Importantly, Jesus did not go to the margins to bring the people there to the centre. It is not about the margins and the centre. Rather he is making every space a centre. Meaning that the experiences of people at the margins are valid experiences and their encounters with God are valid. The margins are active spaces where the church needs to go to learn. That is what I seek to do in my theology and my ministry. Jesus' ideals are love and embrace. I myself know that Jesus loves me the way I am, and so he is inviting me to love everyone and embrace humanity the way they are. I also realize that it is not just the queer people who need love and embrace, there are also other straight people who have been hurt by the system, and they also need the love and embrace of Christ. Every human being experiences some form of exclusion or exploitation or discrimination, and they need love and embrace. So, we do not limit our affirmation to queer people, but also to others because there are multiple forms of discrimination, and there are many victims. So, we make our love and embrace borderless.

Being a religious leader who is openly gay and is promoting the cause of LGBTIQ inclusion has been a difficult and painful journey, but also a beautiful and engaging one. Difficult and painful because recanting those statements that I used to make about myself like, 'I am a sinner', 'I need to die', 'I am not worthy', 'I will go to hell', recanting those statements took me time. Also accepting the fact that it is okay to be gay and Christian was a painful journey. There were moments I was confused, there were moments I wanted to die. There were moments I was depressed. There were moments I tried a lot of things just to heal. But then I had gathered experience in this journey and learned lessons. And so, what I currently do has emanated from my own personal journey. It is because of my own personal story that I am now able to engage with queer people in affirming ways. Like Jesus who is our wounded healer, I have learned from my own woundedness.[5] I know what it is to be wounded, I know how to heal from these wounds, and although some are still scars, I have learned how these scars can be means of supporting people like me. There are a lot of people out here who are struggling like I used to, and they are looking for someone to

---

5. Jalendo here appears to be influenced by the widely circulated book of the well-known Catholic priest and writer Henri J. M. Nouwen (1972).

talk to. They connect with me in very personal ways and allow me to be part of their story, of their journey, which has been interesting and exciting. By listening to their stories, I also discover that I myself haven't yet fully healed, I'm still on a journey of healing myself.

My lowest moments, and they still occur, are those phone calls that I receive from the system.[6] I say system because I am a priest in a homophobic church. By now it is known to them that my passion is in queer theology and pastoral work for LGBTIQ people, and they know that I am not doing conversion therapy, which is what they want us to do. I have heard my own archbishop saying, 'We do not discriminate against queer people; we allow them to come to church so that we preach to them to become saved.' Yet, what they are forgetting is that there are people who are gay and are saved![7] So, I am allowing people to come to God the way they are. After all, a popular hymn in my church sings, 'Just as I am, without one plea.' Meaning, God wants you to serve him just as you are. Yet, they blame me for encouraging people to be gay and to be Christian, saying, 'He allows gay people to sing in church!' Those calls that I get from bishops and senior clergy are my lowest moments. Too many clergy are like the pharisees. The pharisees are the custodians of the system. They want to maintain a Christian tradition that they have received without interrogating it and without attending to people's actual needs. Yet, I am able to use what was used against me for my own good in my ministry. And I believe I can use it for the good of other people. So, the fact that there are many gay people around me is a motivation as those people need a pastor, they need someone to listen to them, and it is a big constituency. I call it a heavy cloud of witnesses: the fact that they are all around me, in the village, in the city, in many church congregations across Kenya. These guys need a pastor, and that motivates me. Also, these days, my theological focus is no longer primarily on scripts and books and articles, but on lived realities, stories of people. I constantly ask myself: How can we draw on those stories and lived realities as important sources for doing theology today?

Transiting from a conservative to an affirming, welcoming expression of faith has been a personal quest. My sexuality used to be a place where I encountered the wrath of God, the wrath of the church and tradition.

6. Meaning: church hierarchy.

7. 'Saved' as in 'saved by Christ', a phrase used in evangelical circles to refer to the experience of accepting Jesus Christ as one's Lord and Saviour.

At that time, before I radically affirmed myself, if I sensed that I was getting attracted to a man I would repent. And I have done everything a person can do to cure themselves of what people have called a disease. I have gone for prayers, I have asked to be exorcized of the demon of homosexuality, I have gone through counselling, I have gone through series of confessions to a bishop. But this time I no longer do that. I no longer struggle with the fact that I am attracted to men. Not because anything has changed but because I have learned that our tradition does not know how to embrace difference, so they call it different names. Difference is called abomination; difference is called error; difference is called heresy. Many of us in the Christian tradition do not know how to embrace difference. But where I am today, my faith in Christ and my sexuality as a gay person, are not separated. It is one and the same thing because my sexuality becomes a space where I encounter the grace of God, the goodness of God, the love of God in very special ways. I have come to recognize that my faith is anchored in my sexuality and my bodily expression which God himself gave. And it is a good space to be in, I am enjoying it.

When I got saved, I wanted to remove the thing that makes me gay. Yet, Christ refused to remove it. It is like St Paul in the Bible, who wrote about him having a 'thorn in the flesh'.[8] Like Paul, I went to the Lord and asked him to remove it, but he said, 'No – my grace is sufficient.' Since then, my sexuality has been a source of struggle and pain but also of great experiences. Calling it a thorn does not mean that I hate it. I just identify with Paul, that he had something that disturbed him, but Christ said, 'It is okay to have it, my grace is sufficient for you.' All the prayers that I did, all the counselling I went through to remove this thing from me, they did not work. That is when the journey of reconciling my faith and sexuality began. I wanted to be a person who loves the Lord without homosexuality, and so every prayer I made, every repentance I went through, my issue was homosexuality. But later in life, I recognized that it is something that is not going to leave me. In fact, this thorn is something that Christ loves about me.

I have come to appreciate that there are multiple expressions of faith and Christianity. The one I grew up in is one that I call conservative, but I have come to identify with what I call, not a liberal but an affirming Christian expression of faith – basically where everybody belongs.

---

8. In this paragraph, Jalendo refers to and cites from the passage in 2 Cor. 12.6–10.

Where everybody is called before God, where our bodily selves are not demonized but celebrated. Our body and sexuality have to be celebrated even within the Christian space. Having radically affirmed myself means that I have confidently and proudly accepted that I am gay, I am Christian, and I am African. These are things that ordinarily do not appear in the same statement in our context. You normally cannot say you are gay, born again and African – it is a struggle in our context. So, to appreciate and proudly make it known out there that I am gay, I am Christian, and I am African, is radical. Whatever other people think of it, I do not care because I have learned that these three things can exist in the same statement. For me that is to be radical.

Earlier, I mentioned the photo that captures my ministry as a queer priest. I have actually another photo, which is my favourite. It is one of me in my clerical vestments, giving Communion to LGBTIQ folks. This is in Cosmopolitan Affirming Church in Nairobi, where I currently serve as support minister.[9] The photo demonstrates that queer people are part of the church, they share in the body of Christ. It is also a reminder that partaking in Communion, or the Eucharist, should not be determined by the terms of any church traditional – it is Christ who invites us! Within many congregations in Kenya, I may not be perceived as a priest in good standing. Yet here I am, serving Communion as a queer person to other queer people. I am a conduit of God's love regardless of my sexuality. I am fulfilled because I can minister and be a blessing to people. And I am empowered because through my ordination I am allowed to be a conduit of God's love. This image speaks to the nature of the future church which will carry out its mandate without the limits of tradition, a church where everyone can serve as conduits of God's grace regardless of their 'standing'. It is a church where everybody becomes a part of Christ. As I said earlier, Christianity has multiple expressions on this continent. This image captures my belief that with time, queer affirming expression of Christian faith will also find home here in Africa. In fact, they already are finding a home!

9. See also the story of fellow CAC pastor, Pastor Caroline (Story 1), in this book and the website of Cosmopolitan Affirming Church, https://cac-kenya.com (accessed 7 June 2023).

Story 3

PASTOR TREVOR: 'IF THERE IS ANYTHING THAT HAS TAUGHT ME ABOUT GOD, IT IS MY SAME-SEX ATTRACTION'

Pastor Trevor is an assistant pastor at a Pentecostal church in Nairobi, who identifies as gay and believes that God has called him to a life of celibacy. Born and raised in the rural Eastern Province of Kenya, he describes himself as a front-row Christian since Sunday school days who has struggled to accept his sexuality. In this story, he narrates how he came to unapologetically identify as a gay man and how he understands celibacy as allowing for platonic friendships with intimacy. He also reflects on his ministry as a pastor, which centres around the values of honesty and vulnerability, allowing others to share their vulnerabilities and struggles with him.[1]

I was brought up in the Methodist Church where I served as a youth leader, but then as a student I started to attend the Christian Union (CU).[2] I found the CU more charismatic than the rather formal and structured Methodist Church, with powerful preaching, speaking in tongues and so on. That is how I became born-again.[3] I served in the CU branch on campus and became a leader, rising through the ranks into the executive committee. During my studies, I had these sexual attractions, but I could not share them with anyone as there was a lot of

---

1. This story is based on an interview with Pastor Trevor (pseudonym) on 13 November 2022 in Nairobi, Kenya.

2. CU is an evangelical and charismatic Christian student movement.

3. Becoming born-again is a notion commonly used in evangelical and charismatic Christian circles to refer to the process of committing oneself to Jesus Christ in faith and becoming saved from sin.

control from the CU membership, closely watching whether any of the leadership were doing anything bad.

I am part of the LGBTIQ community because I experience same-sex attraction. I came to acknowledge these feelings when I was in Form 3.[4] Back in primary school in grade five, I knew there was something that I did not understand, but it did not disturb me then. I would check up men, but I thought it was connected to the adolescence period. Only in Form 3, I properly realized that this is who I am. Strangely enough I had committed myself to chastity from early days, from grade 5 in primary school. This was after at school, our teacher had taught us about sex, showing us movies about HIV and early pregnancies and so on. So, I got scared and I said, 'You know what, Trevor? You are not doing anything.' I kept this promise in secondary school. And as I grew in faith especially in high school, I realized that this is what God wants me to pursue. I decided not to live out my sexual feelings and desires. And when it came to my same-sex attractions, my greatest battle was what to do with these feelings. For a long time, my desire had been to follow God in the way I know. There has been peace when I manage to do that, and no peace when I do not do what is right.

When I became born-again, I had to properly confront and consider my sexual identity, because it was impossible to avoid it. As a saved person, I was constantly in front of this God who knows everything. I was also part of the CU leadership, and this forced me to be upright. There was a lot I could not understand, and I still remember looking for answers on the internet. I fasted and prayed, asking God to take this away because as time went by, it was becoming more intense and stronger. It was a struggle. From 2010 to 2018 it was a season of praying, fasting and confessing. When I transitioned from high school to university, I confessed to a pastor when I was in first year and again in my third year and later when I started working in ministry. I tried everything, hoping that my gay desires would go and that God would just wipe them away.

In my third year (2015–16) while everyone at university was coupling, I felt I needed to have a girlfriend. I thought that having a girlfriend was the only way to end these feelings and have a normal life. So, I tried for some time, but it did not work. In 2018, I realized this was not going to change. It was a bad time to have this huge realization because I was serving in a Christian ministry full time, for one year, and

4. Form 3 refers to the third year at secondary school.

I was feeling out of place. I was sure of my Christian faith, I was also sure of my calling, but I also had these feelings that are very real, and no matter what I was doing and trying, I was not successful in dealing with them. I felt I was not Christian enough and I also felt a hypocrite within my religious community.

In my mind being gay meant to be promiscuous. I felt I did not belong as I did not want to be gay and at the same time I did not feel fully accepted as a Christian. That was a bad place to be in psychologically, because I felt that I did not want to be a Christian, but I did not want to be gay either. Yet I could not stop being a Christian or being gay. I despaired of life, and I was asking myself, 'How can I live in this way? There is no place for me on earth.' I remember writing a letter to myself where I was considering quitting everything, quitting the ministry and even quitting my life. I just wanted to end everything; it was a dark moment. I sent a letter to my pastor, who was aware of my internal struggle, telling him that I wanted to conclude my one-year-long internship and leave the church. This was because I realized that those feelings were not going away and there was not anything else for me to do. I started to have suicidal thoughts. It was a terrible, terrible period. I hated the person I was becoming, I hated being a Christian, I hated the fact that I was different from others. I was in despair, and I did not see any future for myself.

There are two reasons why I did not pursue those suicidal ideas: one is because of God and the other one is because of my mum. My mum had brought us up after my dad passed away when I was young. She is the woman that I love. I love her so much. I could not bear to think of what would happen to her if she were to remain alone. Then miraculously, God came through. I was just scrolling through the internet one night when I bumped on a book called *Washed and Waiting*, about Christian faithfulness and homosexuality.[5] That was like my turning point. The author shares the story of his Christian calling. He explained that he experienced same-sex feelings from the time he was young. He then graduated and became a professor of New Testament and a priest in the Episcopal Church. I believe that was the first time I saw someone who I could relate to. I came to realize that it can be possible to be born-again and experience these feelings; even more, it is possible to pursue a Christian ministry and experience these feelings. Honestly, it felt like God had spoken to me. It was so clear; it was so real!

5. Hill (2010).

I started an online blog discussing the intersection of faith and sexuality. The first piece was like a piece of creative writing where I featured myself as a pastor, and a congregant had come and told me that he was gay and I was trying to speak to them – it was my story, but I was trying to make it creative. I have continued to write. But some people read it and felt that I was not condemning homosexuality enough; they have told me to choose which side I am on. Are you for us or are you against us? I say to them, I am here to say what I need to say. So, the blog had given me a space of personal sharing, about my reflections on Christian faithfulness in relation to my experiences of same-sex attractions. The blog is not very active at the moment due to several reasons, but I hope to restart writing after completing my masters.

In 2018 I came to realize that these attractions, these feelings I am having, may never go away. So, I started to wonder how to live a healthy and satisfying life, nonetheless. I then asked myself, can I read the Bible differently? But my answer was no, I could not read the Bible differently. The verses that say that a man should not lie with another man, in my view they could not be read differently. I then asked God how I could live according to his example. That is how I came to live my current life, where I acknowledge my same-sex attraction and live them out in a way that is not sexual, but not lacking love, not lacking intimacy. Some people believe in conversion therapy and becoming ex-gay. I do not. Of course, God is able to do anything, but for many of us he has allowed us to remain with our same-sex attractions and it is most likely to be there until we die. So, I am not currently waiting for my same-sex attractions to go away. All I believe is that God is able to make me honour him even with these attractions.

Saying that I am committed to chastity does not mean that I live it perfectly. Theologically, sexual relations have to be enjoyed in a marital union between one man and one woman. That is what I believe, and I try to live that out as much as I can. Given that I am not married to a woman, how do I live that reality as a young man, especially given my feelings? I try to live it out through friendships, I champion platonic friendships. The other disclaimer I want to make is that just because I hold this theological truth does not mean I live it perfectly. I am on the journey of seeking how to live as God would want me to. There are moments I fail, moments that I fall, moments where I am not doing it right. But my realization over the last few months has been that my relationship with God has higher priority than the prohibition on having sex. I do not want to be occupied by the latter. My focus is God, that is a priority. My belief has been that I come to God first and then while walking with God I can figure out things. The truth is that one will never be perfect, but God makes our relationship with him perfect and complete. I ask myself, how can my life flow from that?

I do not believe that the Bible was written as a script against gay people. Rather, it is God revealing himself to his people. The Bible is not a constitution against gay people. And the verses that condemn practices by heterosexuals are many more, compared to those about homosexual people. So, the Bible is for everyone, offering all of us guidance for life. Obviously, many in the LGBTIQ community have been hurt by the church. They have heard of the clobber verses – these are the verses that Christians use to pin down LGBTIQ people, such as the texts in Leviticus and the story about Sodom and Gomorrah. And because they are hurt, talking to them about Christianity is difficult because it brings back painful memories. Also, others feel that they cannot reconcile their sexuality and Christianity, so they end up prioritizing their sexuality and mental health. I tell them that it is possible to reconcile their sexuality and Christianity and, if they do not have a personal relationship with God, I try to bring them back to faith. Yet, often they feel like I am just another Christian who is trying to push my ideas on them. So, I try to create relationships with them, so that if the Lord wills, he will bring them back to him. However, with me still holding traditional beliefs on sexual ethics, some members of the LGBTIQ community feel like I am on the side that is against them. But I just keep going. Sometimes when I share my views, especially my commitment to sexual celibacy, I feel alienated. Even within the LGBTIQ community we need to respect diversity, including diversity of views. When a person says they hold certain views which do no harm anyone, we should be willing to listen. Especially in Kenya I hope we accept diversity of views if our main aim is to see the progress and flourishing of LGBTIQ persons.

My favourite characters in the Bible are David and Jonathan. They loved each other sacrificially. Jonathan was supposed to be king, but David came from nowhere and became king. David is set to be king, and Jonathan's father is like, you are the one who is to ascend and be king – can't you see this? Are you a fool and you are literally giving it up? I think they have taught me what love is. Sacrificial love, a same-sex love that sends a message about love to all people – heterosexual and homosexual people alike – showing that people can love each other sacrificially. Their covenant was so strong that even when Jonathan died, David took care of Jonathan's son. David was one of those women-loving guys out there, yet when he describes his love for Jonathan, he says it was more wonderful than the love for women. When I read their story, I see what love is. Those Christians who try to run away from my same-sex love, I tell them, see this thing narrated in the Bible and see how God honours it. That argument is beautiful. I think I love Jonathan. Because David was not really giving up anything, but Jonathan was literally sacrificing. I usually look at this boy and think, he put his heart in it while David was more the passive guy in their friendship. The story makes me reflect on how I can give up something that I think I deserve? How can I try to also explore love? If I end up being deprived of sex, my prayer is that I do not end up being deprived of intimacy. By intimacy I mean that you are known and loved and intimately known by someone, not superficially. Intimacy is where someone knows me, cares for me. My relationships are not superficial, they are intimate, meaningful and so sweet. Especially platonic relationship where people are devoted to each other, they share their joys and their pains, and they truly know one another. It is the opposite of superficial!

I have learned that me being vulnerable with people is a way for them to be vulnerable and open up to me. In the church community there often is a desire to be plastic – to show high spiritual experiences and mask the things you don't want others to see. My desire has been to be real, to be honest about my choices and my struggles. As a leader in my church, I try to see people not as members but as friends. That is how our church has created a community of people who know each other very well and are able to relate with each other. I have a lot of heterosexual friends who come to me and confide in me and say, hey Steve I am facing this and this issue and I cannot tell anybody – what would be your advice? So, just creating those friendships based on honesty is something I am trying to pursue and some of it is already fruiting.

Religious leaders who are opposed to LGBTIQ inclusion in church, I think they are like the pharisees. Jesus is always at logger heads with the pharisees not just because of their hypocrisy but also because they are uncharitable to the poor and marginalized in society. He is just telling them, you white-washed tombs, outwards you are looking good but inside you are not. And I think he would say the same to those religious leaders who know the truth about LGBTIQ people but they are so much concerned about their positions that they do not speak out, and cannot even empathize. Others know what being human entails, and how complex it is. They accept this complexity for everyone except for the LGBTIQ community. So, I think of them as pharisees, and one of the issues that Jesus had against the pharisees was that they were not so much concerned with the love for God. If you look at the twelve disciples, the diversity among them is not something you would find in our churches. They included a zealot and a tax collector. The zealots had tried all their lives to overthrow the roman government and a tax collector was the quintessential helper of the Roman government – because of the taxes. And Jesus brings them together and calls them into one mission. The mission of reconciliation as people to God.

Some religious leaders use the story of Sodom and Gomorrah to say that if we allow LGBTIQ people in society, God will send floods to destroy our country. But can we please read this story again and ask, what is God really saying? It's a story about homosexual gang rape, inhospitality, violence and injustice. I can tell you, the average LGBTIQ person is not thinking about raping people! So, using this story as the number one text in relation to LGBTIQ issues does not make sense. Religious leaders who do this deliberately misinterpret the word of God to just block someone from God when even at the very literal level the text is not speaking to the experience of that person! I think they are just looking for an excuse. So, my message is, let us wrestle through the understanding of these scriptures together.

Another thing that I find off-putting is when religious leaders make jokes about gay people from the pulpit and ridicule them. Hearing these jokes and see people laugh is painful. You are abusing a God-given gift to fulfil the agenda of men, thinking you are building the kingdom of God. When they make these jokes, do they think of the LGBTIQ person in the congregation who has come to the church to encounter God? Do they serve their needs, or fulfil their own needs? Once I had an encounter with a religious leader who read a post I wrote on Facebook. The post focused on faith and LGBTIQ people. He summoned me, trying to understand what I was up to. And he said, 'I know you are not a mole in our church with a desire to destroy us.' Yet, although he said, 'I know you are not a mole', the very fact that he used that word made me realize that it is possible for him to think of me as a mole. If there was a time I felt betrayed by my Christian community, it was then. I was like, I am one of you! You should not be gossiping about me, and even if other people do, he as the lead pastor should not build on that. At that time, I wondered, why I was still part of the church when I was not being accepted? Situations like these is what makes the low moments in my life.

Thank God, I also have some happy moments through my faith, such when I cross the path of likeminded people. I am part of a group of gay Christians. We are very close and support each other. We hold to the same faith and sexual ethics, and we are very honest with each other. It is one of the things that keeps me going in life, knowing that they are there for me, I can call them anytime and they understand me. When I go through some low moments, the members of this group help me to process through life. We have formed a group that is one of my greatest sources of strength. I can also count on a few people who are straight and who are in ministry who know me very well and listen to me without condemning me as such. It gives me hope that I have friends like that.

I have a photo of a seed that is transitioning in the process of growth. It shows a seed that is buried in the ground, but it does not remain there. There are six or seven stages of growth. The first stage looks like the seed is all gone and will never be seen again. At the second stage no one knows what is happening, but you can see something is happening. Then on the third stage we see like it is going down – you can see the roots sprouting downwards. But before long we see something starting to happen – the root that was going down becomes something like an anchor. Before we realize it, we have a beautiful plant. For me this symbolizes how my life in many ways was closer to death. The reality that you have same-sex feelings and the realization that they may not go away feels like death. It feels like I am in this life and I am doomed. And especially in the initial stages, I had these the experiences of disappointments, trying to figure out life. But over time, what I thought would cause death has become life. It has been life-giving in many ways. It has given me a stand, values and all that. I feel like that seed. Everyone thought that it had been pushed down and ended, but I have arisen and come to give life to many others. So, whatever I thought would lead to death has now given life. I thought I was condemned and doomed when I realized my same-sex attractions, but now if there is anything that has taught me about God it is my same-sex attraction. If there is anything that has taught me about caring about others genuinely, it is my same-sex attraction. If there is a thing that has taught me compassion, it is this. I have become a better person because of this. Because I think that otherwise I would be a very selfish and proud person, because God has given me privileges – for example, academically, God has made me sharp. I would be the proudest person in the society. But my same-sex attraction has 'slowed me down' to think about life, to think about God and to think about others and ask, how do I live? The photo of the seed reminds me that stage one – of death and despair – is not all there is. I have the joy of knowing that beyond that, there is life.

Story 4

MAMA ANNETTE: 'MY EXISTENCE AS A TRANS PASTOR IS A MANIFESTATION OF GOD'S LOVE'

In her early thirties, Mama Annette is the founder of a transgender women-led inclusive ministry in Kampala, Uganda. In addition to being a place of worship, the ministry also provides a shelter for homeless transgender women. Seeing herself as a mother in her community, Mama Annette is committed to providing a supporting environment and an affirming spiritual space for trans women who face so much hatred. Referring to the many talents that trans women can offer, she underlines that the church and the wider society are missing out on benefitting from those. In this story, she reflects on the need for queer spiritual spaces within the church and on her role in shaping such a space.[1]

I am Mama Annette, the founder of a black inclusive ministry led by transgender women in Kampala. My fellow pastor, Aggie,[2] was on the streets when I found her, but I brought her to this shelter where we are staying right now. I helped her to find God again, as she had lost her faith after everything she had gone through. Together, we sat down as transgender women, because as you know, women are mothers of the nation and we believe that when women stand in any project, we are always winners. So, we came up with the initiative of a ministry led by transgenders.

Unfortunately, the hate we face in society is real. Recently one of our ministers was attacked because of being a transgender woman – she was on her way to this shelter and was attacked by hostile straight people.

1. This story is based on an interview with Mama Annette on 18 January 2023 in Kampala, Uganda.
2. See Story 5 in this book.

In addition, on Sundays we fear to host our service online because of people who intimidate us calling us men or say that we confuse people. The need to create this ministry came out of the realization that as queer Christians when we go to mainstream churches, they start to preach against homosexuality as soon as they see us. And sadly, even in the LGBTIQ community, transgender women receive insults. We therefore came up with this ministry so that we can provide holistic spiritual growth to our members, and we help them to reconnect with God. With time, this church has become a safe spiritual space for all queer Christians. Here they do not only receive spiritual nourishment but also counselling because some of our members live with HIV and we feel they need counselling.

I believe that it is very important for queer Christians to read the Bible so that they understand it and when we stand in front of a congregation, we can preach a gospel of love instead of a gospel of hate because love conquers all. Moreover, if we learn to love ourselves, we will be able to love others – our neighbours. If you do not love yourself, you will not be able to love your neighbour and your God. For that reason, we hold Bible study sessions every Wednesday. We read the Bible to gain knowledge and also to learn how to preach. This is important even when we go out on to the streets, showing people that the Bible preaches love and not hate or discrimination.

Before starting this ministry, we were facing many challenges. We used to get insulted and discriminated when entering mainstream churches. It was a challenge to go to churches when we were dressed in our gender-affirming clothing. For me this means going to church dressed as a woman, putting on my clothes as well as my make-up, because I believe I am a true woman. Last time I attended a service in a mainstream church, I dressed in a manner consistent with my gender identity. When I went, people started pointing at me and staring at me, asking, are you a woman or are you gay? So, I decided to leave and not stay in that church. And this is the experience many queer and transgender Christians have every Sunday. These types of experiences make us feel targeted and excluded.

I am a mother and as such I feel very protective towards my queer Christian fellows, it is my responsibility to ensure they are safe. That is the reason why I came up with this fellowship; I wanted a place to support them with their physical, spiritual and mental health issues. Sadly, many members of our community have tempted to commit suicide, and we try to support them in whatever they are going through. It gives me great joy to see how our girls are highly motivated and are willing to engage with Christians who come here to the church, how enthusiastic they are in the service, how they support and encourage each other. And to me, what is more important is that they do not give up on life even with the difficulties we transgenders face.

As a transgender woman and a mother of my community, I am here to give hope and to support people's faith because we have a lot of queer Christians who have lost faith. Some no longer go to church. When I sit with my fellow transgenders and other queers, I talk to them with a voice of love, helping them to find love and regain their human dignity. I am here to encourage people; they must not lose hope. I believe in queer Christianity and I have hope for the future. It is our responsibility to promote love and if we continue with our advocacy the future will be great. As a mother, it is important to me to ensure that people who come to this shelter are welcomed, are mentored and coached; we help them to sow the seeds of their future success. We do what we are doing to secure a better tomorrow. We have to put a strong foundation so that the next generation can benefit from that.

Since we started this ministry, we have experienced many changes. We learnt how to pray and how to do charity work together as a fellowship. We promote love and sexual health; we promote security so that our queer Christians are safe and also healthy. We make sure that they eat healthy food as many of them have been thrown out of their family homes and need a home and people who take care of them, especially those who live with HIV. And our fellowship is a home. Being a transgender woman does not impact on my humanity as I am still a human being and I can do anything that other humans do; I can stand in front of people and preach, I can be a mentor and guidance to others, I can help other transgender women to feel empowered.

As an inclusive ministry we welcome everyone – no matter who you are or what your background is. Whether you are LGBTIQ or not, you are welcome here. In this ministry we believe that we are all created in God's image and that nobody is cursed or unwanted. It is part of our journey to welcome everyone. This is an inclusive space. We need everyone no matter their differences; we welcome everyone even though we ourselves are not welcome in other religious spaces. We want to offer a religious space where people do not have to hear tormenting verses such as the story of Sodom and Gomorrah.

One of the aims of our ministry is also to challenge other religious groups. Our call is to show them love, even if it is difficult for them to reciprocate. For us as an inclusive ministry of queer Christians, hating, discriminating excluding people is not our business. They may consider us as the most dangerous people, but our call to follow Christ requires us to show everyone love, including those who do not love us back. They may see us as sinners, they may confuse sexuality with sex and what we do in private; they may not even think of us as people who know God. But we are Christians, we read the Bible, and we love God. Our existence is a challenge to their capacity to love. Being a transgender does not mean that I cannot minister to people, in fact my existence is a manifestation of God's love and that is why I have been called to this ministry as a transgender woman.

As a mother of our community and founder of this fellowship, I feel the need to prepare for tomorrow. Just like Noah in the Bible had to prepare for the upcoming calamity, I do not know what is going to happen, but I need to prepare for all scenarios. I should sensitize people on how to prepare for tomorrow, for the future. We should work to reduce the LGBTIQ homelessness in our community. You can see that people do not want us in society: when we rent a house in the community and people find out about our gender identity, they chase us away. We cannot live like this, hence the need to lay a strong foundation for our future. We need to put up permanent spaces for our people because landlords are always chasing us away. But if we prepare ourselves, we need a permanent location that is a home and welcoming so that even if someone is chased, they know that there is a place they can run to and be welcomed.

Transgender women can make a great contribution to society. Discrimination does not bring us anywhere; it just means that the talents of our community cannot benefit society. For example, we have a land project, and we distribute the produces that we grow to anyone who is hungry, not only to members of the LGBTIQ community. It is written in the Bible that the more you give, the more you receive. The gospel of love is encouraging us to help others. If I am walking and see someone on the streets who is stranded, I will come to their help because the gospel of love is telling me to do so. I also know that our community is very talented. In doing business, dancing, reading the Bible, doing service to the community. We are blessed even if they do not know how blessed we are. Our purpose right now is only to prepare for the future and train our queer Christians; teaching that being a queer Christian should not stop people living their lives to the fullest and realizing their potential. Even with the current insecurities for queer people in Uganda, we still hope in change. Of course, if they were to consider us as full citizens, we would be creative and contribute to the growth of the country. But right now, we are denied opportunities, yet they are also denying themselves and opportunity to receive taxes from us. There are people who commit suicide – these are talents the society is losing for no reason. Being a transgender does not mean that I cannot put up a hotel or a business centre that can employ jobless people. In a way, our loss is also their loss, but it should not be that way.

I think a lot about the future because as Christians we believe in change. I know that right now we are enduring a lot of problems, problems that I would not wish to my worst enemy. Nobody should be put in the situation of being hunted by those challenges. Working for a better future is what motivates us. As a believer I know that in five or ten years from now we will see the foundation for the next generation. I do not want the next generation to face the same challenges that I am facing right now. The generation that will come after us shall not suffer the same way we are suffering – enough has to be enough.

Story 5

PASTOR AGGIE: 'I AM LEARNING TO ACCEPT AND LIVE WITH MY SCARS'

Pastor Aggie is one of Uganda's first openly transgender religious leaders. At the age of twenty, she is also among the youngest pastors in the country. Disowned by her parents and kicked out of high school because of her gender identity, Pastor Aggie has experienced trauma and suffering, which she compares to the biblical character of Job. Yet, as she narrates in this story, encouraged by the image of the risen Christ still having the scars of the crucifixion on his body, she affirms her belief in survival and her hope in a better tomorrow. Co-founder of a church for queer and trans people, Pastor Aggie is passionate about creating a world that is more diverse and inclusive.[1]

I am widely regarded as the first openly transgender pastor in Uganda. I am a woman, a mother and a religious leader. I come from a very strong religious background, and I am passionate about creating a diverse and inclusive space for queer and transgender people; I am passionate about working for a more inclusive and diverse world for all of us. I have been serving in church since I was young because I come from a family with a strong Christian background. In high school, I was in the praise and worship group.

Unfortunately, I was expelled from school before I could complete my high school studies, because of my gender identity and sexuality. And people at that school were like, 'this thing is from the devil', 'how can you be in church while doing *a-b-c-d*?', 'it is the devil coming to us in church'! I was really heartbroken and cursed at church in those days.

---

1. This story is based on an interview with Pastor Aggie on 18 January 2023 in Kampala, Uganda.

I swore never to be part of it. Because I was like, 'God, if you create me like this, why then would you let me go through all these sufferings in this world? Why Lord?' I had to come back home but my dad kicked me out, so I had no choice but to live on the streets for several weeks. That is when I met Mama Annette, founder of a fellowship of transgender women here in Kampala.[2] When I met her, she offered me a hand of hope and brought me into the community as her child. I was lucky to meet a trans woman who brought me into a place where I can freely express who I am. I am happy to be able to express who I am. Mama is also a very good Christian and that renewed my faith in God. I had lost faith and hope in God and did not want to look at God anymore. Because I was blaming God for all the things happening in my life. After all, the Bible says that God knows everything, he knew me even before I was born. So, if God knew that I would go through all this torture and suffering, why would he let it happen? I had all those questions, but Mama Annette used to remind me that I am where I am are right now for a reason, and that all I need to do is figuring out my purpose in life. So, that is where my spiritual calling comes from.

When I sat down and thought about it, I realized that the bad things happening to me did not just happen because I was hated or discriminated against, but rather helped me to leave the place where I was, in order to come and serve the community and prepare the road for those who will come after me. There are many trans folks who will come after me, and God brought me from where I was in order to pave the way for those who will come after me. There is a purpose behind it all. It is not going to be easy for us to have our rights or be accepted in this country. It will take time, but I believe that when we are together in this journey, when we are together as one force, we can achieve it. Life has not been easy, I have lost friends, but I know we shall reach where we want to reach. Right now, I am learning to accept and live with my scars. Ever since I started studying queer theology and reading the Bible from that angle, with support from a few friends, I have learned that when Christ rose from death, even in his divine form, he still had the scars of the crucifixion. These scars mean that he died on the cross and rose again but is still wounded. It is a promise that we will survive death and will be called to life, even when we are still wounded. Therefore, me having the traumas and the scars from the beatings, from the torturing I have gone through, even having been thrown into prison – if I have

2. See Story 4 in this book.

managed to go through all this, it means that whatever next storm comes my way, I will survive.

I should not cry or regret anything about it, because if these experiences had not happened in my life or if God had come to my rescue at that time, now I could not serve as an inspiration for queer and trans folks. I would not be the Aggie that I am, and I would probably be living in denial and in the closet, with the truth tormenting me deep down. Thus, I am proud that I can now stand up and say, 'I am trans, deal with it.' Love me or hate me for it, but as long as Christ loves me, I have all that matters. When my parents disowned me, I felt like I was not worthy of love. So, I would fake this personality so that people would love me; I would be this boy that people would want to be in a relationship with and then inwardly knowing that I am transgender. I would fake life and not even do my hair or makeup or nails just to keep them happy. But deep inside me, I was not happy myself. When I accepted myself, I also wanted to inspire others and give them hope for a better tomorrow. Even if the whole world has neglected us, God has not. Because I have seen it here in my chosen family: I have a mother in this community, who has accepted me and looks after me. That experience gave me hope that God still exists and loves me. I began trusting God again and growing spiritually, although it was not easy after what I had gone through. But luckily, God gave me people who were supportive and shared with me their scenarios of life, so when I joined them together with my scenario, I realized that God loves me; he brought me from a place where I was not loved to a place where I am loved.

We started this church so that it can be of inspiration and an icon to others not to lose hope in God. If you ask queer, trans, gay and bi people things concerning God, many will tell you, 'No thanks, we do not want anything to do with God because the church has done nothing but harm us.' It is because of the church and its teachings that most of us have lost homes, have lost love, have lost our lives and friends. So, most people do not want anything to do with the church. Yet, as it turns out, they are still looking for God. That is why I – no, I should say 'we', as we are a team doing it together – that is why we thought, let's just create our own inclusive space. Because the Bible says that we can come to God the way we are, and that nothing can separate us from God's love.[3] Thus, we do not have to do anything to claim God's love, I do not have to pretend

3. Rom. 8.38–39.

to be straight. Not even church leaders or any rules can take us away from God's love! God's love is already there for us.

Someone told me that we are brainwashing people, trying to turn children into queer folks. However, no one is trying to turn anyone into a trans or gay person. We are just trying to put an end to the suffering and death that happens in our communities. Because many of us are committing suicide because of the terrors happening to us. While if we all grew up in an inclusive and affirming space, no one would have mental health issues or suffering from depression or being gang raped. No one would be going through that. But because we grew up with that mentality of heterosexuality – that marriage is between a man and a woman exclusively – and that mentality of being created male *or* female – that our body defines our gender identity – in our community we end up struggling to accept ourselves, we even come to hate ourselves. We are not brainwashing anyone, but we have to teach the youth because they will be the leaders, pastors and bishops of tomorrow – teach them to accept LGBTIQ people and love them for who they are.

I feel happy because being a religious leader at the age of twenty is a big achievement for me. There are people in their thirties and forties who come to me for spiritual guidance and counselling. I feel happy that people trust me with their secrets and open their hearts to me. Getting someone to trust you is hard, but loosing someone's trust can easily happen. So, I do not take it for granted when people trust me, I take it very seriously. There is a phrase that repeats itself over 365 times in the Bible, and it says, 'Do not be afraid.' So, I am not afraid of anything in the world. But people who are against us should instead be afraid of me. I am not going to do anything to ask for respect or love, because I know that I deserve respect and love, as a human being and as a Christian. I deserve to come to God to pray, to minister and worship. Jesus said, either be hot or be cold.[4] Thus, I cannot be in the church and pretend to be straight. I would be living a double life and not living the kind of person I am called to be. And in that case, God will be like, I do not know who you are. At times, even I did not know who I was, because today I would be this kind of person and tomorrow this other kind of person, as I constantly wanted to please people. Until I realized it is not about them, it is about me and how I feel. So, I chose to be hot instead of being both hot and cold, so that I can fit exactly in the way I am supposed to be fitting.

4. Rev. 3.15.

My favourite character in the Bible is Job. This is because when I look at Job, I can easily relate his experiences to mine. Job had it all but then he lost it dramatically – like, his children, his property, even his health – only to gain it again. I also had it, I lost it – I was kicked out of school, I lost everything including my family, my mum did not stand up for me, my friends let me down – but now I am getting back to where I was. Amidst all the friends I lost, there were a few who stood with me, and they accepted me for who I am. Luckily enough, they address me as Aggie and not by my dead names. They address me as she, not he; they respect the fact that I am trans. When reading Job's story, I can look at him and see myself. I can read my own name instead of his. Instead of a story about Job crying and cursing God, I find myself crying and asking God, instead of helping me out, why have you have forsaken me? The Bible is like, 'Call my name and I will be there for you.'[5] But I have had so many times when I prayed to God, saying, 'I am in need of your help, answer my prayers.' However, what I have learned from Job, as part of my spiritual growth, is that I need to be patient and wait for God's time. Because if I had not been patient enough and I would have gone by what my parents wanted me to do – go to church and be prayed for, be the boy they wanted me to be – I would not be sitting here with you today. I was patient enough to endure everything I passed through, from the time my parents denounced me to this point where God has brought me. Job inspires me to always rely on God, put my trust in God and know that there is a brighter tomorrow even when things seem to be a mess. At some point, Job's wife is like, 'Why don't you curse God and die?'[6] But Job trusted God, and likewise I learned to trust the process, I trust the process of God. I do not have to put on this image everyone wanted me to be.

It still hurts me that my parents have failed to reach the point of being proud of me, but instead still see me as a disgrace to the family. But anyway, that does not matter because I have learned in life to always let go. Because if I cling on to the past, I am going to go down five steps instead of climbing ten steps ahead – I may even develop hatred for them, which I shouldn't. The gospel we preach is of inclusive love, so why would I dwell on the past traumas of my life and have hatred in my heart? Recently, I called my dad and wished him happy Christmas and happy new year and told him that I love him. I hanged up and blocked

5. Jer. 29.12–13.
6. Job 2.9.

his number because I did not want him to call me back and tell me his opinion about me; I do not want to hear his opinion. All I can do is forgive him and let him go and then focus on myself and what I can do best. What keeps me going is the love and support from my chosen family. And other friends of our church, who are not from Uganda but work with us as part of the movement of inclusive and affirming ministries. They keep me going, because they also tell us how even in their countries things are hard. So, they remind you: nothing is easy, just have hope and keep fighting for what you know to be true and to be right; keep fighting for truth, and the truth will set you free. I am not a criminal, I am not possessed, I am just me being me. And people should learn and accept the truth about me.

I have this image that symbolizes the work that I do in this community, it is the image of a dove. When God sent the big flood and Noah was in the ark, he sent out the dove and it returned with a leaf. The way I interpret it, this green leaf was a sign for Noah that there was hope for the world to come to life again. Although the earth was flooded with water everywhere, the green leaf symbolized hope for the world to be restored and have a future. This means that there is hope, even in the midst of hardship that we face. We are going to reach a time when people will be like, 'The message this pastor is preaching is powerful and inspiring!' Even when someone asks, 'but don't you know that this pastor is trans?', they will be like, 'I do not care whether she is transgender or not; when she is preaching, she is preaching to me, I feel moved and I feel touched. When she prays, I feel like my burdens are being lifted; I feel the touch of the Holy Spirit.' Every morning when I wake up, I wake up smiling. I do not wake up with a sad face like before. How can you be sad when you have beautiful people who love you and accept you? This has happened because I have trusted the process of God. People are like, 'Aggie we love you, we are proud of you.'

Story 6

PASTOR RIA: 'WE NEED TO REMEMBER THAT GOD DOES NOT MAKE MISTAKES'

Pastor Ria identifies as gender non-conforming and is a member of a lesbian bisexual and queer women advocacy group based in Kampala, Uganda. She works as a chaplain in affiliation with The Fellowship of Affirming Ministries in Uganda and as country director for Wawa Aba Theological School. Claiming to be a natural leader, her ministry is motivated by the belief that God has chosen her as a vessel of his inclusive love. In this story, she shares her religious journey, her understanding of scripture and of LGBTIQ ministry.[1]

Since I was young, I have been deeply rooted in the Christian faith. As a family we used to go to church regularly. My parents were very committed Christians and they also sent us to Sunday school. All the schools that I went to were Christian schools. When I grew up and went to Makerere university, I yearned so much for God that I got saved in 2006.[2] After my studies I continued to walk the journey of faith, coming to know God deeper. Rather than being told who God is, I wanted to encounter him personally, receive revelations from him directly instead of through intermediaries.

In my whole life I never thought of becoming a religious leader. But when you relate so much to someone, your relationship gets deeper with that person to the extent that you want to move the relationship to another level. You will grab any opportunity to move to a deeper

---

1. This story is based on an interview with Pastor Ria (pseudonym) on 18 January 2023 in Kampala, Uganda.

2. 'Getting saved' is a common phrase in evangelical Christianity used to describe born-again conversion.

level with this person. That's how it is in my relationship with God. And because I am also a leader by nature, I felt the need to guide people and be there for them to 'stand in the gap' as we say in church.[3]

During your salvation journey you are encouraged to preach about the goodness of the Lord. That was all I could do. I had become active in LGBTIQ inclusive faith circles, and the leaders there noticed my passion for God and the gospel. They would encourage me to enrol in faith trainings and religious programmes. One day, I was invited to attend a training event organized by TFAM Global in Rwanda, as they needed representatives from Uganda.[4] At the event, we ended up talking about launching a TFAM (The Fellowship of Affirming Ministries) church in Uganda, and they identified me as someone who could serve the community as a chaplain. When I was called to this ministry, I asked myself, who am I to refuse to serve Gods people? If God has seen that I have the skills, I should be available. This is a calling I cannot decline. This was back in 2017. It was the start of a journey of leadership, which has been amazing. Challenges are there but you keep going. I can say that since I became a chaplain my faith has grown because I have chosen to relate to Christ at a deeper level. Before becoming a chaplain, I was a regular faith community member. When I got saved it was not about leadership, but about my personal growth in faith and spirituality. It was about me getting to know Christ at a personal level; it was about me and Christ, and I did not care too much about the rest.

As an LGBTIQ identifying person, I know that there are religious leaders who are not inclusive in their faith spaces. That is why I moved from traditional religious practices[5] and what is taught there, and I came to this space where I can see and relate to God personally. There are no brokers or commissioners between me and my God. The God I serve and know is a God who is irrespective of titles, class, colour,

3. 'Standing in the gap' is a phrase commonly used in evangelical and charismatic Christian circles to refer to the practice of intercessory prayer, where a person of faith prays on behalf of somebody else, to restore their relationship with God.

4. TFAM Global is the global arm of The Fellowship of Affirming Ministries, a US organization with African American roots aiming to promote a progressive and inclusive form of Christianity (see Lewin 2018; van Klinken 2017).

5. Traditional religious practices, in this context, refer to the established mainline churches, as compared to the newer Pentecostal-Charismatic churches.

sexuality or whatever. Because we are all part of God's creation, and we are all created in God's image. So, to me I believe that you cannot start saying, this person does not deserve the love of God or hear the word of God because he or she is like this, or because their sexuality is like that. I do not believe it. Two, I do not believe that God makes mistakes when he creates people, he does not. He is a perfect God and does not make mistakes. So, you cannot tell me that someone is a mistake simply because of their sexuality. The God that I serve is a perfect God. He does things at his perfect time, in his perfect way and we cannot question him. So, when someone says that another person is not supposed to be this way, or is not supposed to be serving God, I am not buying that. We are all God's creation. I believe that we are all in our father's house and we are all entitled to the privileges of being children in that house. So, the privileges that everyone is entitled to are for everyone, irrespective of whether you are tall or short, LGBTIQ or straight. None of that does matter. We all have these privileges in our father's house.

When I read the Bible in my own understanding, I know that for as long as you are in Christ Jesus, there is no condemnation.[6] That is what the Bible says, and my interpretation is that I am in Christ Jesus, so who is condemning me? My God is not condemning me! That is where religion has played a very bad part, like people misinterpreting the scriptures according to their ideology and thinking of how the world should be. The gospel of Christ is supposed to bring more and more people to the house of God. Thus, I do not agree with a gospel that chases away someone from the family of God. The gospel that people have to hear is the gospel that should bring more and more people closer to God. So, any gospel – in fact, I should use the word preaching because what I am talking about is not a true gospel – that is chasing people away from God is a selfish teaching that takes God's own away from him. It is not a gospel. That is what I believe.

I believe people who are homophobic are not inspired by the scriptures, because the scriptures say there is neither male nor female in Christ Jesus.[7] God sees one's soul, not one's gender, and in eternity we are not going to be male or female. It is patriarchal culture that is causing all these problems. Yet at the end the question we shall all be asked by God is, how did you deliver on my Word? The look of a human being's gender, or the sexual acts they are involved in, is irrelevant to

6. Rom. 8.1.
7. Gal. 3.28.

that question. Of course, there is also the issue of religious doctrine. You find this pastor using the scriptures and interpreting them in a hateful way because they have this doctrinal teaching or tradition in their church. Yet they read the Bible selectively. Because in the Bible you find many things mentioned, such as rape, incest and injustice. Yet these are not talking about these; most pastors are only obsessed with homosexuality.

When people preach hate they are not taking people to God. They are really pushing people away and that to me is not the gospel. The true gospel is about preaching the good news, so any message of hate is their own news. When you tell me that God is good, how he has been faithful, generous and has never failed you, I will come and see who that God is so that I can also know and taste the goodness of this God. That is bringing people to Christ. If instead you start preaching hate, you're putting people off and push them away. The problem is that most people in our society look at these priests as if they are God themselves. Because most of these pastors have turned the tables – they are not preaching about God, but about themselves and presenting themselves as lords to their followers. Yet, we only have one Lord who is our teacher, and that is Jesus Christ.

Reading the Bible myself, I have several favourite stories that have come to speak to me with age. I love the story of Jonathan and David. The loyalty that Jonathan shows towards David, added to the fact that Jonathan was from a privileged background yet had true love for David, is just so beautiful. Mutual trust was key in that relationship. How I wish all human beings would have that – the world would be so much better! I also like the story of Naomi and Ruth. They clearly portray the character of people who are standing and believing in you and loving you even when you are down. They are people who will not forsake you. If human beings were like that in their relationship with each other, we would be in a better world.

Also, Job's character moves me. Job's faith remained strong in God, yet he was tested – it was a faith that is tested beyond faith. Job's faith was really strong! If people can have such faith, even us as spiritual leaders, it would be great.

One of the elevating or high moments in my life and ministry was my ordination. When I was ordained as chaplain it felt like I was tapping into God's glory. You cannot touch God's anointed, so it makes me feel safe. I felt the weight of the ministry on my shoulders, but I also knew that God would be the lead for me I am just used as a vessel. Another high moment was my recent graduation from the Wawa Aba theological training school.[8] When I graduated, I was amazed at how far God has brought me. Since then, I have become the country coordinator of the school. It was another confirmation that people trust me and recognize that I have skills in this journey of leadership.

My work with Wawa Aba has made me grow and has strengthened my confidence as a leader. There was a time when we were not yet set up properly because the institute was still young and we were the pioneers in leadership. We overcame many hurdles, and in the process, I grew in my chaplaincy and leadership skills. Given the task to organize some events, I organized faith gatherings and we saw them through. I was grateful to God for the wonders that he did. Yet, you cannot talk of elevating moments without discussing low moments too. For me as a leader this relates to situations where I encounter indifference and lack of teamwork. Sometimes you want your church to move far, and for this to happen you have to move with others. If you move too fast, you end up moving alone. To me, moving far is key, but you do not want to move fast and end up just moving a short distance. I was taught that if you want to make progress in this work, we have to move together. But there is always the challenge of those ones who do not support teamwork or are not cooperative, that is challenging. Then there is also indifference among people, or they have their personal issues and bring them to the ministry in an unprofessional way. Yet people have different personalities and even if you are their leader there are things you cannot do. You cannot force yourself into their personal lives, even if their issues are hindering the professional work.

Scripture has taught me that whatever hindrances come before you, kindly stick to God's principles. Continue loving God and do the work God would love you to do. Remain focused. Because if you divert, you are going to lose it. Maybe God is saying, trust in me, and even if challenges will come, I trust my daughter to be able to overcome these challenges. People will talk bad, homophobia will come, and they may chase you around. Just remain focused. As a leader, it is such challenges that keep me rooted and that influence how I relate to my friends and to my God. As religious leaders we are vessels of Christ,

8. Wawa Aba Institute is an initiative linked to TFAM, aiming to use the womanist theological tradition to develop leadership skills of lesbian, bisexual and queer women. See its Facebook page, www.facebook.com/Wawainstit ute. See also the interview with Pastor Caroline who is involved in Wawa Aba Institute Kenya (Story 1).

and we are in people's lives because God has put us there to be used so that the people can reach God. It would be very bad to be chosen as a vessel and then not being available for others; your purpose won't be fulfilled. Even when we talk about homophobic people and the way they challenge us and our work, we have to remember the biggest commandment that Christ left us with, which is love. So, for the kingdom to get filled, we need to show and preach love. Can we be a little more accommodating just like how our God is, for the purpose of God's kingdom?

We need to remember that God does not make mistakes and if God wanted only heterosexuals or only homosexuals in the world, he would have created it without sexual and gender diversity. God is not boxed in the way humans box God and want God to be like them. We need to have faith. Faith is key because no one has ever seen God, but he has spoken to us, and we have read the Bible and therefore believe. We are then gradually nurtured into that faith. If people start saying, God should be like this, they are forgetting that God is a designer, and he has created us the way he wants us to be. So, homophobic preachers bring their reasoning and biases and impose them on God. It seems that these preachers deliberately do not want to understand. They may even be reading scriptures, but they deliberately do not want to understand God's love and be inclusive. It is however important to add that LGBTIQ people do not need to seek sympathy or justification from religious leaders. Sympathy for what? The love that God has for LGBTIQ people is enough for us. That love is like a miracle that cannot be explained physically or medically. God is the perfect designer! He created everyone differently. So, how can you question how he created this one? The Bible says that we were all created in the image of God in our diversity![9] That is the beauty and the blessing of God.

My hope is in Jesus Christ. God expects me to be the servant of his people. All promises are there in the Bible, and God speaks at every point of our lives. Faith gives me hope as well as perseverance. You know that you will be hit, but do not put your trust in human beings, instead put it in God. Those are the words God has given to me. If God is at the centre of every Christian in this world, if he is really the centre, hate will go down. The homophobic hatred and preaching, the killings and violence against minorities, it will go down. Because love can capture and overcome everything, the jealousy, the homophobia and all that. If

9. Gen. 1.27.

love is at the centre of every Christian affiliated to Jesus Christ, hatred will have no place.

Lastly let me say that in the LGBTIQ community many people have come to hate God because they have been presented with a God who is a hater. I would love them to know that God is not like that. God says, 'Come to me the way you are'. Even before he created you, he knew you in and out, and hence he says, 'Come to me whoever you are and with whatever you have'. God has never said to us, 'Go away!' Yet, our people are chased away from the church. I would love so much that our people would come to know God; that they could have hope. In order to do our work as faith leaders, we have to bring people to God and teach his principles. We need more spaces, gatherings, workshops and seminars for LGBTIQ people where they can learn that God loves them.

Story 7

PASTOR DERON: 'THE LORD HAS A REASON WHY I AM A TRANSWOMAN'

Pastor Deron is pastor at a ministry led by transgender women in Kampala, Uganda. Knowing of the many difficulties and burdens that trans people, and LGBTIQ people more generally, face in Uganda, Pastor Deron is committed to building a fellowship of healing and love where members can regain their faith in God. In this story, she speaks about her strong sense of calling and her strong faith in God who is on the side of the vulnerable trans community. She expresses a firm hope for the future out of the conviction that 'the Lord will win the battle for us'.[1]

I am Pastor Deron. I am a transgender woman of twenty years old, and a minister of God. I call myself 'the chosen one'. I am a pastor at a ministry led by transgender women in Kampala, the capital city of Uganda. I serve God's people. I live at a shelter[2] because my parents wanted me to leave home, as they could not understand what I was. The way my mum used to look at me … She always had that expression like she was thinking, 'Deron, there is something wrong about you.' So, at least now, when I meet her, I can tell her that I am a minister and a preacher, and I hope she will respect me for that.

My journey of becoming a religious leader began in 2022. When I was at secondary school, I was not much interested into the LGBTIQ community. But when I finished my senior fourth grade, I became curious, and I approached the community. I wanted to see how other

1. This story is based on an interview with Pastor Deron on 20 January 2023 in Kampala, Uganda.

2. Shelter refers here to safe spaces organized by LGBTIQ community-based organizations that offer accommodation and support to community members.

people were doing there. But it was a bit of a shock, especially to see what people from my fellow transgender community were going through and to listen to their stories, very difficult stories; some were discriminated, some had been beaten up. This is particularly true when you have started taking hormones but you have not gone through surgery yet. You take hormones in order to become what you want to be, but at home people beat you or kick you out of the family. Some families may even try to kill you.

Our LGBTIQ community has many problems; we do not seem to fit within society. At times, when one of our transgender fellows dies, when we go to their home for the burial; on arrival, family members see us as the ones who led their child to live the life they did and the ones responsible for their death. Then they call the community to stone and kill us. Even in churches, pastors preach against LGBTIQ people and it is just painful to be a church member. It does not matter that we, LGBTIQ individuals, are full of love for people. In society, even people from your own community, they only see you as their downfall and they hate you for what you are. It is not possible to have a stable life in our communities.

I became a minister of God in order to address some of these challenges. I have been standing up with the ministry as a transwoman. In our own ministry we do not discriminate against anybody. This ministry has been created with the intention of welcoming any kind of person to the church. As the Bible says, we should be friend to everyone. So, the purpose of this ministry is to bring everybody to God and to be a place where there is no discrimination against transgender women or anybody else. My fellow trans people should be free to live the life they want, without suffering or being discriminated. This is particularly true for LGBTIQ people in Uganda, as we are people who love God and are the most likely to attend churches. Now, in our fellowship, we are free to encounter God. I am a pastor because I am part of God's plan. I joined our ministry because I have agreed to serve God. You cannot stand at the pulpit unless the Lord has called you. If the Lord tells me to go and speak to someone, I will have to go, regardless of whether I am their friend or enemy. The Lord also has a reason why I am a transwoman, and that reason is what will make me go forward. If I was pretending to be cisgender, I would not move forward. I know we shall all rise up and say 'Hallelujah'. And it is only God who drives all of us to live the lives that we live.

When I look back at my personal journey, thinking about how I grew up, I would not say that it was terrible as such. It was only when

I became a religious leader and heard other people's stories that I fully realized the magnitude of the challenges that trans women in Uganda face by being denied the opportunity to be who they are. Insecurity and hiding are the hallmarks of our lives; yet in God's presence there is no hiding. Security is so important to us and that is why we need more safe religious spaces where we can be ourselves. This is what motivated me to become a preacher. I often say that the Lord will take care of our enemies; that is why sometimes we see changes and even see parents coming to us, saying they are sorry for what they did when we were young. In my preaching, I tell my transgender women that even if society says that we are cursed, we have to know that we are not cursed, but instead we are a blessed.

There are joyful moments in my life, especially when I am with my fellow transgender women. Having people following me online for what I am, also gives me much happiness. I can be discriminated in my everyday life, but my online pages are growing and growing. On Facebook people are showing me love for who I am. We are ministering to a lot of people online, and there are also fellow pastors who love me the way I am. When people accept you the way you are, all the problems vanish. These are some of my happy moments. I also experience happy moments through the encounter with God, when the Lord talks to me and through me, he also speaks to many other people.

It causes me sadness not being able to advertise our religious events online. This is because if we do make public the place where we meet, people will search for this physical space and that would constitute a huge security risk. We do not want people showing up and questioning our ministry, or risk being visited by the police. Being arrested is a tangible risk to avoid. So, we manage those security risks by distributing invitations only through emails, which we send to those who we know, asking them to invite only people they know very well. This is limiting our growth as a church, but it also limits risks. We would love to be 'out and proud' but it is simply not possible in the current environment. We go on with our struggle while prioritizing security. I feel much pain when I find out that people who allegedly are friends, behind our back are scheming against you. One day I went home with my fellow transgender friends, some of whom had dressed in their gender conforming ways.[3] Personally, for security reasons, I did not. But when

---

3. Deron uses the term 'gender-conforming' here as meaning, conforming to one's gender identity rather than to one's biological sex.

we got there, people around started whispering to one another and we felt very insecure. When you dress in conformity with your gender identity, you feel so insecure. In that specific situation we had to ask everyone to be vigilant but even then, we were beaten by *boda boda* drivers.[4] It was so bad. Another story that bears much sadness to me, is about a fellow transwoman. She was coming to church on a *boda boda*. The driver called his fellow *boda boda* colleagues at the drop-off stop of the transwoman. These guys were waiting for her. When he dropped her, they drugged her and they beat her, undressed and humiliated her in the most extreme way. She was eventually taken to hospital and all we could do was praying for her.

My favourite message in the Bible is the command to love one another, even those who hurt us. We cannot force everyone to be our friend, but the Bible commands me to love you as my neighbour, so I have to do that, no matter the situation. If I have a neighbour that I love and she loves me in return, we have fulfilled our call by God. But even if you do not love me, I still have to love you. The book of Amos describes how it is impossible for everybody to be friends.[5] Nonetheless I have to love everyone. One day you could become my enemy, but that is part of the divine design. I am glad that there are haters because the Lord uses them to teach me and guide me. I have trust in the Lord. Even on my social media, people abuse me at times and say hateful things. So, I say to myself that these people are insulting me while I am ministering in God's presence and their action must be part of God's plan. Everybody has to have an enemy to guide you into the right direction because these people are being used by God in one way or another to bring me back to my right path. We must thank God for our enemies, as they are the messengers that God will use to guide us to the right path.

When I think of religious leaders who are against LGBTIQ inclusion, a particular personal experience comes to my mind. Someone once preached to me on a verse in Leviticus that says a man cannot lie with another man, but I stood up against that preaching. The Lord knows me as I am, and the Bible tells us what to do next. And the Bible says you are not the one who appointed yourself. God is the one who appointed you,

---

4. *Boda boda* are motorbike taxis used to carry a passenger and/or goods. They are commonly found in East Africa, where they are popular as an efficient and affordable form of transport.

5. Am. 3.3 reads: 'Do two walk together unless they have agreed to do so?' (NIV).

the one that gave you different gifts. There are ministers and bishops who oppose LGBTIQ people. All we need to do is to stand up and not pay attention to such leaders. We do not look at other people when we are serving God, we only look at God. When our spirit is filled, we stand up. I have to stand with my baggage of responsibilities and fight the battle for my Lord. Belief is the answer; if you believe that the Lord is with you, there is nothing else to worry about. A friend of mine from the western region of Uganda, came to church when I was preaching, and at that time she was going through a lot of pain. As I was praying in church, she was itchy all over her body. She then told me that when she surrendered her life during the last song, she got healed. From that experience we learned that the Lord only wants that we surrender our lives to him, and he will save us.

Some members of our community have given up their faith and may even have come to hate God. It is because they did not dedicate enough time to get to know God personally. What they were told about God in church affected their ability to really know and love God. We are all born loving God, but growing up we sometimes learn to hate him. We need to relearn to love, and when that happens, love will overcome all the pains that we face, and we will come back to the Lord. The Lord is using me and other pastors to teach LGBTIQ people to love again and to bring back faith into the life of people. LGBTIQ people should not pay attention to those religious leaders who oppose them. This is because the Lord knows each one of us LGBTIQ persons, even before we were in our mothers' wombs.[6] The Lord knew that we would be LGBTIQ people and he loves us the way we are. Even if you are a transwoman, God loves you. When I stand and preach in church, they do not attack me because the Lord does not look at my dressing. Instead, the Lord looks at my heart and wants that I fully love him and surrender to him. The dressing and the walking style do not matter but the heart does. So, all LGBTIQ people need to do is to surrender their hearts to God and all their mind and soul.

We should leave the homophobes alone and focus on serving God instead. We are blessed and anointed but the problem is that people assume that we only think about sex, that we are obsessed with going to bars or taking drugs. They do not see our spiritual side. If only everybody would pass through God's hands and would say, 'God, I am yours now, do everything you want with me; I surrender to you!', the Lord will do

6. This phrase is a reference to Ps. 139.13.

everything for us, and we shall be successful. Let us stop looking at what these pastors are saying about us. They will continue to call us names and say that we are cursed, but we know that we are blessed. So let us not pay attention at what they are saying because in God's presence we are blessed! They think we have nothing to say to God, but we are blessed and all we need to do is to claim these blessings. It is only God who has control over our lives. Therefore, we should stand and be still with our God. We should speak only one word and they would see the light. The Lord operates in LGBTIQ churches, he does not discriminate. To God we are all equal. The Bible tells me that we were all made in his image, how then can they discriminate against someone who is created in God's image? How can they preach against them?

All God's people are equal before God, and we are all made in the image of God. I do not think God will love you if you do not love me or if you decrease loving me. Instead of seeking reconciliation with homophobic pastors, we should invite them to stop discriminating because the Lord knows those who they are discriminating against. If they think that LGBTIQ people are not living according to God's ways, then they should keep loving them anyway, instead of fighting them. They cannot say they love the same people they are fighting. Moreover, they will never win because we are praying to God and God is fighting for us. As long as we continue serving God, they won't win their battle. We shall remain in God's presence until the very end. I want to be a voice of prophecy for LGBTIQ people, they are going to get a big ministry and many blessings so that they can see what the Lord wants them to be. Being transgenders does not mean that they cannot be great. Let them stand still. In this inclusive ministry the Lord will ensure that all forms of discriminations will be eliminated.

In my life I have gone through many challenges. When you begin to be successful, the Lord may bring some temptations to see if you are strong in your faith. But if you stand strong, he also fights with you, he cannot leave you alone. The Lord is there for us. We may not have money, but we can remain strong against the power of the evil one. The Lord will be there to support us. All these problems that we have been facing, the Lord will wipe them away regardless of the strong forces against us. Whether they are parents, presidents or politicians, the Lord will win the battle for us. And everything will be wonderful. Our parents will come to us, and they will love us the way we are. Even if a person does not have parents, the Lord will be there for them. I believe that those who have caused suffering to the LGBTIQ community, whether parents, family members or others in the society, eventually they will come back to us and ask for forgiveness as the Lord will answer their prayers. Everything happens for a reason and there is a reason for what we are going through. God already knows what will happen next. It is all in God's plans. All we need to do is to surrender to God. We need to look to God and follow his commandments and all will be well. I look forward to praying to God so that we can get a church that is inclusive for everybody, where transgender women will be able to minister to all the people in society, not just to LGBTIQ communities.

Story 8

BISHOP JAMES: 'SOME OF US ARE MARTYRS BY DOING THIS WORK'

Bishop James is the founder and presiding bishop of a Pentecostal church in a rural area in the central region of Uganda. Since founding his ministry in 2003, his church grew, and Bishop James rose to being an overseer of a network of churches in the district. Closeted at that time, he started ministering LGBTIQ youths attending his church and gradually became involved in the movement of inclusive and affirming ministry. After being outed, he lost his position as a district bishop and the membership of his church dwindled. Yet, despite many challenges, Bishop James narrates in this story that he remains committed to his calling. Invoking the history of the Ugandan martyrs, he suggests that LGBTIQ leaders such as himself are the martyrs of today but may one day be respected and celebrated.[1]

We planted our church in June 2003. That is when the ministry began – almost nineteen years today. Before that, I was pastor of a church in Kampala, which I left out of the conviction that I had to move to this place in the rural area. I came here and started the church. We started in a humble way and by the grace of God we bought this land and managed to put up this cathedral. At first, we were praying under a tree, then we graduated to a simple shelter which we built with our hands – we were involved in making the bricks and I was being helped by a group of youth. My work has been so much inspired by the youth, and this is the gift that God gave me, because most of the people who come here are the youth. The place is amazing, as you can see, but this has

---

1. This story is based on an interview with Bishop James on 19 January 2023 in Central Region, Uganda.

been our own sweat. God gave us this opportunity of building a place where to praise him.

We also had been working with fellow born-again churches in the area. Finally, we had come together and decided to create a leadership body that could coordinate the work. My name was proposed and before I knew it, I was elected as the overseer of the council of born-again churches in the district which I led for seven years. At that time, I did not expose my sexuality to anyone, nobody here knew that I was gay, and I never talked about these issues. But as the work in our church was progressing many youths came and joined our ministry. During my work of pastoral care, I came to know that some of them were gay. I could not share this with the others, as of course it is confidential. Yet it is how I slowly started my advocacy, undercover because I had still not come out. Among the new youth members was a group of about twenty who were LGBTIQ. So, I started handling them differently. I got to know them, and I would encourage them to remain focused and serve God. Our mission as a church is to love God and all his people, demonstrating God's character as we go forth to reveal Christ to our community. That is our mission, we love God and all his people irrespective of their gender, their sexuality and other such characteristics. Our church is a welcoming place for all, a very special place of worship and home for all to experience the love of God. Everybody here feels free, welcome into Christ's family and allowed to respond to his grace.

In 2016, I had an opportunity to attend a meeting in Kampala that was organized by St. Paul's Reconciliation and Equality Centre.[2] There I came into contact with other LGBTIQ inclusive religious leaders in Uganda, one of whom was a Catholic priest. I was very encouraged to see other religious leaders doing the same work I was doing and some of whom identified as LGBTIQ. After that workshop I received a phone call from the Catholic priest telling me that he had been invited at the US Embassy where he had given phone numbers of religious leaders who are inclusive of LGBTIQ people in their congregation. He wanted to inform me so that I would not distress should I get a call from the Embassy. After a week I received a call from the Embassy, and I was invited to a meeting with the cultural officer. At the meeting the cultural

2. St. Paul's Reconciliation and Equality Centre was founded in 2010 by Bishop Christopher Senyonjo in Kampala, Uganda, to provide pastoral counselling to members of the LGBTIQ community. At the time of writing, it is no longer active.

officer told me that they had identified me as one of the church leaders in Uganda supporting minority groups and wanted to know more about that work. I explained what we are doing here, including supporting orphans and youths who have been thrown out of their homes, helping them to live dignified lives. Besides, it is my greatest desire to see the future generation of youth knowing that they can be whatever God has designed them to be. On my way back home, I received a call indicating that I had been selected as one of the religious leaders to participate in the International Visitor and Leadership programme to take place in the United States in August 2016. The theme was 'The role of faith-based organizations in a diverse democracy'. In total we were seven Ugandan religious leaders who participated in that workshop. That programme turned my life around. I gained greater understanding about LGBTIQ human rights. We visited several cities in the United States, such as New York, San Francisco, and Washington, DC, and got connected to so many people, one of whom was Bishop Joseph Tolton of TFAM.[3] After my return from the United States, I organized several meetings with LGBTIQ religious leaders and allies, and out of that the Universal Coalition of Affirming Africans (UCAA) was formed, which was fully registered as an NGO on 30 June 2017. I served as a co-founder and have stayed involved up today.[4] UCAA's mission is to advocate for and promote LGBTIQ rights through changing people's mindset about LGBTIQ+ realities, engaging with their different faith denominations and cultural beliefs.

For a long time while serving as a pastor and even a bishop, I had not disclosed my sexual orientation to my family or even my wife. But as I ministered to the LGBTIQ youths in my ministry and later got connected to other LGBTIQ inclusive religious leaders, it was inevitable that word would get out. Actually, it was my wife who brought it out. My wife discovered that I was gay and that I was supporting gay people here in the church and that I also collaborating with others outside. She went public about it, and it was horrible. So many of the members said that I should step down. I stepped down as the presiding bishop of

3. Bishop Joseph Tolton is part of The Fellowship of Affirming Ministries (TFAM), a US organization with African American roots aiming to promote a progressive and inclusive form of Christianity (see Lewin 2018; van Klinken 2017). Tolton is in charge of TFAM Global, spearheading TFAM's work in various African countries.

4. TFAM.

the district but not here at this church, which after all I had established myself. Although I first denied that I was gay, with time I decided to come out. First, I disclosed to my children because I thought it was better to start with my own children. While the small LGBTIQ group in the church already knew, the majority in the church did not know. Their initial reaction was not so bad – they said that it was OK. But my wife took them aside and told them not to side with me, and then they left me. Many members of the church left when my wife disclosed it to them. I remained with a few faithful members, most of whom are not even gay, but they continued to believe that I, Bishop James, am a man of God. They said that it was the devil trying to divide the ministry. We remained with about thirty members. There were those who were asking me to leave and forget about this ministry because now the entire community knew that I was gay and was collaborating with other people in Uganda, and they feared that I may be killed. But God has called me to stand here and create space for young LGBTIQ people to feel celebrated, empowered and joyful. I do feel grieved for the childhood I did not get to live. I do know very well that the homophobic and transphobic people are ready to accuse and attack us, but that cannot stop me. Also, here I had these LGBTIQ people who were now helpless – how could I leave them? So, up to this day we continue with the work. The journey has been challenging but we believe in God, and we are still believing that God will show his goodness in this land of the living. Yes, we only have a few members, but they are committed members. This congregation is not only for LGBTIQ but it is for all, we have people from different backgrounds.

Even through all these challenges, I do have happy moments. One of these happy moments was when we organized a gathering and invited many of our fellow LGBTIQ community working in different parts of the country. They came here and it was like a large get together. Some people from the local community, and even some local government and political leaders, joined us at the event. It was a wonderful moment, and we celebrated a lot. Another happy moment was when this church was officially opened in 2021. It was a wonderful moment to see that despite everything, God had seen us through. Here we were and the work is done and the people coming here know who we are – it is not that they do not know or understand. We frequently welcome new members who come to join us. Some of them only come for one service, and then they disappear – especially when some neighbours taunt them, saying, 'Have you now decided to join those people, those are gay people. Do not you fear they will indoctrinate you or spoil your kids?' People fabricate all kind of stories about us, but God knows the truth. The more unfounded hate they spit in my face, the stronger I become.

When I look at scripture, I find my favourite story in the Bible to be of Joseph and of David and Jonathan, about how they were so close. Even after Jonathan had passed on, David could not forget his close friend and the vows they had exchanged. Then, there is also the story of Joseph and how his family turned against him and persecuted their very own, not knowing that this guy would be the saviour of the entire family. These stories have really shaped my life because when you see Joseph for instance, he never cried for the pain that was inflicted on him by his own family. He decided to let it go and serve them. It resonates so much with my story, given what I have gone through, and the pain inflicted on me by my own family – the person I thought would be my close friend, my wife, as well as my children – and my church members and see them turn against me. This could have caused a mental breakdown, but I have decided to let it go.

We will continue serving and loving everybody no matter their background. We will continue loving everybody – because that is our mission, to love God and all his people no matter their background. Even these people who inflicted pain on us, if they want, they can still come back, and we will welcome them. We have no problems with them, we do not regard them as devils – we do not see them in the same angle as they see us. Joseph never did. If Joseph could not hold anything against his brothers, we also should not hold anything against our community. We love them and we say they should also love us the same way we do but it is entirely up to them. I also advise LGBTIQ people to be forgiving like Joseph because forgiveness is the best medicine. However, they should not continue going to churches that hurt them. They should instead identify those churches that regard them as human beings. They should go to churches which believe and treat them as children of God, because you are justified by faith not by your sexuality. Gender and sexuality are not issue of primary significance to the Christian faith. No one's salvation hinges on what we do, think or believe regarding gender or sexuality.

What inspires religious leaders who are opposed to LGBTIQ inclusion is the story of Sodom and Gomorrah and the way they interpret it. They call LGBTIQ people an abomination, saying they are the reason why an entire race was wiped out. However, when you read Ezekiel, you find out that it is not true.[5] The sin of Sodom and Gomorrah was not about sexuality was about their hateful behaviour

5. Ezek. 16.49.

towards strangers. It had nothing to do with sexuality but with injustice towards strangers and a failure of hospitality. I have come to realize that religious leaders who are against LGBTIQ inclusion do not want to listen. They come up with their own interpretation and are not willing to listen. So, refusing to listen and learn is a choice. That is why they just come up with their judgement, they humiliate and bring you down so that you do not have anything to say.

But when you see these incidents of Joseph you find that he decided to use the greatest weapon – love. You remember that our Lord Jesus said, 'A new command I give you: Love one another. As I have loved you, so you must love one another. By this everyone will know that you are my disciples, if you love one another.'[6] And the Apostle Paul writes, 'Love never fails. But where there are prophecies, they will cease; where there are tongues, they will be stilled; where there is knowledge, it will pass away.'[7] So, this is the greatest weapon LGBTIQ people need to use: love. I see love as the only weapon we need to use. Remember, 'For God so loved the world that he gave his one and only Son, that whoever believes in him shall not perish but have eternal life.'[8] God did not send his son to condemn the world but for the world to be saved through him. So, if God did not send Christ to condemn us, then who are you to condemn those who are not condemned by God?

There are a few inclusive religious leaders who are like Nicodemus: they do not want to come out and be seen in public as being supportive of LGBTIQ people.[9] Some of them come to tell me, 'We know what you are going through. It is horrible. We do not see any problem with the work you are doing.' Yet, they will not defend me in public. I think they fear to lose the privileges attached to their current work because they tell me, 'This is how I make money to support my family; I cannot cut off the hand that feeds me.' Some of them are even part of the LGBTIQ community themselves, and we work together. But they only come when we organize workshops somewhere else, and they will say, 'Please bishop, do not out me, please.' At first, it made me mad, and I would tell them they were hypocrites. But I now do understand them, because a place like here in Uganda is so hostile, it is not easy unless you have decided, like I did, to accept what may come. I have

6. Jo. 13.34–35.

7. 1 Cor. 13.8.

8. Jo. 3.16.

9. Nicodemus is a pharisee who came to see Jesus secretly at night (see Jo. 3).

decided to stand out, and if I end up becoming a martyr, to God be the glory. We must dare to go where others have not dared to go. You know, we have martyrs in Uganda.[10] Many Christians have come to respect and celebrate the Ugandan martyrs. Today, some of us are martyrs by doing this work. It gives me hope and courage that yes, the ground may not be conducive, but we stand our ground and will not run away from this country where we started our work. This is Africa and as Africans we must stand our ground and do the work and prove to the world that being LGBTIQ is not foreign or evil but Godly. It is how God who has designed us with different colours yet as one people.

There are many challenges facing us as an affirming church but our commitment to LGBTIQ human rights remain the same. We are dedicated to being the church that God has called us to be. We shall continue to be dedicated and we appreciate whatever support we receive from people who are standing with us, some of them may not even be in Uganda. They are a great encouragement. It gives me hope to know that I am not alone. We have a crowd of witnesses who support and pray for us – even if they are not able to support us financially, they are standing with us nevertheless. I see a bright future for Africa. In those olden days, we did not use to see many people being open about their sexual orientation, and we did not even have churches of our own. An openly queer person could not open a ministry and head a church. But now things are different. I have begun to see pastors and bishops supporting us. So, I see the future is bright even if it will not be a one day or one year event. Things change slowly, but change will surely happen. I do have hope and faith in what I am doing and what others like me are doing out there serving the minorities. I know they are really giving out their lives and their best. The ground may not be conducive as of now, but we cannot just fold our hands and wait for that land to be ready.

10. Bishop James is referring here to the martyrs of Uganda, who are recognized by both the Anglican and the Catholic churches. They were pages in the royal court of the Buganda Kingdom and were among the first converts to Christianity in Uganda, in the late nineteenth century. They were executed on orders of the Buganda King, for reasons linked in some sources to their refusal to meet the king's sexual demands. The shrines of the martyrs in Namugongo, Kampala, are sites of pilgrimage and their memory plays a complex role in current discourses regarding homosexuality in Uganda (see Rao 2015).

Part 2

STORIES OF LGBTIQ-ALLIED RELIGIOUS LEADERS

Story 9

PASTOR SILVANA: 'MY ROLE IS TO BE A TREE THAT BEARS FRUITS'

Pastor Silvana ministers in a Pentecostal church in coastal Kenya. Thanks to a training about sexual and gender minorities, she has developed her understanding of LGBTIQ persons and has come to include them in her ministry. This is inspired by her renewed reading of the Bible, which tells her that God's creation in all its diversity is fundamentally good, and that Jesus's ministry was inclusive towards the marginalized. Having been raised in a Muslim context, Silvana converted to Christianity against her mother's wish. This has strengthened her belief that people should be able to identify and express themselves the way they choose. In this story, she narrates how she sees her role as a religious leader as a tree bearing fruits of justice and freedom in society.[1]

I was born in Kilifi County in coastal Kenya. My father was born as a Christian, but my mother was a Muslim, so my father converted. We were raised in an Islamic setting. As a young child I was brought up as a Muslim, but my heart never was really into Islam. Even the rites of worship and fasting, my heart was not responding to it. Instead, I was attracted to Christianity from childhood. At secondary school, when I could hear young people in the Christian Union (CU) singing gospel songs and praying, I knew that was where I belonged.[2] One day, my father reconverted to Christianity, but my mother remained a Muslim. Because she had named me after her own mother, she felt that of all her children, I was the last one who could become Christian. At

---

1. This story is based on an interview with Pastor Silvana (pseudonym) on 20 December 2022 in Mombasa, Kenya.
2. CU is an evangelical and charismatic Christian student movement.

school I would find it hard to resist participating in CU meetings, and when my mother would hear of it, she would beat me with a big cane. Later she assigned one of my brothers the role of caning me every time I joined CU meetings. I could be caned but still found myself singing and praying. It was not an easy journey. When I joined high school at a boarding school away from home, I took my chance and converted to Christianity. I gave my life to Christ. When I went home, I told my mum that I was now a born-again Christian and that is my stand, regardless of the outcome. I also prayed for my mum so that she could become born-again. I did not want my mum to die before accepting Christ as her Lord and Saviour. Luckily, she accepted Jesus Christ in 1993 and in November the same year she passed on. So, I glorified God because my prayer was that she knew Christ before she would pass on.

Even before I converted to Christianity, I could just see myself leading worship songs and doing service in the church, but I never thought of it as leadership in the church. It was just a feeling. But after converting to Christianity, the CU patron at my school saw something in me and he gave me an opportunity to serve as Bible study coordinator. I would be coordinating Bible study for form one and two pupils. I also initiated prayer and fasting meetings every Friday, and early on Saturday morning we would gather to pray for the Lord's presence in our school. Through all these activities, the CU became very strong. So strong that the patron commented how since the establishment of CU in the school, our class had done tremendous work. By the time I was finishing high school, I was already a preacher and I had gone through some Bible trainings. Indeed, the CU patrons presented me with a Bible as my parting gift.

After high school, I returned home and stayed there for about five years before joining college. During this time, I was serving in the church by teaching Sunday schools, leading praise and worship and participating in the intercession group. I liked serving God. I knew that I would serve God in the church. What I did not know is which role in the church I would major in. This is because I was a very good singer, but I was also a very good organizer. It was not until I got married and had children, and had joined another church in Mombasa, that a fellow church member asked me a question, 'Silvana, do you know you are gifted and your area of work is in the body of Christ?' I responded by saying that I only knew that I was good at singing and worship. But he said, 'No, you have more to offer.' He then asked me to look at the gifts listed in Ephesians and he said, singing is not mentioned anywhere, yet it does mention prophecy and evangelism.[3] So, he made me think, and he encouraged me to fast for three days so that God could reveal to me what role I could play in building the kingdom of God. After the third day we went to a *kesha*,[4] and it turned out that the pastor and his associate were not there. It was just a handful of us present. So, the friend I was with said, 'This is your time, you are going to lead the service and preach.' I initially refused, but he said that God wanted me to do something. So, I preached and the *kesha* was so successful that by morning no one wanted to go home. When the pastor heard about this later that day, she called me and said that she had been given testimony that I was a powerful preacher. She then instructed me to preach the next morning in church. So, that is how I began serving, and how God started using me. And with time the senior pastor gave me so many opportunities to preach, and God was using me in a powerful way. I became assistant pastor until I began my own church.

Now it happened that one day I was called by a bishop, a friend of mine, and he told me that he had been invited to a meeting in Mombasa which, because of other commitments, he could not attend. He asked if I could go and represent him. I asked him what the meeting was about, but he did not know. He asked me to just go and later give him a report about it. When I went to the meeting, I found many religious leaders present. The meeting was being moderated by Ishmael, the PEMA Kenya leader.[5] There were also several young men and women at the meeting. Ishmael began by discussing discrimination and judgement that many marginalized groups face. This was well received by the religious leaders, and they were willing to listen. But when he introduced the issue of LGBTIQ and began to open up, people actually realized that this is what the meeting was about, and hell broke loose. Religious leaders became very angry, shouting 'Why did you call us for this? It's a blasphemy!' People were making lots of noise. I found myself pleading with my fellow religious leaders, asking them, 'Can we keep quiet and listen to what we have been called for? If at the end of the meeting you decide you are not interested, you go your own way and do

---

3. Eph. 4.11: 'Christ himself gave the apostles, the prophets, the evangelists, the pastors and teachers.'

4. *Kesha* is a Shahili word for overnight prayer meetings which are popular in Pentecostal-Charismatic churches.

5. PEMA Kenya is a Mombasa-based organization advancing the rights of gender and sexual minorities.

not come back again. There are so many things we can learn here if we listen.' So, they listened to me and from that point, Ishmael was looking at how I was pleading with my fellow religious leaders and managed to calm them down how and make them stay until the end.

When I went home, I sat down and asked myself, 'Am I really up for this? Will I be able to listen and support LGBTIQ people and other things that the Bible has actually prohibited and condemned?' Yet, I also realized that Jesus does not mention anything about homosexuality. I like to research, so I went to see what the Bible says about it and tried to establish what God's attitude about it is. I found that little was mentioned about LGBTIQ people in the Bible. But Genesis made me think twice, even thrice.[6] This is because after God's creation, the Bible says he looked at all his creation and he saw that it was good. God looked at all his creation, that is everything he had created, and saw it was good. I asked myself, where did the homosexuals come from? Where did the intersex come from? Are they not part of God's creation? After that I began to challenge myself to appreciate everything that God has created. Because if God appreciated whatever he did, who am I not to? I also needed to appreciate everything that God has created, provided that it does not get me out of God's will. From that moment I began to make an effort, working to make sure that we all live in a safe place and secure environment. Later I received another invitation from PEMA Kenya to go for a five-day training, which is when I came to learn about the reasons why some people are gay, lesbian or intersex. I never knew. When I went for that training, I got a lot of information which helped me up to today and that is where my journey began. So, when religious leaders were asked to be human rights defenders and support LGBTIQ persons I found myself there and I remain there until today.

What continues to motivate me is in doing this work is God's word which says that we should not discriminate. God does not show partiality. He loves everybody. So, who am I to discriminate? Who am I to say, these people are from God, and these are from the devil? I am not called for that. Judgement belongs to God. There is a parable in Matthew where Jesus compares the kingdom of heaven to the owner of the farm who went to plant good seed but at night, an enemy came and planted the bad ones.[7] When the farmer was asking God what to do, he was told: let both grow together until the harvest, there will come

---

6. Gen. 1.31: 'God saw all that he had made, and it was very good.'
7. Matt. 13.24–30.

a time when God uproots the bad ones and stays with the good ones. So, I am not here to judge. Whatever was planted, it is not me who planted it. It is God who planted and even if it is not God, it is not my business to know who planted. There is also the story about that young man who was born blind in the Bible and after Jesus prayed for him, he got healed.[8] The disciples were asking Jesus, now between this young boy and the parents, who sinned? Who contributed to this young man being born blind? And Jesus said, none of them, neither the mother nor the son, but this happened so that God can be glorified. So certain things are happening so that God can be glorified and for us to know the purpose of God in our lives. So, what makes me to continue this journey is the realization that I am not here to judge. I am not here to discriminate or to side-line other people and to make them more or less important than others. We all are created in God's image and likeness, no matter whether the person is intersex, lesbian or not. I normally say, somebody's sexuality is not my problem. My concern is to make sure that regardless of one's sexuality and everything, you embrace God, you value God and you walk according to God's law.

My association with LGBTIQ people and the rapport that we have built with them is actually wonderful because they trust me as a religious leader, and we are able to walk together. One day I opened up to them and I told them that I do not discriminate against them but am ready to accommodate them. From then on, we have shared so many stories and we pray together. They now trust that this pastor can pray for them, and they take me in confidence. If I cannot give moral support to those that need it most, then I have failed as a pastor. Even with the joy that comes with being an inclusive religious leader, there is pain that comes from being discriminated against by those who criticize LGBTIQ people. Sometimes I get tagged in messages saying, you know, nowadays pastors are spoiled. When that happens, I go home and meditate, wondering whether I should leave this work. Then another thought comes in telling me to just press on. There are times I feel like I should abandon this work, but then God comes in and I just soldier on. What inspires me to soldier on is the story of the prodigal son who had left his father's house.[9] The father had all reasons to tell him not to come back to his household because he had already given him everything he wanted. Yet when the young man passes through

8. Jo. 9.
9. Lu. 15.11–32.

difficulties, he realized what he has done, and he remembers his father who always looked after him. So, he said, let me go back to see if he will accept me as a servant. He came back to the father not to be received as a son, but as a servant, yet the father had mercy and compassion. He was a caring father, and the reception was so encouraging, 'I thank God that my son was dead, but now he is alive. He was lost but now is found.' So, if the father in this parable could actually forgive his son instead of judging him, who are we to judge others? This story helps me to understand that Jesus could walk with any person and even visited Zacchaeus' house.[10] If he could walk with these characters, who am I to choose who to walk with? If he could provide the services that were needed at the time, who am I to refuse to provide the services needed today? The father of the prodigal son accepted the son back, then who am I not to embrace the LGBTIQ people and give them the support they require? These stories encourage me to be a person that accepts diversity. It does not matter where you come from, your tribe or your sexuality, but your joy brings me happiness. When you are sad, I cannot be happy. The Bible asks us how we can love God who we cannot see, if we cannot love the people that we see every day.[11] The first thing to show love to God, is by loving any other persons. So, their joy has to be my joy, their cry is my cry, and this is what love is.

Some pastors who say they want to convert LGBTIQ people are actually torturing them. Instead of torturing them, we should try to understand and interpret the Bible correctly. In Leviticus for example, we do not know the context when these verses were written. In many cases when we interpret the Bible, we have to know the context. You do not just read one verse and interpret the verse independently of other verses. Instead, you read other verses before it and after it and then try to derive the message of the writer.

When I look at the Bible, many verses speak about love, coming together, that we are one body, and that you should not discriminate. It reminds us that everyone one of us has a part to play in the kingdom of God. So, if we think LGBTIQ are bad people, who will help them? If anything, should we not embrace the LGBTIQ and bring them closer to Christ? Should we be the ones discriminating against them? Is that what we are really called to do? Are we not using these scriptures to justify

---

10. Lu. 19.1-10. Zacchaeus was a tax collector working for the Roman occupier, and thus despised by his Jewish community.

11. 1 Jo. 4.20.

our own hearts of hate and discrimination? For me, I think we should sit down with them and understand why they are the way they are.

When I gave my life to Christ and was called to be a pastor, I was not told to be religious leader for straight people only. I did not get any specification that only straight people will follow Christ. We have been told to never get tired of doing good, of helping because that is where God is. Many a times, minority groups are the ones we are obligated to embrace unconditionally. This is because they do not have hope. Who will come to their aid and give them hope if we do not. They have passed through so much trauma. Who can help them to overcome these traumas and live a hopeful life? It is us religious leaders.

This is because we preach the word of God that gives hope. The word of God does not discriminate; instead, it embraces love. The story that encourages me very much in this work is the story of the good Samaritan, about the guy who was beaten by thugs to a point of death. The priest ignored him, someone else also comes along and ignores him, while they belonged to the same group. It is only when a Samaritan, who had no relationship with him, passes, that he receives help. A priest is the one supposed to be a helper, yet in this story he does not. Imagine, what does it say about me as a religious leader when I hold a Bible and preach life to the people, but I ignore an actual person who needs life support? Is that just, is that truthful? If I cannot help you, who needs me? If you read the Bible and you understand it, you get to many insights that you need to help the LGBTIQ and not to discriminate against them – precisely because they are already discriminated against in society. I have been in situations myself where I needed help and did not receive it. It was after I had completed school and needed money to continue at college. My dad had the money, but for some reason he did not want to support my studies. Perhaps because I was a young woman and he thought I would get married soon. At that time, I felt no one cared or loved me. Even God seemed to have forgotten about me. In the end, my brothers helped me to go back to college, but I had a lot of pain in my heart. God healed me of my pain. But still when I meet someone who is in pain, I am reminded of what I went through. I cry on their behalf even before they start crying. The pain of being neglected, of being discriminated against. It is painful and that is what LGBTIQ people go through. They need us, they need us to embrace them.

If I can use an image, it would be of a tree. A tree has green leaves, and its flowers are all bright. This is because of the coordination between the trunk and the roots. The roots are tapping the water and nutrients and they make the tree to blossom. My Godly foundations are the roots, and this foundation is what helps me to bring the nutrients – spiritual energy and support – to the trunk and branches. After this, there will be fruits. Fruits are when I see LGBTIQ persons being happy and pursuing their lives, not being discriminated in access to services. They are living full human lives, they are not hiding or fearing in the society. My role as a religious leader is to be such a tree, and to help bear such fruits. I see the energy that God has given to me as a root cause helping LGBTIQ people to live good lives in freedom and in wholeness. We are already seeing some fruits. For example, we have gone to service providers, police and even the chiefs, making them aware of the needs of LGBTIQ people, and the message is being received. In the future, I hope to see more fruits coming through. LGBTIQ people will be accepted in every part of society – they will get jobs and not be discriminated and will be treated as any other person and their sexuality or gender identity will not matter at all. That will be a very good situation. May the trees be bearing an abundance of fruits!

Story 10

PASTOR NEEMA: 'MY TASK IS TO RESPECT DIVINITY AS REFLECTED IN EACH OF US'

Pastor Neema is an ordained minister in one of the mainline Protestant denominations churches in Kenya. As a single mother in a patriarchal institution, she has had her own struggle with the church. Perhaps for that reason, she sympathizes strongly with LGBTIQ people. She is committed to a method of biblical interpretation that does not take the Bible literally on issues of gender and sexuality, but that approaches the text critically in its historical and cultural context. As she narrates in this story, in her theology and pastoral ministry Pastor Neema seeks to affirm what she believes is the Bible's core message – the message of God's unconditional love.[1]

My journey to become a pastor started very early, when I joined Sunday school. There I developed an interest in all issues related to the church and faith. But since my parents were very poor, they did not want me to become a pastor; instead, I did accountancy courses and worked at a bank. But deep inside, I really wanted to become a pastor. At some point, I resigned from the bank and went to university to read theology. That is how my journey started. I am really passionate about being a pastor and helping people, especially those who suffer. I was ordained in my denomination about ten years ago, and I have really enjoyed pastoring ever since. It has not been an easy journey because our churches are very patriarchal and women in leadership are not always appreciated. For me, personally, it has been especially challenging to go to the church elders and having to tell them that I am a single mother

---

1. This story is based on an interview with Pastor Neema (pseudonym) on 13 January 2023 in Nairobi, Kenya.

with a child. It was very hard to go through. I interviewed for so many positions before I managed to become a minister.

As a pastor, I like to preach because it allows me to speak to people directly. I thank God that I am a trained theologian because 98 per cent of pastors in Kenya have not been trained theologically and their reading of the scriptures is literal. What I mean is, if you read the Bible in a literal way, you easily make mistakes. But when you do exegesis, you are able to get the key meaning of the text.[2] A good example is when the Bible says that women should not speak in church.[3] It is very important to understand the history of that text, its background, what the mood was at the time of writing, and why Paul was saying that in that precise context. Only in this way you can really understand what Paul meant when he said that women could not speak in church. And from there, you can begin to think about whether or not it is applicable today. I do not think this single verse should be taken as a general rule that women are never supposed to speak in any church setting.

Look, for example, at the story of Lydia in the Bible.[4] Lydia was distributing food and clothes, that was a leadership skill in her society. She also assisted Paul the apostle. So, that means that women could be leaders. When you say that women should not be leaders, you have to know that Lydia was given leadership responsibilities. Another example is Priscilla, the wife to Aquila.[5] Of the six times that the couple is mentioned in the Bible, five times Priscilla is mentioned first. It shows that she must have had a leadership role in the Christian community. The prominent mention of her name may have been because she was the head of that district or cell group. Probably the Bible wants you to consider Priscilla as the key person. You remember even when Paul came from Rome, he stayed with Pricilla and Aquila. So, Priscilla was a teacher to Paul, and she was also a teacher to Apollo. Therefore, you cannot disregard one gender and say that women should not do this or that. Then you do feminist hermeneutics, you get to know that women were leaders at some point. This way you will understand that when you say women should not speak in church, that is a wrong reading of the scriptures.

2. Exegesis is a technical term for the process of interpreting a text, specifically of scripture.

3. 1 Cor. 14.34; 1 Tim. 2.12.

4. Act. 16.14–15.

5. Act. 18.

The problem we are having today in Kenya, is that many religious leaders do not go to theological universities, so they are not trained and as a result they are reading the Bible literally. If the Bible says remove the eye, they remove it; or the story about Sodom and Gomorrah, they read it at face value as being about homosexuality. While even Jesus in the New Testament does not mention that at all when referring to what happened to those cities.[6] When you go to school and study exegesis, you start to recognize that biblical texts have developed before they were written down, and even when they were written down, we ended up with slightly different versions as they were copied, because it was all handwritten. So, the meaning is not always as linear and obvious as it might appear at first sight.

If you are not trained as a theologian, you will bring so many things into the text which have no relevance, and you end up victimizing people, who should not have been victimized. Because when you look at the story about Sodom and Gomorrah, homosexuality was not actually the sin. Instead, it is a horrible story about rape of guests who came to visit these cities. Yet, many untrained pastors use this story to claim that the Bible says that homosexuals do not belong to God, and that homosexuality will incite God's wrath. That is very wrong. But once you have been trained theologically, you will be able to understand what these verses really mean. You will look from the Old Testament to the New Testament and see what the text means without fighting with other people. The background to the story of Sodom and Gomorrah is a tradition that when guests would be visiting you, your neighbours would come to meet your guests, welcome them and share a meal with them. That was the background, but in the case of Sodom and Gomorrah, this tradition is disrespected in the most terrible way. Lot's neighbours come to his house, not to greet his guests and welcome them, but do demand that they sleep with them! This is why the cities are destroyed, not because of homosexuality but because of inhospitality and cruelty towards visitors. When you are doing exegesis, you want to know where the text is coming from and what its cultural background is. But in popular interpretations today, instead of doing exegesis people are doing eisegesis, that is, they bring their own meaning into the text. Thus, instead of pastors extracting the real meaning from the text, they impose their thinking on it, their own homophobia, which leads to very poor theology. Then it becomes a story about how God is finishing the

6. E.g. Matt. 10.15.

town because of rampant homosexuality. We should not do theology
that way.

I feel dispirited when our senior pastors start preaching about
LGBTIQ people and say that they do not belong to God. I ask myself,
why did God create them in the first place? In Jeremiah we read that we
were created long before we were in our mother's womb![7] If God never
wanted that community to exist, then they would not have been here.
But God has created them, and in fact gave them great attributes, like
many of them are musicians and artists, and many of them love God.
So, who are we to judge them? It is only God who can judge. I have
to say however, that like many others, before I became theologically
trained, I was also condemning LGBTIQ people. But when I went to
university and began interrogating the texts, I found the story to be
different. For instance, when I looked at Genesis and read about God
creating a man and a woman, I asked myself, what about the intersex
people? Who created the intersex? I then also learned that in Genesis
we have two parallel creation narratives, from the Yahwistic tradition
and the Elohistic tradition; one talks of a woman being created from
man's ribs while the other does not have hierarchical sequence of
creation but rather says that God created humankind as male and
female.[8] I interrogate the creation stories as an African person, because
as Africans we also have our own creation narratives. As a result,
even though I am a Christian believer, I look at these biblical texts
critically – where does it come from, where is it going, what is the
mood, the background, the history of these texts? If we say that woman
was created from the rib of man, that text is often used to bring women
down, claiming that men were first. Yet, the same story also says that the
breath of God gave life to both man and woman. So, I take that to mean
that all human beings share things equally because we are dependent
on the breath of God, regardless of whether we are male or female or
intersex, and regardless of our sexualities. This is also highlighted in the
other story, from Genesis, which says that human beings are all created
in the image of God.[9]

7. Jer. 1:5: 'Before I formed you in the womb I knew you, before you were
born I set you apart.'
8. This refers to the stories of Gen. 1 (the Elohistic tradition) and Gen. 2–3
(the Yahwistic tradition).
9. Gen. 1.27: 'So God created [hu]mankind in his own image, in the image
of God he created them; male and female he created them.'

What I am underlining is the need to do critical rather than literal analysis of the biblical scriptures. Because reading the Bible literally can be risky. For instance, there is a text in Genesis saying that we have to give birth, multiply and fill the world. But in the contemporary world, this does not mean giving birth to fifteen children! Because you will not be able to educate them, we have no land or property to give them, the circle of poverty will increase. They will end up becoming thieves; then we say that God does not want thieves, and yet it is you who created the situation forcing them to become thieves. I have learned to say this verse is not about giving birth through anatomy but through the brain; educating them and giving them the skills for a good life, that is an alternative meaning of giving birth. It is not about quantity but quality. It is important to realize that it was not God writing these texts himself; instead, they were written by people who had their own culture, historical milieu and even biases. But if you read the Bible critically, you will get the correct word of God out of those stories. It is like smelting gold – you get the gold and leave out the stones. So, we have to dig to get the correct word of God, and the correct word of God is love. It is not about who you are, where are you coming from, who did what. The word of God, fundamentally, is love and everything else follows from that. Therefore, we should read the Bible for this core message and not be judgemental. It is wrong to judge others and to discriminate against LGBTIQ people. Instead, we should listen to them, know their abilities and learn about the stories of their lives.

Listening to their stories, I feel very bad when hearing about their individual and collective experiences of discrimination. These stories are so painful, of family rejection, eviction from schools, being fired from their workplaces and so on. I have witnessed cases of mistreatment, even by our police officers. In one instance, I visited a group who had been locked up by the police. I was called as a pastor to negotiate their release. And the police in turn asked me, who are you? I told them I am a pastor and they asked me, do you know the kind of congregants you are having? The police started telling me about them because the police thought I did not know they are LGBTIQ. So, I stayed at the police station until the group had been able to raise money for bond and get a lawyer to represent them. In the meantime, I tried to sensitize the police so that they could learn more about this community and stop harassing them. Yet, instead I was mocked by the police, 'What kind of pastor are you? How can you be close to people like this? Do you not know they are criminals?' They harassed me with their questions and comments. It was a very bad experience.

I think there is a lot of ignorance in the way society treats LGBTIQ people, including among pastors. Thus, in addition to doing good theology, there is a need to build the capacity of pastors on LGBTIQ issues. I recall a training we held at a university. Before the training, many pastors were looking at LGBTIQ community members as animals. But after the training the pastors were able to understand they were wrong. By the time the training was coming to an end, all those pastors had become allies, me being one of them. We were able to sit together with LGBTIQ people, eat together and share stories with each other. We need to come together as a community, with the religious leaders, eat together, sing together, share together. Only that way, we can begin to question all the assumptions and stereotypes, such as about inhuman nature, the association of homosexuals with rapists and so on. Only through such personal encounters, pastors will be able to understand that they are wrong.

What inspired me to become an inclusive pastor, is my understanding of everything as God's creation. If everybody is God's creation, regardless of their diversity, my task is to respect the divinity that is reflected in each one of us. We are all created by God. Thus, I will push on because God is love and if I do not love people then I am not a Christian. And since I will remain a Christian, then I must love people. Not only those ones who are thought of as good and decent and acceptable, but rather everyone. If I do not do that, then I am not a pastor, I am only pretending.

Currently there are few openly LGBTIQ affirming religious leaders in Kenya. However, there are many more who are hiding because they do not want to lose their jobs, or because their families or children would judge them harshly. I know a few bishops who are my friends, and they are inclusive, but they cannot state that publicly. Even many women pastors, who have struggled with patriarchy in the church themselves, they do not have that courage to come out and say, 'I am LGBTIQ inclusive.' Many are hiding because if they are known, they may lose their jobs or authority and they may be rejected by fellow pastors. They also fear the baseless accusation that they became LGBTIQ allies because they were given money. So, these are the reason why many pastors are not coming out openly; if an LGBTIQ person goes to them, they are able to help at a pastoral level, but it will remain between that person and the pastor. We also do not talk about it with our congregations otherwise they will talk about us badly, while we depend on them as our source of income. Even some of our children may judge us, so somehow, we end up alone. But we have already formed a WhatsApp group of pastors who are inclusive, and we know ourselves – we know which pastor we can refer a client to, in case there is a need.

Lastly, I would like to say that we need to go back to the scriptures and do exegesis properly. We need to see the people who have been rejected and who are wounded, physically and emotionally. We need to provide spiritual nutrients to them. If we remain shallow in the way we look at scriptures, we will look for passages to justify discrimination. On the contrary, if we are rooted and embrace faith deeply, we shall realize that the passages used to wound these people, actually, have been misinterpreted. When I deal with members of the LGBTIQ community, I am happy when they open up and we pray together. I am so happy when they come to me, I do not even ask them to change. Theologians or pastors do not tell people what to do. I am just so happy to be amongst them. They are not bad or demonic, as many people seem to think. I am always surprised to find just how gifted and talented these guys are, and how cheerful their company is. They do not reflect the common stereotypes that people have against them.

Story 11

EVANGELIST VINCENT: 'MY HOPE IS THAT LGBTIQ PEOPLE WILL KNOW GOD'

Vincent is a Kenyan Catholic lay evangelist inspired by both liberation theology and charismatic renewal. He takes the task of evangelization very seriously, but not in a judgemental way as he wants to show people the love of God. This shapes his approach to LGBTIQ people, who he first encountered while at university. As becomes apparent from his story, he is not explicitly affirming of same-sex sexuality from a theological point of view, and he refers to it as a 'choice' and a 'sin'. Yet, Vincent's position is that we should leave judgement to God and should follow the example of Christ who did not condemn people.[1]

I am Vincent, a lay Catholic evangelist. I am a member of the Catholic charismatic renewal movement, a movement within the Catholic Church that puts a lot of emphasis on the Holy Spirit, similar to the Pentecostal experience. I started my ministry in 2004 just after completing high school, and I am still going.

In my life, I have met many people who either do not believe in the existence of God or who doubt the presence of God and say 'God never cares'. Experiencing this disbelief in God's existence or in his interest in our life, changed me deeply and made me become an even stronger believer. My approach is rooted in liberation theology.[2] There are different ways of living one's religious experience. Some people may

---

1. This story is based on an interview with Evangelist Vincent (pseudonym) on 21 December 2022 in Mombasa, Nairobi.

2. Liberation theology emerged in Latin America in the 1960s as a movement emphasizing that God is on the side of the oppressed and that the church is therefore called to be in solidarity with the poor and marginalized and

see God as a punitive deity that undermines your dignity and freedom. For me, through liberation theology, I perceive Christ as a friend who liberated me, someone who let people be themselves and enjoy what they believe in. It is through this lens that I have encountered the LGBTIQ community. Some are friends, some are acquaintances. They may be different from me, but they are rightfully created by God, and they bear the image of God. They are who they are, it is their choice. Humans have free will; people choose who they want to be in life. Who are we to judge or to inflict punishment? The scriptures make it very clear that vengeance should only belong to God.[3] My mission is to work and speak through validation, speak true and liberate individuals. Everyone should have an encounter with and experience a friendly God. Christ said that he will no longer call us slaves but call us to be his friends.[4] My mission is to help people to experience such encounter with Christ, as a friend, a brother and a liberator.

Being a lay evangelist has been such a wonderful journey. The 'aha! moment' was when we were in Dar es Salaam for an evangelization seminar. We had three days to go out and speak about Christ like street preachers. I was taken to brothels where we were asked to convince female sex workers to convert and learn about Christ. At the time I was only nineteen years old. We were in groups of three and I went with two other partners. It was not an easy task, but a fun one if I reflect back, because the sex workers were very clear; they asked us, 'So you want me to change? But this is where I get my daily income. If you marry me, then I will change.' But my mission was not about marriage. If we had to talk about marriage in that case, it would have been marriage to Christ. I really did not know what to do and how to behave in that situation. I simply said, 'I will pass by tomorrow and we see what will be your reaction. Just think about it, Christ loves you. I wish you well and good luck in your work and let us meet again tomorrow.' We went back the day after, I looked for the same sex worker, but she wasn't around. I had her phone number and, even if we did not meet in person again, we stayed in touch and talked for five years or more. Recently, I spoke to another

support their struggle (see Gutierrez 1973). It has had a considerable influence on African theology.

3. Deut. 32.35: 'It is mine to avenge; I will repay.'

4. Jo. 15.15: 'I no longer call you servants, because a servant does not know his master's business. Instead, I have called you friends, for everything that I learned from my Father I have made known to you.'

evangelist in Tanzania who told me that this woman had actually joined the praise and worship team in his church and is now married with children. What if in that occasion we had condemned her and told her that Christ does not love her? We need to consider her experiences in life. She had to live in a city, had to pay rent and feed herself. How could I have changed her life if I did not have an alternative job to offer her? All I could do was listen to her and tell her that Christ loved her. There is satisfaction in experiencing transformation, to see that now she is off the streets and has a family of her own and she belongs to a church community.

When I was at university I had another eureka moment while I was interacting with fellow students. At the time, I used to write some preaching for an inter-faith monthly publication. I was staying in a hostel. A good friend of mine, a renowned transgender activist, who was not understood at the university, was there as well. There was no information on transgender rights at the university, no one wanted to share a room with her; even being in the same hostel was viewed with such stigma. So, I used to say 'hi' to her. It happened that people started to ask, 'Why are you talking to that person?' I would reply, 'Do you mean that she is not a human being?' I was interested in the evangelism of presence,[5] an approach to evangelism that goes beyond holding the Bible, but instead encourages to see Christ in each person, genuinely care for the person in front of you. It encourages you to relate to that person and see them in a different way. Meeting that well-known transgender activist was something new to me. The experience of talking to her, understanding her life without judgement and stigma, was important. I was studying psychology at the university, so I knew the harm that negative sentiments and attitudes could cause.

When I started working, I was in Turkana and some of my friends were LGBTIQ. They had not come out and initially I was not aware of their sexual identity. One of them was a boss of mine and the other was a donor. I was working as a child protection officer, and I also interacted with international staff from the United Nations. When other people came and told me that I was friend with such and such person and ask whether I did not know these people are gay, I would ask them how that information should change me. How does it affect me that one of my

5. Evangelism of presence, or presence evangelism, is an approach to evangelization centring around mere presence among people as a form of Christian witness (see Reid 1998, 13).

friends is gay? Will I refuse to seek funding to implement protection for child refugees just because one of the donors was gay? So, later on, when I moved to Mombasa and then to Nairobi, should I have refrained from becoming friends with LGBTIQ people? Should I limit my friendships just because some of them are gay? It is similar to someone who does not believe in Christ. The person can be your brother, your sister. Will your relationship with them change? No, your relationship will remain. They will be still your siblings without knowing or believing in Christ. Similarly, if someone has a different sexual orientation that does not change anything. That is their personal life, in the same way you also have a personal life. What brings the two of you together is friendship; stick to that. Moreover, the ones you know are those who have come out, but what about those ones who are still in the closet? In churches there are so many who are in the closet. You could be shocked to find out how many more there are if God were to call out everyone. Maybe up to 60 per cent would be either LGBTIQ or have had same-sex experiences at some point in their life.

I do not directly preach to or for the LGBTIQ community. I did not have a seminar with, or preached to the cohort, but I have friends and we share the word of God in our interactions. There is a way of speaking of God. I have attended PEMA Kenya's trainings where members of the LGBTIQ community talk and speak about problems they may have with religion.[6] We just share and discuss. In my everyday life, in the community where I belong, I treat LGBTIQ individuals as full human beings with rights and a sound mind. They have a soul like I do, and a heart like I do. They have red blood like everyone, but the only difference is their choice. You have your choice, they have their choice, and each of us makes choices out of their own consciousness. You cannot convert someone who is not ready to make that decision. You can only reason. You need to understand why they are the way they are. What matters to me is sharing Christ, share general information about Christ. Do you really have to speak about sin and condemn every single time? Where is the gospel of hope, of affirmation, of love? Why is it always about, 'You will die if you do not do this'? What about saying instead, 'Even in the midst of your troubles, there is God. Talk to him the way you are talking to me as a friend, talk to God.' Evangelizing and preaching should be a friendly activity, not a condemning one. Because if you condemn at

---

6. PEMA Kenya is a Mombasa-based organization seeking to advance the rights of gender and sexual minorities.

every instance, every day, then I do not think people will ever come to your church.

Some of my evangelist colleagues know about my acceptance of LGBTIQ people. That is because when I teach, and I specifically focus on the Catholic Church's social teaching, I would say, 'Christ has opened his arms to everyone, including those who have committed numerous abortions, everyone is welcome. Whether you are gay or lesbian, Christ's arms are outstretched towards you. Come! Come to talk with me.' That is what I would say. We are all children of God so let them be. But that does not stop sin from being called sin. When someone repents, they become part of Christ. It is better to have a clean ending than a clean beginning. People might repent just before their death, or they might fall into sinful situations just before dying. You can go to heaven, or you can be condemned to hell; just like the thief at the crucifixion of Christ, the good thief. It is not about the beginning, it is about how the ending goes and we should always be conscious of our ending. You may despise a person, and then you find that they are the registrar in heaven; what will you do?

I really like the story of Mary Magdalene in the Bible. She was not an interesting person to meet, you can imagine she would even fetch water when the sun is up at noon, when other women are not at the well. But look at her transformation. She used expensive perfume to wash the feet of Christ. And while the religious leaders were murmuring around him, Christ said, 'I came to your house, but you did not welcome me. Yet, this woman poured perfume on my feet. Woman, get up. Go in peace and live right.'[7] Those were strong words from Christ. Imagine, Christ is righteous, but he would not condemn a known sinner! Think about his body, he accepted to be touched by a blemished person. Would that not be a sacrilege in our normal way of looking at things? He let his body to be touched by a woman, and one who was a public sinner! He never judged. He was on earth to teach us how to live in the right way. If it was just about saving, he would have used one word and saved us all from hell, just like he used one word at the time of creation. But he came to teach us through his actions. This is the powerful lesson that we religious leaders should learn, not just in relation to LGBTIQ people, but with everyone else in society. There are many religious leaders who cannot even hug a sex worker. How do you think they will treat LGBTIQ people? This story teaches us that we should not judge

---

7. See Luk. 7.36–50.

and discriminate. If we read through the story of Mary Magdalene, we can see that LGBTIQ people too want to be close to Christ. We will not go to heaven with our attributes, but with our soul. You do not know what pushed Mary Magdalene, to walk into a meeting full of men and go straight at the feet of Christ. This is the same Mary Magdalene who went also to the tomb to take care of Christ. So, even LGBTIQ people have a place at the feet of Christ. If they need a relationship with their maker, who are we to be an impediment to them? Just bring them closer to Christ. If Christ did not push this woman away, then I do not think we, who are representing Christ and his mission, should do it either.

Religious leaders who see LGBTIQ people as demonic are probably inspired by the passage where the disciple Peter tells Jesus that he will not face any suffering. Yet Jesus saw it was not Peter but the devil who was speaking through Peter, so he said, 'Go behind me, Satan.'[8] Others may say, Jesus insulted Peter, but in fact Jesus was addressing the devil. Many religious leaders would want to scold the sin, but they end up turning to scold the person instead of the sin. Sin will never be baptized and receive another name. Sin is sin and will remain sin. But we should not condemn the person. We, Catholics, believe in purgatory; will God forgive those ones that are so busy condemning? Let us leave God to be God in people's lives – he knows his creation better than we do.

Helping other people excel in their spiritual life, gives me hope. My hope is that people who identify as LGBTIQ will know God. These are people who are hungry for God's interventions in their lives. They are the same people who pray when they go for job interviews. They still know God is there in their life. The bad encounters with religious leaders they had in the past should be forgotten. As long as they know God and they do not feel discriminated in church, their life in Christ will continue.

8. Matt. 16.23.

Story 12

PASTOR STEPHEN: 'I ARRIVED AT THE POINT OF REPENTING FOR MY HOMOPHOBIA'

Stephen is a youth pastor at one of the independent Roho churches in Kenya. The church is known for its beliefs in dreams, visions and prophecies and for its positive approach to indigenous culture and tradition. Since the church places an emphasis on the direct guidance of the Holy Spirit, Stephen's decision to study theology was met with suspicion. He however testifies that it has enriched his knowledge and understanding, including about issues of sexual orientation and gender identity. He advocates listening to the stories of LGBTIQ people and repenting for the wrongs the church has done to them.[1]

My journey to become a religious leader started at a tender age, when I sometimes assisted the Sunday school teacher at my church and stepped in for her when she was not available. I then trained to become a Sunday teacher myself and later entered the youth ministry. After completing high school, I went to university where I studied theology. My formal training in theology has given me a strong foundation in ministry.

I come from one of the independent churches in Kenya, which we here refer to as 'Roho churches'.[2] Our church broke away from the Friends African Mission, nowadays known as the Friends Church of Quakers. As an independent church, our theology is centred on the

---

1. This story is based on an interview with Pastor Stephen (pseudonym) on 17 March 2023 in Kisumu, Kenya.

2. *Roho* is the Dholuo word for spirit. Roho churches are independent churches with an emphasis on the experience of the Holy Spirit; this indigenous charismatic movement emerged in western Kenya from the early twentieth century (see Anderson 2001, 153–5; Mwaura 2004).

manifestation of the Holy Spirit. We recognize the trinitarian God, but we are motivated first and foremost by the belief in the Holy Spirit. We believe in the baptism with the Holy Spirit of adult persons upon repentance. We also do not celebrate Holy Communion like the mainstream churches because we believe in the presence of the Holy Spirit in the believer. We are mainly found in western Kenya, but we also have branches in different parts of Kenya, Uganda, Tanzania and Burundi. The centrality of the Holy Spirit means that we have prophesies, revelations, ecstatic experiences. We also remember and celebrate the founders of our own church through ceremonies; we venerate them as our spiritual ancestors. We also have seers, that may be called diviners; they are like prophets who guide us and tell us about the future. They are also able to identify our past sins in order to encourage us to repent. We choose our leaders through prayers, as the Holy Spirit will indicate the chosen people to lead us in this way.

During the colonial period, schools and hospitals were mostly run by the European mission churches. If our *Roho* people[3] would go to those schools and hospitals, they would be sent away. So, leaders of our church decided that we shall not be going to hospitals, and instead would practise faith healing through prayer. Until this moment, some of our members do not go to hospital for medication, they just believe in prayer. Initially our church law was that we could not go to hospitals but when the church officially registered, the government required that children are allowed to be vaccinated. Thus, the agreement was that children can be immunized and that church members have the freedom to go to hospitals if they want to.

I thank God that I was able to study theology, because I come from a very humble background and my church did not have the means to support me financially. I did public fundraising and relied on partial scholarships from the university. My theological studies both at an undergraduate as well as at a postgraduate level represent some of the highest moments in my life. People in our community are also very proud of this accomplishment. However, there are still members of my church that are disappointed by my decision to study theology. You see, I performed well at high school and thus it was natural for me to pursue university studies. I started to fundraise in my village, but I would use a general acceptance letter into the university as proof of my intentions without mentioning theology studies. In my village, there is a belief

3. Meaning, members of the Roho churches.

that people who do theology do so as they were not good enough for other kinds of studies. They used to ask me, how is theology going to help you? How will it pay your bills? Moreover, in our church, academic theology is not appreciated. We believe that the Holy Spirit inspires us what to say; therefore, people think you do not need to learn theology to be a minister. So, there was this resistance, yet I was convinced that I had a call to serve the Lord, and I wanted to study theology. I found it to be a broad subject which is very instrumental in my journey. In fact, after studying theology, I became even more convinced that I had made the right choice. Of course, there are people who criticize the fact that even after my studies I am still unemployed, while if I had undertaken different studies, I may have had a job by now. But I had this conviction that I needed to study theology to better understand my call. Currently there are five people with a theology degree in my church and we are working towards reshaping the misconception of what theology is and how it could serve our spiritual community. However, it is a slow process that will require time.

Nevertheless, I am receiving some recognition in my community. Even though I serve in the youth ministry, the elders invite me to their functions and sometimes ask for advice. Our women's group ask me to attend their church events to serve as facilitator. Other churches, too, invite me. I also work as a tutor in a growing Bible college, and I help with the training of pastors there. I am, therefore, not just serving in our church but also doing service to other denominations who know the resources I can bring in. People in my area often look down on members of my church, because we use to wear white turbans and a cross on the top of our clothes. They think of us as being primitive, illiterate and people who did not go to school. Yet here I am, coming from this background, dressed in this way, and yet I am educated; people look at me differently. Even the Quakers are beginning to invite me to their events, something that never happened before, because they thought that illiterate people could not offer much. This for me is the highest moment of my ministry: being able to invert the dominant narrative about our church and my life generally.

My personal journey to become LGBTIQ inclusive began at university. I can remember that we had a number of workshops and seminars where some LGBTIQ people were invited to share their stories. We would listen to their stories, and we could read their stories from a theological perspective. For example, we would discuss intersex people in relation to the creation story, the story of God who created male and female. We would ask difficult questions. Is the biblical distinction of creation as male and female contradicted by nature? If this distinction is the reflection of God creating in his own image, are the intersex people also created in the image and likeness of God? And for gay and lesbian people, should we condemn them and send them away from the church? If homosexuality is a sin, why should we treat this as a sin of higher magnitude than say a corrupted person, a thief or an adulterer? Why do we send the former away from the church and exorcize them, while the latter are believed to receive divine mercy, compassion and forgiveness? If being LGBTIQ is a problem, who do we blame? Are these people possessed by a demon? Or are they created in the image and likeness of God, just the way they are? Through such conversations and interacting with them something clicked in me. Before condemning and rebuking, we need to sit at the table and listen to each other. As much as we need to look at sexual orientation from a biblical point of view, we need to listen to people's stories and life experiences.

I normally use the analogy of the hospital. Because as religious leaders we are like spiritual doctors – when someone sick comes to you, you cannot just inject medicine. You need to collect a kind of 'spiritual history of the condition', so that when you are making a spiritual diagnosis and recommending treatment, it should be after you have done a proper diagnosis. This is what we need to do; we need to bring them on board so that the solution we recommend is coming from a place of information and knowledge. Generally, we need to offer training so that religious leaders can learn and can be able to listen. So that when they exorcize or pray for an LGBTIQ person, they do it on the basis of a good understanding. If we say, '*riswa* in the name of Jesus',[4] we should say it in a way that brings blessings to all concerned.

You see the problem that many religious leaders have is one of misinformation and lack of knowledge. When you speak about LGBTIQ here, what comes to people's mind is men having sex with other men or ladies and having sex with other ladies. However, it is about much more than sex. They lack information on the whole issue of sexual orientation and gender identity. If we were to take time to understand before going on a pulpit and preach against LGBTIQ people, we could offer an amicable solution. Especially after the recent Supreme Court ruling on the right to association,[5] you see religious

4. *Riswa* is a Dholuo word meaning 'go out/depart'.

5. On 24 February 2023, the Supreme Court of Kenya ruled that the National Gay and Lesbian Human Rights Commission must be allowed to officially register as a non-governmental organization.

leaders and politicians speaking without being properly informed. They are reacting to something that they do not understand, or maybe they are wilfully ignorant. Because when you listen to the information that they give us, or the kind of issue that they are condemning, you realize that this is distant from what they would know if they engaged with LGBTIQ communities and tried to understand them.

I arrived at the point of repenting myself when I realized through conversations and spending time with LGBTIQ people that I had been condemning and preaching against them wrongly, because I was not properly informed. I wish more religious leaders would reach that point after careful self-reflection. Our church has yet to take a formal position on this issue. We recently had an executive committee which brought together leaders from Kenya, Tanzania and Uganda and one of the issues on the agenda was the question of LGBTIQ. We were to develop a statement, but we did not get to it. I was curious to see what our church would say and what would inform the position they would take. I suspected that their decision was going to be informed by the general view that this thing is so bad without having real information on the matter, as in other churches. However, within our church we have heard many stories of homosexuals. The church at some point even wrote down their names and came with a list of people to excommunicate. I remember the meeting of the executive committee that wanted to excommunicate those people. It is then that I intervened and asked whether they had evidence. Someone replied by saying, oh we all have heard those rumours! So, I told them that they could not put people on such a list without evidence. And in any case, they should instead talk to them and try to understand them, without condemning first.

I love the story of a guy called Jephthah in the Bible who made a vow to God; if God helped him to win a battle, he would offer to God the first thing that comes to him when returning home.[6] So, he went to war and he won, and he came home celebrating but as he was coming into his compound the first person who came to meet him was his only daughter. He had made a covenant, thus he had to offer his only daughter to God. I tell people in my church, whenever you make a covenant, sit down and look at that covenant very well. The promises you make, ensure that you have thought through them very well. Applying this to the question of LGBTIQ people, we should think twice before making superficial vows saying, I will never allow my daughter or my son to be like this, or I will

6. Judges 11.

never allow a person like this in my church. Now you are making vows and promises and yet one day there will be an LGBTIQ person in your church or family, and you realize that your covenant will cause suffering to this person, and you will regret it.

We need to look at LGBTIQ issues critically, carefully and prayerfully. Moreover, we have to discuss sexual orientation and gender identity scientifically. Are we willing to learn from science, or do we just quote a verse from the Bible? I believe that we have to look at both, the Bible and science, to get a better understanding of scriptures on this issue. As science evolves, our understanding should evolve as well. For instance, we know from science the earth revolves around the sun. Yet, the person who discovered this was condemned by the church as being blasphemous. It is only later that the church repented and accepted his position. Science has contributed to our understanding of many phenomena; we say that science complements the scriptures. So even as we read the Bible, our understanding of the scriptures is enhanced by the contribution of scientific knowledge. No one today believes that the earth is held upright by four pillars. Today, science is giving us new insight in sexual orientation and gender identity. Why would we cause people to suffer, instead of looking at these issues carefully, critically and prayerfully, and with an open mind? Let us allow LGBTIQ people to correct us, to teach us.

Honestly, for me this has been a very lonely journey. It requires a lot of perseverance and motivation because when you speak about it and ask people to listen, they immediately accuse you of being one of them.

Story 13

PASTOR DORCAS: 'I PERSEVERE WITH MY CALLING TO PREACH LOVE IN THE COMMUNITY'

Pastor Dorcas is the lead pastor of a Pentecostal church in coastal Kenya. Since participating in a training about sexual and gender minorities, she has become a vocal ally of this marginalized community. Taking inspiration from biblical prophets such as Isaiah and Jeremiah, Pastor Dorcas has a strong conviction that she has been called by God and been given the spiritual power and authority to do great things in society. As reflected in her story, this motivates her to preach peace and love and to advocate for the inclusion of sexual and gender minorities.[1]

I was born a religious leader. By saying that I mean that I noticed I had this vocation right from my childhood, when I was supporting the Sunday school teachers, first as a participant, then as a teacher and then as an overseer. In 2010, I gave up my formal employment to become a fulltime minister. I want to thank God because since I started engaging myself as a Christian leader with sexual and gender minorities (SGM), I have learned many things. I have grown as a person and as a pastor. The journey started when I joined PEMA Kenya.[2] I was invited to some of the training courses they offer for religious leaders. Before that time, I did not want to hear anything about gay and lesbian people. But that changed thanks to the training, and I have now become a champion. We

---

1. This story is based on an interview with Pastor Dorcas (pseudonym) on 21 December 2022 in Mombasa, Kenya.

2. PEMA Kenya is a Mombasa-based organization advancing the rights of gender and sexual minorities.

continue to work together on matters of human rights advocacy and to create a safe space for the community.

Many men of God do not want to participate in this work because they have not looked deeply into what the word of God tells us. The Gospel of Matthew states very clearly that we should not judge.[3] The way you judge others is the same way you will be judged. I learned that as a minister of God we are not supposed to judge other people, and that is why I have become a champion and advocate of gay and lesbian people who are constantly judged and discriminated against in society. As a woman of God, I want to be a voice for their security. Because the Bible tells me that God has ordained us to be partakers of peace and to be partakers of love. That is why I am here as an advocate of the SGM community and try to protect them, to make sure they live in peace as part of the community in which I am based.

For example, sometimes I find a person being beaten up or harassed because of the way they are dressed, and people assume that they are gay or lesbian because of their dressing. In such cases, I will stand like a woman of God and tell the crowd, 'This is a son just like your son, or a daughter like your daughter, and we need to protect them!' I recall a sad incident where community members brought a boy to my house who lived in our neighbourhood. They were a gang comprising of both Muslims and Christians young men shouting, 'This young man is a homosexual and we hear that you know him.' They were ready to beat him up. I first asked them to calm down so that we pray before engaging in any discussions about the young man. I asked them to sit down since I have a big compound at my home. Once they had sat down, I introduced myself as a woman of God and I preached what the Bible is telling me, which is that God has ordained us to love all. I reminded them of that story in the Bible, where people bring a woman to Jesus who apparently had been found in adultery.[4] Like Jesus in this story, I asked them, 'Who of you is without sin? Who is ready to throw the first stone?' Of course, they all stayed silent. So, by the grace of God, I became a winner. The boy is now living safely in the community.

There are places where it is difficult to introduce yourself as advocate for gay or lesbian people. I have come to learn that it depends on the entry point you take. I want to thank God because I am a member of an interfaith group that works on child protection, which is how I got

3. Matt. 7.1: 'Do not judge, or you too will be judged.'
4. Jo. 8.1–11.

to meet PEMA Kenya. And since then, I have learned that I can be a voice in the country to advocate for peace. I thought my work was to preach in my church and be a mother. But God wanted me to do more than that. With time, I have come to appreciate the work I am doing. I am a very strong woman and I use the work God has called me to do, to be a voice of change in Kenya, an oracle. And the Bible tells me that I am given power and authority to be an overcomer. Still, doing church ministry is very demanding. This is because I am a married woman and a mother of four children. It is difficult to balance space for the family and space for the ministry. It was especially difficult when my husband was not yet born again. He was a man like any other man, drinking beer and coming home at late hours. Those were moments when I was very down as a wife and mother who is also a church leader and a role model in the community. I have learned to be dependent on God because the work which God has called me to do is voluntary work, we do not do it for compensation. It is a calling, and you volunteer to do this work with money or without money. Thank God, my family is doing well, and my husband is supportive. I have engaged my son in secondary school, and my daughter is finishing university. They have no problem with me working with the SGM community.

In the scriptures, I am very much inspired by the stories of women whose lives are turned around. Take Rahab the harlot.[5] Born as a beautiful girl, she becomes a prostitute, but God turns her life, and she ends up changing the community. God saves her and brings another face out of the prostitute. There is also the story of Jesus meeting the woman at the well.[6] Powerful. This woman has been married multiple times and is now living with a man who is not her husband. Yet, Jesus encounters her and turns her life around. She later was ordained an evangelist who brought change in the community. Those stories in the Bible remind me that any person can become anything, can become a greater person in the community. They encourage me as a woman of God, to help any person I meet to become a strong person in the future. Any woman or man I meet, I make sure that there is a turnaround in the life of that person.

The Bible tells me that God has called me, and therefore I should not be afraid. The words of the prophet Isaiah mean a lot to me, where God says, 'You are my servant; I have chosen you and have not rejected

5. Josh. 2.
6. Jo. 4.1–42.

you. So do not fear, for I am with you.'[7] Therefore I will not despair or be afraid of anything while working with gay and lesbian people. As a woman of God, God has given me the mandate to become a mother to all. I have not had any problem working with these people. I have even adopted one as my daughter, who is working as an activist. I love her and she has become part of our family. Likewise, the prophet Jeremiah feels that he is too young and not ready for the task God has given him.[8] Yet God reminds him that he has been given power and authority to pull down any obstacle, and to set up new foundations. I count myself as a champion and an overcomer like Jeremiah because the authority God has given me, and I am using it very well in the community.

Those who are opposed to diverse sexualities seem to get their inspiration from the story of Sodom and Gomorrah in the Bible. That is why many men say to me, 'You cannot advocate for these people, they are cursed.' Yet the Bible tells us we must love everybody. And Galatians puts it clearly to me, and that is what I stand with, 'Let no one cause me trouble, for I bear on my body the marks of Jesus.'[9] It reminds me of the cross of Jesus that tells me Jesus finished it all. So, I ignore those who tell me I should not be doing this work and I persevere with my calling. I have been called to be a mediator within families and to provide a safe space for gay and lesbian persons. Those who are fighting SGM do not know whether among their own children, or in a next generation, they have a gay or a lesbian in their own families. These things are left to God. Our work is to preach peace and love in the community and above all to pray for SGM and protect them as members of our family. That is why, when I found this girl neglected because she was a lesbian, I took her up in my house. And in my church, I have a young man who sings in the choir; am I supposed to send him away because he is gay? No way!

In my church community, I take things slowly. But I have begun to engage people who are pillars in the church. And when they talk about me, they say, 'our mother is an advocate for all people', that is how they put it. I take pride in that, because I am comfortable with the calling that God has put in my life. As a woman of God, I am not called to judge anyone, or to change anyone. I am instead called to pray for them and that is what I do. I want to thank God because I am

7. Is. 41.9–10.
8. Jer. 1.6–10.
9. Gal. 6.17.

seen in the community as a dominant voice. God has given me power and authority, so I can have an influence in different areas. Working on SGM issues has shown me that nothing can bring me down. I can conquer any challenge with the help of God, and I am coming out as a strong woman, a woman of God working without fear. And gay and lesbian people in my community know that they have a woman of God who will keep them safe in her house when they are being fought and who will fight on their behalf. I am looking forward to being one of those who advocate for their peace and protection.

Story 14

EVANGELIST JOSEPHINE: 'AS A MOTHER IN THE COMMUNITY, I SHOULD HAVE NO BOUNDARIES'

Josephine is a lay Catholic evangelist living in western Kenya. She used to view homosexuality as an evil thing, but this changed when she participated in a training about sexual orientation and gender identity where she was touched by the testimonies and lived experiences of LGBTIQ people. Having a strong belief in her role as a mother in the parish and community, she realized that LGBTIQ people are our children and, more than that, are children of God. As she narrates in this story, since then she has become a strong ally of LGBTIQ people in her community.[1]

I believe that mothers should play a specific role in the family and the community: we are comforters. As comforters, we should accommodate everybody in the house, in the congregations, in the country. Being a mother myself, when I walk around and see a child lying on the road, I normally stop and ask him or her how they are. If the child is sick, I can even take such a child to the hospital. This motherly love goes beyond our own children. We look after people in our community and congregation. We mothers should be approachable by anybody in the community. We should not have boundaries but protect and care for everybody who needs it.

My calling to this work began while I was at school. I was a staunch Christian at the time. I was in the Young Catholic Students movement, and I was deeply engaged in church activities. In many of these gatherings, it happened that I was chosen as a leader. That is how

---

1. This story is based on an interview with Evangelist Josephine (pseudonym) on 17 March 2023 in Kisumu, Kenya.

I became an evangelist. Doing church activities makes me happy and I enjoy it every time despite the challenges. There are challenges when you are a leader. If you speak the truth, you cannot please everybody, and people may dislike you; but this does not refrain me from going ahead. I also work with children in the parish, which is my passion. I recall an event, a few years ago when I had some money to spare and decided together with my team to hold an entertainment event. So many children came, and we spent the whole day with them. You know when a child hears that we are going out somewhere, they came even with children who did not belong to our church. Working with children is very easy because they are very genuine, they do not cheat, they are themselves and very honest. So, I enjoy working with them, even playing with them – you may think I am their age-mate.

In terms of how I started working with my LGBTIQ children, one day I was invited to an interfaith meeting by Nyarwek.[2] We were with a few religious leaders at that meeting. At first, I was very opposed to the issue when I got to know what the agenda of the meeting was. I thought of it as an evil thing. But I did not oppose verbally to the meeting; I kept those thoughts in my mind. Then, when I had the opportunity to listen to the LGBTIQ people at the workshop, I came to change my views. I am now an advocate. I am not a lesbian, but I learned a lot from interacting with them. Some of them have had very painful experiences as their stories demonstrate. Some have been pushed away and suffered rejection by their own families. As a result of such trauma and the stigma they face, some of them have even attempted to commit suicide.

I studied counselling and psychology, so I empathize with what they are going through. I even been counselling some of them especially those who have been sent away from their families. They faced so much trauma so I could not just stand and walk away. Initially I was counselling them secretly, and gradually I came to terms with it. I realized they are human beings; they are our children and are part of our community. I used to think that they were few, but I discovered that actually there are many of them. So, inside my heart I realized, this could be my daughter or my son. I said, let me not be like the other parents who have chased away their children, because by the time when you chase away your child, what kind of future do you give

---

2. Nyarwek is a network of LGBT+ organizations in western Kenya, which has its offices in Kisumu. For several years, they have been running programmes with religious leaders.

them? Probably that would be a death sentence, because once a child is sent away, he or she will really struggle and might even commit suicide. At the end of the day, you will lose out so much. So, I decided to accommodate everybody as a counsellor. I accommodate them because they are all human beings. People are created differently, and our behaviours cannot be all the same. We have to accommodate all human beings created by God. Even people who are speaking ill of LGBTIQ people, in their houses they may have LGBTIQ children. Even our religious leaders, some are LGBTIQ themselves. They do not want people to know, and therefore they speak out against it so loudly, yet they are one of them. They are hypocrites.

Although I used to hear about homosexuality long time ago, I did not know much about sexual minorities, I was not even sure that they really existed. It is only when I met people from this community at the Nyarwek meeting and afterwards, that I got a sense of what they are going through. They were narrating their life stories themselves and they came out openly, saying, 'I am so and so and I am gay' or, 'I am lesbian.' During these meetings, I learned about the need to ask someone of the correct pronoun that they would like us to use. This is because we learned that gender identity refers to someone's inner understanding of their gender, that is whether one is male or female. I came to realize that these are our children, and above all, that they are children of God. You cannot chase them away. Moreover, you should not point at something happening in your neighbour's house and oppose it; the next day you will find it in your own house, what will you do?

Nowadays, I am very happy when I meet members of the LGBTIQ community and we interact freely. One day when I met one of my friends, she is very open with me and calls me mum. She respects me. I remember I met her at a hotel and she was with her mother. I was with my husband, and she came over to greet me. She even insisted for me to go and greet her mother. So, when I met her mother, I was happy and told her mother: you gave birth to this girl, but she is now my daughter. We laughed and had a happy moment together. However, I have also had sad moments. Such as when we had a meeting in Bondo district and one of the participants narrated his story. It was such a sad story. His parents decided not even to pay his school fees because he was a gay. And he was such a bright boy! I felt bad for what parents are capable to do to their own children. Thank God, he had been adopted by his maternal uncle who looked after him. Yet, others are less lucky. It means that, because of our ignorance, we may preclude the road to future doctors, lecturers etc. We seem to forget that, despite their sexual orientation, they have brains, they are good in school and pass exams, they contribute to society. They are citizens like us.

I am inspired by the story of Jesus feeding the multitudes with two pieces of fish and five loaves. This story speaks to me especially in the current period of scarcity and drought. The situation for many families is very difficult. Sometimes you have unexpected visitors, and they come around lunchtime; you have a small piece of meat and some *ugali*, but in your heart you think: will this even be enough for my family? You may be tempted not to share with your visitors. However, this story teaches us that no matter how small the food portions may be, God will bless them and everybody will be full. I am encouraged by this scripture to share the little I have with everyone. Listening to the LGBTIQ community and sharing love with them is an extension of this kind of sharing. I empathize and sympathize with them, and for me it is a form of sharing the bread and fish like Jesus taught us.

For those who are opposed to social inclusion of LGBTIQ people, I do not know what inspires them. There are scriptures that seem to oppose those acts, and even myself in the past I opposed them. Yet eventually I came to see them differently. The problem is that there is no engagement and there is no knowledge; in this way, it is difficult to understand and recognize their humanity. I was the same before, a real enemy, but when I started to spend time with them, I gradually changed. It may be useful to invite religious leaders into the trainings so that they better understand what sexual orientation and gender identity are. It will be gradual, and it will take time, but it is not impossible for them to see the light. That is what happened to me, after all. If you train two or three, they will influence others; that is how the gospel spreads. Especially after the recent court ruling, people have been wild out there, including many vocal religious leaders.[3] You know, many Kenyans are pretenders, so when you approach people you have to be careful. Many people are pretending to be angry with the court ruling, shouting loudly in public against the dangers of homosexuality. Yet, they know that they have those people even within their own families. When they are outside, they shout loudly just so that people will not suspect that their son or daughter is gay or lesbian. So, they are pretending, keeping up an appearance.

3. On 24 February 2023, the Supreme Court of Kenya ruled that the National Gay and Lesbian Human Rights Commission must be allowed to officially register as a non-governmental organization.

Even with these challenges however, we have to remain hopeful that LGBTIQ people will be included. It will happen one day. Actually, a long time ago they were included in our societies. In the future, I know they will be fully recognized in our society, like in other countries. Also, those of us who have come to terms should step up and reach out to those who are still opposed to our LGBTIQ children. We should tell them that there was a time we shared their views, but we now see things differently. We need to tell our stories of change, as a testimony of how God has enlightened us.

Story 15

PASTOR LAURA: 'I FEEL LIKE QUEEN ESTHER, WHO PUT HER LIFE AT RISK TO SAVE OTHERS'

Pastor Laura is ministering in a Pentecostal church in coastal Kenya. She became involved in the ministry for LGBTIQ persons thanks to a training programme of PEMA Kenya where she was touched by the personal stories of struggle and trauma. Having been in an abusive marriage for twenty years before deciding to divorce from her husband, she is able to empathize with the pain of people who are discriminated and marginalized. Pastor Laura narrates in this story how the biblical character of Queen Esther, who came to the rescue of people who were at risk of being killed, inspired her to become a strong ally of LGBTIQ people, out of the awareness that they are fully children of God.[1]

I became a pastor by chance. You know, sometimes in life you just find yourself doing something that you hadn't planned, but it's the direction God took you in. For me, it happened because I got married to a person who was very religious and who was already serving at church. I joined him, and we ended up going into ministry together. In our church, I became responsible for worship. I love singing with all my heart. When I sing, any pain goes away, and I feel good. When I am leading praise and worship, people like it very much and they tell me I have received a special gift to touch their hearts.

Serving in ministry has its own challenges, however. You meet many people from diverse backgrounds and characteristics, and sometimes they have their own agenda. The most painful was that sometimes false accusations were made against me. And in one case, the person

---

1. This story is based on an interview with Pastor Laura (pseudonym) on 21 December 2022 in Mombasa, Kenya.

announcing false information from the pulpit was my own husband. This happened repeatedly until it came to a point where I could not take it anymore. I had to give up and run away for my life. The marriage I was in had become violent and very abusive, physically, spiritually and financially. So, I had to run for my life two years ago. And I am happy and peaceful now. This explains how I came to understand the pain that LGBTIQ people go through in society. I got exposed to LGBTIQ people through a training my husband and I were invited to at St Paul's University in Nairobi, provided by PEMA Kenya.[2] My initial reaction was like, I cannot do this. Yet by the time the five-day training was coming to an end, I wanted to be engaged in this work. It is not just me who had this initial reaction, many other pastors who had been invited also had that same initial reaction. We thought of the training as being demonic, but by the time the training was finished we all thought it was wonderful. The training followed a very good methodology, first introducing issues of discrimination in general, then discussing LGBTIQ related issues more specifically later. Since that training, PEMA Kenya have been inviting me for many more trainings. Before attending these trainings, I thought LGBTIQ persons were different people from the rest of us.

I remember during the training there was this one person, I could not tell if it was a girl or a boy. She told us of how she always had to be careful of where she rents a place to stay. For example, she cannot live in a place where people share bathrooms, because it has happened that housemates attempted to break the bathroom when she was taking a shower, so they could see how she looks like when naked. Her story really touched me. Being a mother myself, I realized that she is somebody's child. Her story really touched me and I said to myself, 'We should not discriminate against them.' I always feel good when I make new friends. One thing I have realized about the LGBTIQ community is that they are very friendly and they have a clean heart. And I love how they bring themselves out, how they interact with one another and with me. I interact with them easily and we talk about many different things. It does not have to be about sexuality or relationships all the time.

From my studies during the training, and from my personal encounters, I now know that LGBTIQ people are God's children. Moreover, I feel like we should support them and be there for them. We

---

2. PEMA Kenya is a Mombasa-based organization advancing the rights of gender and sexual minorities.

should fight and make people understand. Where I am now, I make sure that everybody knows about LGBTIQ people. Somehow, I always find a way of bringing this topic up in a discussion and use that opportunity as a teaching moment. Just yesterday, while at the hospital waiting for my daughter to give birth, I had a heated argument. I asked those who had come with me how they would feel if we were blessed with the birth of an intersex child. I always find a way of introducing this subject so that I can educate people on it. Then somebody said that he hates men who smack the backside of other men. I asked, what his feelings are when a man hits a lady and why he only gets offended when it is a man. He said, 'When it is a man, then someone may be training himself to become gay.' I used the opportunity to educate him that no one is trained to become gay. It is how one is created. It is God's creation. I made him know of the sexual orientation and gender identity continuums. And then we talked and talked, and I told them what I have been taught at the different trainings that I have attended. I asked them what they would do if our daughter gave birth to a child who is like that – like here we are in the hospital, if our daughter's baby comes out as intersex, are we going to run away? Are we not going to take care of the child until they are grown up? In the end it was fun and they embraced the teaching.

Supporting LGBTIQ people has, however, come with its own set of challenges. I remember one time when I attended a PEMA Kenya meeting, and I had told my husband about it (I was still married at the time). The following Sunday, he suddenly announced from the pulpit that I was attending meetings organized by homosexuals and was promoting homosexuality. From that time, I was baptized a pastor for homosexuals and that is only what I heard. Can you imagine what others were saying behind my back? It was very painful because it had come from my own husband. I recall that we had both been invited to go to the St. Paul's training. In fact, he had planned to attend the training but some other engagement came up so he could not. But when we came back from the training, PEMA Kenya started inviting me for additional trainings. I think that is where he got the idea from, or maybe he felt side-lined as he has that kind of character.

My favourite character in the Bible is Queen Esther.[3] Although this story does not directly relate to LGBTIQ work, I just love how

---

3. See the *Book of Esther* in the Bible, about a young Jewish woman living in the Persian diaspora who becomes queen and risks her life to save the Jewish people from annihilation as schemed by Haman, the king's senior adviser.

she was. Esther put her life at risk to save the lives of others. She goes to the king and plays into the power struggle between Haman and Mordecai, and that way she saves the people who would otherwise have been exterminated. You see, I work with children and youth myself, especially girls, and when one of them is being discriminated against I feel bad. I always try to protect them. Sometimes I will put my life at risk to protect them. The Bible says, 'Throw your bread to many waters, you do not know which is going to come back to you.'[4] That is why I say, do not judge and try to do good wherever and whenever you can. I believe that people do not just meet by coincidence, there is a purpose, there is a lesson and there is a blessing. If there is no blessing then there is a lesson, so do not judge people by their appearance. The training at St Paul's made me realize that LGBTIQ people are human beings and there is nothing wrong with them. And now because people feel that there is something wrong with them, I want to stand there and say there is nothing wrong with them. Most people do not read the Bible as they should. They will just take one line and will not reflect on where it is coming from and what it means in its context. My very basic belief is, we are part of God's creation, and God's work has no mistakes. I cannot judge other people, because today it may be you who is being discriminated against, but tomorrow it might be me.

Many people say that LGBTIQ people train themselves to be this way, others say it is demonic. Even the pastor I currently minister under, he would cast demons out from them. But I have been speaking to him and now he is streamlined. He does not judge like he used to do before, and he does not longer ask LGBTIQ people to come to him for deliverance. He has stopped doing that. Other people blame the parents for their children turning LGBTIQ. They say the parents are the ones who brought up their children wrongly. For example, in our family, I am the first born and I have three brothers, so we grew up together and played together. If I had turned out not heterosexual, then someone would probably have blamed my parents saying that they did not put me in an environment where I could grow up like a girl.

What gives me hope is that one day, LGBTIQ people will be treated with respect like everybody else in society. A journey of a thousand miles always starts with the first step. Maybe we are still on the first step, but it is the beginning of a journey, and we shall get there. One

---

4. Eccles. 11.1: 'Cast your bread upon the waters, for you will find it after many days.' (NIV)

day, one time, we shall come to a point where this will no longer be an issue. By then, you will not need to interview a few inclusive religious leaders as role models, because we all shall have learned a lot and will have changed. My children are growing up knowing that the LGBTIQ community exists, and when they get to my age it will not be hard for them to realize LGBTIQ rights. My mother may not agree, my grandmother even worse, but my children do, so it is going to be ok in the future. And one day we shall stand and say, we started somewhere and now we are here. For example, it was not easy when we started but now, we are holding this interview in a public space. There will be a time when we discuss these issues on TV. Maybe there will come a time when I do not have to ask you to anonymize my story and perhaps, I will be very proud to be an ally.

Thinking of an image that symbolizes the work I do, a crown comes to mind. This is because I feel like a queen. I like working with the girl child and I want them to feel in their own special way, knowing that they are queens, whether straight or not. They should be proud. A queen is never shaken, a queen is confident, a queen will always do what she wants, just like Esther in the Bible who I just talked out. I like empowering the girl child, so they have more confidence in themselves and go for what they want. And have courage and be strong and know that nothing can defeat them. Everything is possible through Christ who strengthens us.[5] I feel proud, I feel wise. I feel beautiful because when you are a queen you will be dressed in the best way possible, with the best make up and because everyone thinks you are beautiful.

5. Phil. 4.13: 'I can do all this through him [Christ] who gives me strength.'

Story 16

BISHOP ROGER: 'WHEN YOU START BEING INCLUSIVE, YOU ARE BRANDED'

Bishop Roger is leading several Pentecostal churches in the Kisumu region, western Kenya. In this story, he confesses that at his first encounter with a gay person, he called for his lynching. But such has been his conversion that he now pays for the schooling of an intersex person who also lives with him. He changed his views and attitudes thanks to a sensitization training about sexual orientation and gender identity. Since then, he has become an advocate among fellow religious leaders, wearing the title 'gay bishop' with pride.[1]

I was born in a Catholic family but around the time I finished secondary school, my father passed away and we were left with my mum. After the burial, I decided to move out in search for a living. I moved to Eldoret town in Rift Valley, and while attending a crusade I received salvation and then also changed my denomination. In Eldoret I was working as an auto-wiring technician. Later I migrated to Nakuru to do the same job, and while there I decided to join a theological school.

After the Bible school, I decided to start a church in Kisumu. And then I started another one, and now I have more than five and this is what I am doing. In 2020, I was ordained as an assistant bishop in the Kisumu region. When I ventured into fulltime ministry after I left my work, the standards of living fell significantly. Having a family to feed can be very difficult because the church cannot support you to meet your needs. Your spouse even become unhappy because what you are getting cannot meet their needs. But luckily, I have been able to

1. This story is based on an interview with Bishop Roger (pseudonym) on 16 March 2023 in Kisumu, Kenya.

educate my children. That said, my work is my passion, I love it. My happiest moment was during a meeting with the late Rev. Bonnke, well known here in Kenya and internationally.[2] I have also met Pastor Peter Youngren who is from Canada and who is preaching here in Kenya even at this moment.[3] These encounters made me happy because so many people were saved and healed.

I was once very much against key populations.[4] There was a time a pastor was caught having sex with young man in my area and I was called to adjudicate the issue. My judgement was very harsh on that person, saying that he should be lynched. Luckily for him, he managed to escape. From that day, I did not want to hear about key populations. If I would meet any of them, they could not talk to me the way we are talking now – I could not even listen. But ten years ago, I met a lady who asked if she could have time with me to talk. Even though I was not comfortable with what she shared in that conversation, she invited me to a meeting of a group of people who are like her, and I went. The first day of that meeting I was very uncomfortable, even the second. The third day I started seeing some sense in what they were saying. Initially I thought I was being recruited into the gay agenda. I thought, these are the evil people who want to spoil our nation. They have been given money to recruit us. And yet, at the same time, I was listening to them and thinking, these words make sense. For instance, they talked about the love of God being for all – and it made me wonder, why would I not love these people even though I think they are sinners? Some of the other pastors and bishops matched out, but me I decided to stay on until the end of the training. Then after that she introduced me to Nyarwek and the trainings they organize have changed my mind.[5]

I learned about other faith leaders like Bishop Desmond Tutu, who talked about gay people and saw them as human beings just like

2. Reinhard Bonnke was a German American evangelical preacher and founder of Christ for All Nations. His ministry was particularly focused on Africa.

3. Peter Youngren is a Canadian evangelical preacher and founder of World Impact Ministries.

4. The term 'key populations' is frequently used in public health discourses about sexual and gender minorities and other groups considered to be at high sexual health risks.

5. Nyarwek is an LGBTQ+ organization in Kisumu, western Kenya, running programmes with religious leaders. See Introduction to this book.

everyone else. And I remember Tutu asking, 'How can you preach to someone that you do not want to talk to?' Then I realized that gay persons may have some problems that they want me to pray for. How will I pray with you if I do not want to see you? How will you reach out to me if you know this bishop does not want you? These are the things that Desmond Tutu made me think about, and I reflected and felt that there were some things we are doing as religious leaders which can make people not to come to God, but instead may chase them away from God. And I realized that I do not own God. Our God is not like my pen or my phone. He is the God of all creation, even trees, thieves, name them. God is their God as well. He is not like my phone that I can switch off and no one will get me. That is not God. As pastors, bishops, imams we are behaving as if we are owning God as our personal property, which is not right.

After the training, at the place where I live, there was a young person who was intersex, and the family members did not want people to know that she was like that. So, they decided to lock the child in the house while the younger siblings went to school. You know, in our community those people are not supposed to interact with other people because they can bring bad omen. After the training, I decided to approach the family, and it was not easy because the mother did not want people to know about the boy (let me not call the person a boy). So, I approached the mother and started talking to her. Then there was a meeting organized by Kwamboka.[6] I went there with the mother and the mother listened; even before the end of the meeting, during the break, the mother decided to call the child and confessed that she had wronged her kid. From that day she decided to release the boy who then came to stay with me, and I decided to take him to school. Currently she is looking more like a girl, and I have taken her to a special school in Nyabondo. Then I said to myself, if I had not gone for that training, I would just be in denial saying that these are bad people.

I like the way members of key populations interact with me these days. If I call them, they can come and talk to me freely. I can recall a time I was with my wife, and we were walking downtown and met three ladies from the community. They met us and hugged me so tightly. Another pastor who was there with us, after walking some distance he

6. Kwamboka Kibagendi is an openly intersex identifying activist working with Jinsiangu, an organization advocating for the well-being of intersex, transgender and gender non-conforming people in Kenya.

asked, who are these, why are they hugging you like this? Then my wife told him, these are our spiritual children. They were dressed in a non-normative manner, but I love them because they are human.

Unfortunately, when you start being inclusive, you are branded. In Kisumu town I am known as the gay bishop. And some people are thinking that gays are sleeping with me. I think because of misunderstanding. It not only happens with gay people, but also with other marginalized groups. For instance, if I go to a bar and order a soda, I may call the prostitutes and talk to them. Yet, other people will say, pastor what is this? Is there no other place from where you can take a soda? You have now fallen, you are backsliding. So, it is not just the gay issue. In our churches even young widows are having problems. A pastor cannot talk to a young widow for a few hours without people saying the two are dating. There is a lot of branding. Even people living with HIV, some people do not want to sit with them in church.

I like the story of Naomi in the Bible. She and her husband moved to a foreign land, because there was drought and famine in Israel. They moved to Moab, but according to the Bible the Moabites were cursed. While living there, Naomi's husband died and her two children also died. She is left with her two daughters-in-law who were from that country, one of whom was Ruth. Ruth insisted on going back with Naomi to Israel, because the famine there was over. Naomi gave her freedom to remain among her people and remarry, but Ruth insisted on accompanying her. The reason why Naomi was having judgemental attitude towards Ruth was because she was from Moab, the cursed people. She did not want to bring Ruth back with her to Israel, the holy land. But remember, when they went back, Ruth met Boaz, and she gave birth, and later David and Jesus come from that blood lineage. So, Ruth is in the genealogy of Jesus, and that is why I am saying that the Jesus I am preaching did not come from holy people. Therefore, I cannot be against a drunkard or a gay person because I do not know what plans God has for them. God's plans are God's alone.

I think one of the reasons why many pastors and bishops are against gays is because of wealth. Some churches are not there to serve God. They are there to serve their own personal needs. They own a number of things, such as houses, huge bank balances, they have shares in many companies. It is not because of God; it is about making money. They think that preaching against homosexuality will keep their churches popular. It is not only about wealth but also misinterpretation of the Bible especially the story of Sodom and Gomorrah. You can use the Bible to bring people together or to drive people apart. Although some of them are theologians, they have decided to misinterpret. Because you cannot make a doctrine with one verse. Many bishops claim to take the Bible literally, but in fact they do not. Because the Bible says that a woman cannot come to church when they are having their period. Are we stopping women coming to church? Even a lame person, according to the Bible, is not supposed to come to church. Yet, some pastors are lame themselves! Paul says that as a servant of God, it is better not to be married. Yet, most pastors and bishops are married, sometimes even to more than one wife. What I am saying is, no one takes the Bible hundred per cent literally. So, picking a verse to scare away gay people, it is a misinterpretation.

While we can organize trainings to sensitize these leaders on who gay people are, there are some people whose views cannot be changed. Even the Bible says that people can be stubborn! You can throw peas in the strongest fire, but some will remain hard. So, we will not change all these people regardless of what! Whether we train them, even if you call them, they do not even want to hear, and yet they continue preaching about it. I have been talking to these bishops here in Kisumu and if they do not want to hear, I leave them alone. Some have changed when I talked to them. I organize a meeting, we share lunch, and I tell them that gays are not recruiting people the way they think. I remind them that the gay community exists, but they say they do not want to hear about that. In Kisumu there was one pastor who was very bitter, not knowing that one of his sons was gay. I tell them to create safe spaces for the community, to give them a hearing and to let them decide how they want to lead their lives; it is not for us to decide for them. I have five kids; I cannot decide for any of them. One of my girls is a friend to a Muslim; if the young man comes to pay dowry it is up to my daughter to decide if she wants to be a Muslim.

What is giving me hope is that change in attitudes is possible. For example, when we learned about HIV in this country, even coming close to people living with HIV was not easy. There was so much stigma and fear. Yet with time, we learned about it and came to understand it. Let us give it time and everything will come to a good end. We have to continue defending, preaching, and telling people that these people are human beings, created by God. They are here to stay.

Story 17

REVEREND KIMINDU: 'THIS CAN ONLY BE A CALLING, OR I WOULD HAVE STOPPED LONG AGO'

Rev. Michael Kimindu is a retired clergy in the Anglican Church of Kenya. In this story, he narrates how he became one of the first Christian leaders in the country to openly support sexual minorities, specifically through the organization Other Sheep Africa Ministry, which he founded in 2003. Having served in the navy as a chaplain for many years, he returned to parish ministry after his retirement, but was soon asked to step down because of his LGBTIQ advocacy. He has continued his ministry in the Metropolitan Community Churches. Belonging to the Kamba ethnic group, which he claims to be liberal on matters of sexuality, he believes that God prepared him for this work from a young age.[1]

The question of how I became a religious leader who is supportive of LGBTIQ inclusion is quite an interesting one. To be honest, I do not really know how this journey started. Having been involved in advocacy for so long, sometimes I also ask myself, how did it all begin? Frankly, I think God was preparing me from my childhood because in the 1960s, when I was young, the Kamba community was quite liberal about

1. This story is based on an interview with Rev. Kimindu on 4 January 2023 in Mtito Adei, Kenya. Kimindu refers to himself as a bishop-elect emeritus because, in his own words, 'although I was elected to be an Anglican Bishop, I was not consecrated as one, so I remain a bishop-elect'. In the interview, he narrated how in 1998 he was elected to serve as bishop of the armed forces but was never consecrated as such because of political issues, which he explained as 'tribalism' in the church.

sexuality.[2] Kamba people have traditionally had an easy time discussing sexuality openly. When I was at school, I can remember witnessing sexual experimentation among heterosexuals, and herdsmen were using aloe vera plant for self-stimulation, and there was even same-sex sexuality. I have talked to many Kamba people, who told me that even in the villages there were people known to be gay, and nothing happened to them. So, coming from a culture that is very liberal on matters of sexuality has made it easier for me to advocate on these issues.

My journey into ministry began at Maseno high school, where they gave us a lot of religious training – every morning we would worship at the chapel, and every Sunday we had a service, often with visiting clergy including bishops. So Maseno was a place where emphasis was laid on our Christian life. When we got to form 4 (fifteen to eighteen years old), I had already made up my mind that I would like to become a minister in the Anglican Church. After finishing school, I worked for three years as a teacher, but in 1977 I was lucky enough to go for my training at seminary. I studied there for three years, but I cannot recall the word homosexuality ever being mentioned at St. Paul's United Theological College.[3] Shortly after I joined the military chaplaincy, there was an incident where two sailors at the navy were found sharing a bed. When it was reported to the commanding officer of the base, he asked me to accompany him to the dormitory to see those boys. We went there and asked the boys what was going on, but they said they were just sharing a bed. So, the commander asked me, 'How can you advise as the chaplain?' I told him that maybe we could look through the regulations of the navy and see what they say. At that time, we were still following the Queen's regulations for the British Royal Navy. There was nothing about same-sex sexuality in the regulations – so we told the sailors to stop sharing one bed and the story ended there.

I was reminded of that episode many years later, when in 1993 I got a scholarship to study for a master's degree in counselling in the US. On the notice board there were advertisements of student body activities, and one of the groups was called Affinity. The convener of this group was the lady who had welcomed me to the seminary, when I first arrived there late at night. Since I knew her, I thought I should go and attend the meeting of her group. Yet, then another white male student asked me which group I had chosen. When I said I had chosen Affinity, he asked

2. The Kamba (also known as Akamba) are one of the ethnic groups in Kenya.
3. Currently known as St. Paul's University.

me whether I knew it was a group for homosexuals. So, I responded, 'What do you mean? Do you mean there are homosexuals in this seminary?' He said, 'Yes, they are here.' I was surprised and asked, 'Are you saying the convener of that group is a lesbian?' You see, I thought to be homosexual one would look very strange and would certainly not be in a seminary. Anyway, I got scared and never joined the Affinity group.

However, I learned that one of the professors – the one teaching us the marriage and family counselling course – was a lesbian, and I liked her teaching so much! While teaching us about marriage and family counselling, she talked about counselling special populations. These were identified as gays and lesbians, alcoholics, black Americans and Hispanics. That is when I remembered my story at the navy base when the two sailors were caught sharing a bed. I said to myself: after studying this course, when I go back to Kenya, I should have an answer to my commander about homosexuality. I therefore included counselling for special populations as one of my courses. And then it happened that I started discovering the LGBTIQ students and teachers. I can remember one time we were in a study group of six students and one of the students invited us to his home for our group work. So, we went to his house, and as we continued with the discussions, tea was served, and the person who served us tea was another man. My fellow student introduced him as his partner – they were living as a couple! Next thing, while studying there, the bishop of Indianapolis attached me to one of the parishes – I would go there and lead the service and preach on Sundays. There were five priests in the parish, two were heterosexual couples and the other one was a single male. I was told that this single priest was openly gay. By then, finding a clergy who is openly gay did no longer shock me, it hardened me. Now I had all the reasons to know more about homosexuality. So, I got a lot of books about the topic and studied them, so that by the time I came back to Kenya, I knew that homosexuals did not choose to be homosexuals and they are not sinners, or bad people. Instead, they are children of God like everyone else. So, when I came back to the navy, I had an answer to my commanding officer. However, the issue of homosexuality never came up again while I was in the navy after returning from the US.

Yet, upon my return to Kenya, while working in the navy, I was also volunteering as a counsellor at a youth centre in Mombasa. That was when I was asked to visit a young girl who had been admitted to the mental health hospital. So, I went there, and while there, another twenty-year-old man was brought to me, who had been committed there as a mad person. Yet when I talked to and listened to him, I did not find mental sickness in him. I told the doctor that I did not think the man needed to be hospitalized but rather should come to the youth counselling centre and could be assisted from there. The doctor agreed and I asked the young man to come to the youth centre on a Wednesday afternoon. Following what I had learned, I asked him whether he had a girlfriend. He looked at me and did not answer, so I did not follow up. We talked about other things, and we continued for a number of weeks until one day he told me, 'You know major, there is a question you asked me the first time we met. You asked me if I had a girlfriend, but I want you to know that I am gay.' As he was sharing this, he brightened up, he became very happy, he became very free. The following week, he came back to the centre, dressed very smartly, very clean, and we continued our conversation. Soon, people at the centre were asking me, 'What did you do help him – he is so bright, he is so jolly and looks so decent?' I told them that this is the secret of counselling!

Then in 1999 one of the army chaplains was rumoured to be gay, and reports were made by chaplaincy and theology students claiming that he was making advances to them. I was called in to counsel him. When this report reached the archbishop, he called me for a meeting and asked whether the things he had been hearing about reverend so and so were true. I responded saying that whatever is shared in counselling is confidential. Yet in our conversation, I asked the archbishop, 'What is the church' stance on this?' At that time, the debates about homosexuality in the global Anglican Communion were just starting. The Anglican Church in Kenya had not yet taken the position they have now with the advent of GAFCON.[4] So, the archbishop at that time did not have an answer to my question, but we agreed that we cannot judge these people, we cannot send them away because the church worldwide has not yet made a decision on the matter. Some years later, the archbishop had retired, and his successor also called me for a meeting as he had been told that I was protecting this allegedly gay clergy. That was in 2003, when Bishop Gene Robinson had just been ordained in America,[5]

4. GAFCON stands for Global Anglican Future Conference. It was founded in 2008 in response to what it perceives as 'moral compromise, doctrinal error and the collapse of biblical witness in parts of the Anglican communion', especially in relation to issues of sexuality (see www.gafcon.org/about).

5. Gene Robinson served as bishop in the Episcopal (Anglican) Church of the United States in the period 2003–13 and was the first bishop in the worldwide Anglican Communion who was openly gay and in a same-sex partnership. His consecration caused huge tensions in the Communion.

and the Anglican Church in Kenya, and elsewhere in Africa, was beginning to develop a firmer stance against homosexuals. So, by the time we were coming to 2008 for the Lambeth conference,[6] the African bishops said they would not go to Lambeth but would go to Jerusalem instead, which is how GAFCON was born. However, it so happened that although Lambeth is a conference of bishops, in 2008 I was invited to attend Lambeth as a voice of witness to the presence of homosexuality in Africa and as a member of the Anglican Church. This confirmed my choice to study about homosexuality in Africa because I realized that the harvest was plentiful, but the harvesters are few. I chose to become one of the harvesters.

Back in 2003, while I was serving as the chaplain at Armed Forces Memorial Hospital at Mbagathi, a friend of mine invited me to come and preach a series of sermons in his parish in Nairobi. He gave me freedom to choose the topics of interest. When I was looking for topics, the issue of Jesus being the shepherd came to me and I opened the Gospel of John, chapter 10, where Jesus says he is the shepherd and talks about sheep. In verse 16, he says, 'I have other sheep that are not in this flock, and I must bring them also. They will listen to my voice, and there will be one flock and one shepherd.' As I have been trained to do when reading scripture for sermons, in doing my exegesis to find out what verse 16 meant, I asked, 'Who are these other sheep?' I got to understand that during the time of Jesus there were Jews and non-Jews. The latter were not accepted in the assembly of believers or in the temple. Also, when you had broken one of the taboos or commandments, or when you were a leper or an adulterer, you would not be allowed. So, that is when I asked myself, 'Who would be excluded today?' And I realized that in the modern world, homosexuals, alcoholics, divorcees, sex workers and sometimes even children are excluded. These are the other sheep of today! So, I went to preach about this on a Sunday morning. Interesting enough, some of the congregants asked the vicar, 'Can you ask Rev. Kimindu to spare some time in the afternoon for us to come and meet with him?' And when I was asked, I accepted. In the conversation that afternoon, although the issue of homosexuality did not come up, other groups like divorced people and alcoholics did. They were asking, what can you do for us? The idea came up for them to start

6. The Lambeth Conference is a gathering of all bishops of the worldwide Anglican Communion, which is supposed to be convened every ten years by the Archbishop of Canterbury.

meeting as peer groups, and the vicar was willing to allow them to meet. When I travelled back home that night, the issue of other sheep kept going round my mind. How come this topic was so important to the congregation? Can I continue with this other sheep business? And from that day, the idea of other sheep did not leave me. I started convening 'other sheep meetings'. Gradually, gays and lesbians started to attend these meetings, and this is how in 2003 the beginning was made of what became Other Sheep Africa Ministry.

Upon my retirement from navy chaplaincy in 2007, I was posted in a parish in Nairobi, but I was there only for one year. I had become vocal on LGBTIQ advocacy, and I was preaching about inclusion of gay and lesbian people in the church. Some of the parishioners were against it and they went to the archbishop to report me, saying, 'The clergy you brought to us is bad, he is talking about homosexuality.' That is how I came to lose my parish in December 2007, having been there for only one year, and I was not even being paid. The archbishop just told me to step aside. It was a very low moment in my life and ministry when I was relieved of my parish duties in the Anglican Church because of my advocacy for LGBTIQ people. However, God turns grass to grace – I have nothing to complain about because God has not asked me to step aside from work in his kingdom. I found another denomination where I could continue practicing my ministry, this time as an openly LGBTIQ affirming clergy. That was the Metropolitan Community Churches, which has its origins in America.[7] In 2008 I was licensed in that church and went for my licensure in Pretoria, South Africa. Since then, I have been a minister in that denomination and I continue my advocacy.

So that is how I developed my calling – this can only be a calling because if it was self-appointed, I would have stopped long time ago! Along the way, I have been inspired by the character of Jesus Christ, because he was very inclusive, and he calls us all to be like him. The message of Jesus Christ should challenge every homophobic person to change their position. This is because Jesus says, 'Come unto me all of you who are tired of carrying heavy loads and I will give you rest.'[8] Note

---

7. The Universal Fellowship of Metropolitan Community Churches was founded in Los Angeles, California, in 1968 and has since then grown and become a global movement of churches, communities and ministries that offers refuge to LGBTIQ people (see https://insidemcc.org/).

8. Matt. 11.28.

that he said, 'all of you'! All of you is ALL of you – it cannot be only the heterosexuals. And then there is also the verse of Jesus about the other sheep. It means whoever is excluded by our human regulations can be included according to Jesus Christ. When it comes to the characters in the Bible other than Jesus, you will find David and Jonathan. They were male friends and very close to each other – the commitment of their relationship was so open, and Jonathan even gave up his father's throne and gave it to David. Another fascinating character is the Roman centurion in the Gospel of Luke who himself may have been gay as he cared greatly about his servant who had fallen ill. He trusted the power of Jesus so much that he told Jesus, 'You do not have to come to my house, just speak a word from where you are and I know my servant will be healed.'[9] And that is what happened. These characters are pillars in my ministry.

Homophobic pastors are inspired by human literal reading of the scriptures. When I say literal, I mean, they do not ask themselves about the context of the writing of the Bible. The Bible was not written as one letter at the same time to all people – it was written over a long period, in specific contexts, and addressing the situation of particular people. Those who oppose homosexuality will quote the Bible saying, 'Let no man lie with another man like a man lies with a woman.'[10] Yet, they will not ask when was it written, what was the situation, what was happening at the time of writing? They will not ask those questions; they will just say, 'It is written!' However, I believe you cannot say that you love God while hating your neighbour, especially not when that neighbour has not done any harm to you. Just because their hair is black and yours is brown, or they are left-handed and you are right-handed, or they are gay and you are straight – that cannot be the basis for discriminating them. In the same Bible, which they are using, you will find verses talking about the only debt – owe no one anything, except the debt of love.[11] So, if love turns out to be the debt that we need to pay, then where do you find a place for discrimination? The other thing is, sex was given to us by God. In my understanding, sex is not about which specific part of the body is being used; sex as given by God has two components – it can be for procreation but also for pleasure. Now

9. Luk. 7.6–7.

10. Lev. 20.13.

11. Rom. 13.8: 'Let no debt remain outstanding, except the continuing debt to love one another, for whoever loves others has fulfilled the law.'

if you want sex for procreation, of necessity it will be about opposite sex interaction. But for pleasure, there are so many ways of having sex for pleasure. Moreover, same-sex orientation is not about choice, it is about attraction. Attraction is inbuilt, and you cannot fake it.

As much as I have faced many challenges due to my ministry, I have always been encouraged to persevere. When I receive Christmas greetings from a gay or lesbian person who I counselled years ago, and they call or write to me to say what it meant to them, I feel fulfilled. When the parent of a gay child calls me to find out what is happening to their child, and I can talk to such a parent, so they come to understand, I am fulfilled. This is because I feel that the message of the other sheep has been communicated and a soul somewhere may be saved. The work for LGBTIQ inclusion is like burning a candle. You do not light a candle and put it under a bowl.[12] If you support LGBTIQ inclusion, then you should stand out like a light – let people know that for you, LGBTIQ people are human and do not portray any form of ugliness or danger; they are a comfort to you in every respect, they are jolly people especially when given a safe space to be themselves and encounter Christ.

12. Matt. 5.15.

Story 18

FR. ETTORE MARANGI: 'I DO NOT SUPPORT LGBTIQ PEOPLE AS AN ACTIVIST, BUT AS A CHRISTIAN'

Originally from Italy, Fr. Ettore Marangi is a Franciscan friar and a Catholic priest who has lived and worked in Kenya for the past ten years. Initially working as a theology lecturer at Tangaza University College, Fr. Marangi lost his job because of a Facebook post suggesting that we could encounter God in the faces of lesbian and gay people, among other excluded communities. Working in a slum area in Nairobi, for him to be socially engaged with marginalized groups such as LGBTIQ people springs from his Franciscan spirituality and from the gospel itself. In this story, he shares the insights he has developed through his ministry into sexuality in Christian traditions and in African cultures.[1]

I am a Franciscan friar originally from Italy but now living and working in Nairobi, Kenya. I always wanted to match my academic studies with my religious vocation as a Franciscan. That is why I wanted to do theology for the poor with the poor, and to share my commitment with them. After my graduation, I worked for a few years as a teacher in Italy, but then I applied to be transferred to Kenya, because at the time, the Kenyan Peace and Justice movement was very strong. I taught in Tangaza University College, but I was not impressed with the Nairobi suburb, Langata, where it is based. There are so many Catholic priests and churches there; more masses are being said there than in the Vatican! There was not a real need for me. That is when I decided to move from Langata to Westland's in Nairobi, more precisely in Deepsea

1. This story is based on an interview with Fr. Marangi on 1 March 2023 in Nairobi, Kenya.

slum[2] where we started a community project. When I arrived in the area, there were so many street children that I had to do something. I have started to match children to women in the community who raise them as their own. The idea of taking care of non-biological children in larger family units is something that is shared across Italian and African cultures. The project developed and now we take care of the children's education. We offer a boarding school for primary school students and a day school for high school students. In the 'I care school', our vision is informed by the pedagogical approach developed by Paulo Freire in Brazil.[3] We also have activities aimed at women. We do Bible study, using stories from the Bible to promote social action. We provide microcredit and run an NGO through which we provide health support in the community. We also have a network of volunteers coming from Italy to help. I have been working here for ten years.

I became a Franciscan brother to follow the spirituality of St Francis of Assisi who went back to the principles of the gospel by selling everything and donating it to the poor. My journey has been quite unique because when young, a teenager, I was not interested in religion. On the contrary, I was part of a gang of boys who bullied other boys. Then, one day, I felt something in my heart, I understood it was wrong, so I left this group. My brothers and sisters used to go to church in the month of May – the month of the Virgin Mary in the Catholic calendar. Once I went with them to church, to be honest, to look for friends, not for spiritual concerns. But while there, something happened that changed my life forever. It felt like Jesus was talking to me. It was then that I felt I had to make a choice between continuing with my shallow life, or to embrace spirituality for good. After May, when my siblings and friends stopped attending church, I decided to continue. I went everyday early in the morning. In joined a church group for youths committed to many issues including prayer and meditation but also social and ecological issues. So, this social commitment was something that I developed from the perspective of faith – the vocation to become a priest came after.

The Franciscan order has no seminary. Instead of a seminary we have small communities – not more than twenty people per group. While I was in this community in the south of Italy, we were studying at a theological institute. So, there was theory and praxis being related

2. An informal urban settlement.
3. See Freire (2018).

together daily. I studied philosophy, then theology, then went to the Gregorian University in Rome and after my PhD I taught for some years in Italy, dogmatic theology. Then I left everything to come here to Kenya, and I had to learn everything, including Kiswahili. I became a friar because I found people within this order very open to others. You know, Francis of Assisi had a very good relationship with the world, and also with his own body, at a time when the body was seen as a source of sin. Women were considered to be something sinful, and temptation was seen everywhere. Francis was a saint because he taught people to love themselves and to love others. Within the Franciscan order there is no hierarchy but brotherhood; that is why I was attracted to this order. And Franciscans have always been engaged with the prophetic needs of society.

Being LGBTIQ inclusive for me sprung from the gospel itself. I have not been supporting LGBTIQ people as an activist, but just as a Christian. Here in Kenya, talking about homosexuality is almost an obsession. People say that there are no homosexuals in Africa, yet they talk about homosexuals all the time – this is a contradiction! If there was a problem to discuss and tackle in churches, that would be rape and violence. These are real problems. I have been working here for ten years and heard many stories of rape from women living in slums or from middle-class women. I would say that around 50 per cent of the women I have encountered have experienced some form of gender-based violence. This should be at the centre of public debates but instead all they talk about is homosexuality.

The risk of being openly homosexual here is very high; I would not go public if I was homosexual. However, I use Jesus and his radical inclusivity as a way to initiate important conversations. For example, when I am in Italy in order to provoke an audience, I would mention the fact that Jesus welcomed prostitutes and tax collectors. If I am with white supremacists, I would speak about black people. Here in Kenya, talking about Jesus being poor would not be provocative. For people to understand the inclusive way of Jesus, you have to look for those who are excluded in that society, and in Kenya, that are the homosexuals. In my community work, I have had children where from a very young age you could see that they had an issue in terms of gender. So, we had to protect them. I am still in touch, checking in on them to see how they are doing, and telling them to be careful … This is how I became engaged in this work – they are wonderful young people. We need to protect them so that they do not end up being stigmatized forever.

I have always been struck by the hypocrisy in many Christian congregations, because there are homosexuals everywhere, but they do not talk about that. Once I wrote a post on Facebook, it was not a big deal to me, but it became an open scandal. After celebrating a mass in a convent that focused on the closeness of Jesus to those who were marginalized in society, I was discussing with the nuns over breakfast about the people who were kept at the margins of society nowadays. With regards to the US, we said that black people were marginalized. Disabled people are marginalized in many contexts. Women are kept at the margins in Iran, for example. Homosexuals are kept at the margins here in Kenya. But on what side is God if not with those excluded, those ones at the margins? When I went back to my room I kept reflecting on the manifestation of God's justice and on the image of God. I asked myself, who is the person that can claim to be closest to God today? I was also thinking eschatologically, about what is the real image of God that we will discover in the afterlife? Because biblically speaking, in the present day, we only know God partially, but in the future the full mystery will be revealed, and we shall see God as he is.

Thinking about all this, I came up with a joke that I put online, saying, 'The biggest surprise in the life of a priest happens when he dies because he discovers that God is a woman, she is black and she is a lesbian.' When I discussed this post during a lecture with my students, they suggested that I should have also considered to add in 'disabled' because we find God amongst the most excluded in society. But this joke caused a drastic response. Hell broke loose! I was dismissed from the college where I taught, without the possibility of explaining myself. Surely the problem was not connected with me saying that God was a black woman – it must be because I said God is a lesbian. Yet, my point was that those who are most excluded in society, show us the face of God. Instead of being considered demonic, because of their experience of exclusion, homosexuals may actually be the tabernacle of the presence of God.

I learned the hard way that in Kenya, homosexuality has become a deeply political and ideological issue. I have been here for many years, and I can confidently say that regular people in the street do not discriminate. In Deepsea settlement there is a Ugandan LGBTIQ refugee, and everybody loves him. He has been there for many years. He is usually invited to play the drums at church. I think people in this country have always been welcoming but now homosexuality is used in ideological ways, a way to define a collective identity, with 'homosexuality not being Kenyan'. But what does it mean to be Kenyan?

What is surprising is that not so many people actually discriminate. However, those ones who do are very vocal, emotional and not flexible. They will not reason! They create an environment of fear. There are teachers in Tangaza University College who cannot speak up on my defence because otherwise they would lose their job, too. So, the environment of fear is very much present, and it allows people to advance these homophobic arguments without being challenged.

Historically speaking, Africans did not have an issue with homosexuality, look for example at the Ugandan martyrs.[4] Perhaps people did not speak about it, but they certainly knew about it. Homosexuality has always been present. In some cultures, maybe homosexuality was seen as something bad. But in others it was tolerated and in others it was celebrated until Christianity came to Africa. Now we have this public obsession with it. Going deep into the issue, the problem is that the Christianity we practise here is a heritage of colonization. We talk a lot about inculturation,[5] but we have not managed to develop a form of Christianity that links to our cultures, our feelings and our needs. We need a decolonization of the mind, not just in the church but also among the political class. Because what I see is that we took a piece of Europe and we put it here.

Many of the popular arguments against homosexuality, culturally speaking, centre around family and marriage. They say, 'We are defending family values.' Yet, I discovered that African cultures have many different forms of family. Marriage often was polygamous. There are ethnic groups where women in certain circumstances could marry women. And the family functioned as an extended and open family model. So, in Africa families were never like the nuclear family of Mary

4. The martyrs of Uganda are recognized by both the Anglican and the Catholic churches. They were pages in the royal court of the Buganda Kingdom and were among the first converts to Christianity in Uganda, in the late nineteenth century. They were executed on orders of the Buganda King, for reasons linked in some sources to their refusal to meet the king's sexual demands. The shrines of the martyrs in Namugongo, Kampala, are sites of pilgrimage and their memory plays a complex role in current discourses regarding homosexuality in Uganda (see Rao 2015).

5. Inculturation is a term often used in African Catholic circles to refer to the process where Christian faith and African cultures come together in a productive way to create a more authentically African form of Christianity. See Magesa (2004).

and Joseph with the child Jesus. Even in Europe, this family model only came after the industrial revolution. So, this nuclear form of family life has never been there in Africa. One of the women in my Bible study group, because we have reached a level where we can share everything, she said that in Kenya every woman is practically single. This is true for several reasons: many have been disserted by their husbands, others have travelled far for work, and even if husband and wife live together, they often do not share that much. So, from a sociological point of view, Africa has many different experiences with marriage and family forms. *The* African family does not exist.

In my class you would not find many people that discriminate homosexuals, in fact many share the present teaching of the Catholic Church that to be homosexual is not a sin. But the few that are against it, they are very determined. I try to teach them that being Christian should mean to be open to others, to even challenge your own identity. Indeed St Paul said, 'I became a pagan to the pagans, a Jew to the Jews.'[6] You must lose your identity in order to recognize yourself in those ones different from you. But here the opposite is happening. For them the identity issue is becoming stronger and stronger without understanding that those cultural traits that are used to define this identity, they have actually been produced externally. This explains those strong emotions as they fear the idea of losing their own identity. It becomes a question of life or death for yourself. You do not know who you are anymore. But Christianity is meant to be the opposite – God became human. That is what the theology of the incarnation is about. The journey between divinity to humanity, I think, is bigger than the journey between being heterosexual and homosexual, or for a heterosexual to understand a homosexual.

Even beyond Africa, for me today homosexuality is a focal topic in the church. The acknowledgement that homosexuality has nothing to do with the devil, but it is part of God's creation is pivotal. If homosexuality is accepted, then there is space for everyone in the church! Those ones who read the Bible in a fundamentalist way, they shut any opportunity for inclusion. There is no coherence in a fundamentalist reading of the Bible because anyway the reading goes through a process of selection; for example, even if the Bible says so, we do not stone women; they chose what they want to hear. The fundamentalist reading of the Bible is not so much a Catholic problem, more an issue within Protestant

6. See 1 Cor. 9.19–23.

churches. Instead in the Catholic Church there is a tendency of not talking about sex at all because there is a lot of hypocrisy, amongst the clergy and churchgoers alike. They preach in one way, and they behave in another. For example, there are a lot of people having extra marital sex … but nobody talks about that. So today the reality is that we are not saying anything valuable in terms of moral theology related to sex.

I think the current pope, Pope Francis, is doing a lot to try to initiate important conversations. But in the local church there is silence. We have good pastors and even bishops that are welcoming, but they do not take position. They are open in their pastoral ministry, but they do not stand up in public. We should not treat people in different ways because they love in different ways. Nobody should live in fear. To my fellow clergy I say, do not be afraid of being LGBTIQ inclusive because in the end we are only accountable to God and not to human beings.

Story 19

SHEIKH DAWOUD: 'I DO NOT PROMOTE HOMOSEXUALITY, I JUST PROTECT PEOPLE WHO ARE PART OF OUR COMMUNITY'

Sheikh Dawoud is a devoted Muslim and a human rights defender who lives in Mombasa County. He works with PEMA Kenya delivering training programmes to fellow religious leaders across the country. In this story, he shares his experiences of the resistance they encounter during this work, but also tells how bridges can be built when religious leaders really listen to LGBTIQ people and learn about their experiences. Sheikh Ibrahim is frequently accused of promoting homosexuality, yet in his own words, all he seeks to do is to protect the human rights of minorities in society. Doing so, he is inspired by Quranic verses underlining that judgement belongs to God.[1]

I am a devoted Muslim believer and also a human rights defender. Over the years I have dealt with different human rights issues such as advocacy in favour of HIV and AIDS treatment and care, child protection, Do-No-Harm for people who use drugs, and as well as LGBTIQ inclusion, in this case with a particular focus on violence protection. LGBTIQ inclusion, however, has been far more challenging than the other human rights issues that I have worked on previously. This is because there are so many stereotypes about this community, so there is a lot of resistance even among fellow religious leaders who are completely unwilling to engage with this issue.

My journey to becoming inclusive towards sexual and gender minorities started back in the early 2000s. One of our family friends is

---

1. This story is based on an interview conducted with Sheikh Dawoud (pseudonym) on 20 December 2022 in Mombasa, Kenya.

a Christian reverend, Rev. Kimindu,[2] who has been working in this area for a long time. He is the one who invited me and other religious leaders to a dialogue with our LGBTIQ fellows, who often are disowned by their families and unheard within our communities. He was concerned that religious leaders most of the time are just dismissing these people. Thus, he had started a programme where religious leaders could explore verses from the Bible and the Quran relating to human sexualities. His vision was that creating understanding of these issues would help to change the situation on the ground, especially reducing the high levels of violence and discrimination that LGBTIQ people face in society but also in faith communities. I participated in that programme, which he delivered together with PEMA Kenya.[3] We first started discussing the situation of HIV and AIDS in the community, then we moved on to discussing gender-based violence, then drug abuse, and it was only at the end that the issue of LGBTIQ people in our churches and mosques was brought up. The intent was to show religious leaders that all those issues are interconnected and how they are letting down those various people. The training really empowered me, as it removed the ignorance and stereotypes that I had about LGBTIQ people. The moment I learned that these are our brothers and sisters, and they are fellow human beings, I started to recognize our shared humanity. And if they are human, who am I to judge them? So, that is how my journey began, and I have been working with PEMA Kenya since then.

But this work has not been easy. I can recall, for example, that on one occasion we brought together 250 Muslim leaders from both Mombasa and Kwale Counties. The meeting started well, since we first discussed with them the issues of HIV and drug users, and then stopped for a tea break. Upon reconvening we initiated the LGBTIQ discussion, but unfortunately the scene became very hostile and volatile. They were angrily shouting at us, 'Why are you coming here to teach us about homosexuality? We have no interest in this seminar of yours!' After some time of chaotic shouting, many of the participants left. With the few that remained we continued the meeting. From that point on, we decided to focus on other regions instead of the coastal region. We went to Kisumu, Nairobi, Migori, Garissa and so on. The only other two areas we got into problems were Garissa and Isiolo, which both have quite

---

2. See Story 17 in this book.

3. PEMA Kenya is a Mombasa-based organization advancing the rights of gender and sexual minorities.

a strong Muslim presence. On one occasion, we had gathered sheikhs and elders, and we started the meeting by introducing ourselves. Unfortunately, the lady who was co-facilitating with us introduced herself as a lesbian, and at that point the meeting turned chaotic. We were lucky that the convener of this meeting is a well-respected human rights defender in the area, so she urged the participants to listen and if they did not agree with our message, then no one would compel them to change their views. So, people calmed down and the meeting went on. They became so accepting and understanding, that when the meeting was over, they were willing to take photos with the lesbian lady they had earlier so loudly rejected.

Another meeting I will never forget was in Garissa County. We hardly had the opportunity even to introduce ourselves before all hell broke loose. Some elderly Somali men started shouting and even threatened to beat us up with their *bakoras*.[4] We were really scared for our lives. There were only five of us, far away from home, and here we had angry locals threatening to beat us up! But thank God, the handful of instigators who wanted to beat us were requested to leave the meeting, and the organizer managed to calm down the crowd and we felt safe again. I also remember an incidence in Mombasa where the meeting deteriorated into a heckling match. They were telling us to go away, saying, 'What things are you bringing here? Don't you know that God has cursed these people? What are you coming to tell us?!' We remained silent without answering them back, hoping that our silence would calm down the situation. After the insults many of them left the meeting and it is only after they left that we were able to continue with the few who remained.

Travelling to other parts of the country such as the western region in counties such as Kisumu and Migori made me realize that LGBTIQ communities are not unique to Mombasa. The long-term narrative in Kenya had been that LGBTIQ people are only to be found in the coastal region.[5] But when we got to places like Migori, Kisumu and Homa Bay in western Kenya, we found that they are there, too. Religious leaders in those areas told us that they have LGBTIQ people in their midst. They were therefore happy that we were building their capacity on how to minister their needs. So, for me this was a happy moment realizing

4. Traditional walking sticks.
5. The Swahili coast of East Africa has a long history of same-sex sexuality (see Amory 1998).

that these people are everywhere in society and they are human just like anyone else.

My approach to this work should not be seen as if I am promoting LGBTIQ people; what I am trying to do is to emphasize that they are human beings, and we should not subject them to judgements or deny them their rights. My stand is that if they need to go for medical, police or whatever services, they should feel free like anybody else in society. If they go to a police station to report a human rights violation, then the focus should be on the violation of their rights not their sexual orientation. If on the other hand they commit a crime, deal with this person as you would any other criminal but not any worse on account of their sexuality or gender identity. If they go to the hospital, treat them like any other sick person without denying them any essential services. So, it is not about promoting them, but rather about ensuring that they get equal treatment without discrimination. Even when they themselves talk to society, they say they do not need special treatment but just want equal treatment without any form of discrimination. That is why I do this work, on the grounds of equality and non-discrimination.

I am inspired by the positive changes that we bring in society. For example, when we were in Machakos, we sat with religious leaders there and we educated each other; at the end of the session they were asking if we could come back and educate them some more. I had expected that we would get harassed like other places we had gone to earlier, but in Machakos they were so keen to listen, and they saw the benefits of our conversations. They felt that a one-day training was not enough, so they were asking for three to five days so that we can discuss the issues in-depth. I can also recall a time when we went to a mosque in Makindu and leaders there said that they had children in their schools who are LGBTIQ, so they asked us to share more as they wanted to understand and support them. It gives me great joy to see LGBTIQ people being treated as human beings in society. I can give you a recent example, of an incident in Mombasa. Some LGBTIQ people had organized a birthday party and local youths wanted to beat them up. The area police commander was called to calm down the situation, but instead of offering protection he wanted to arrest the LGBTIQ folks. However, the chief of that area had participated in our training, so he told the police commander not to arrest anyone. Instead, the chief called me and together with PEMA Kenya we evacuated the group to a safe place. The ideal situation would of course be that these guys could just have a birthday party like anyone else and not be bothered; but at least we were happy to know that the chief and the local elders came to their defence.

In all these engagements I am inspired by two Quranic verses. The first one says that the Almighty God created Adam, the first human, in his own image.[6] For me, this applies to humankind as a whole, and it means that God does not discriminate for we all are created in God's image. Second, the Quran also tells us not to examine each other, because the Almighty God is the only one who gives judgement.[7] He has not given anyone permission to judge. All judgements are given by Allah. Those who judge others have taken on the work of the Almighty God. I often feel like many religious leaders do not want to reflect on these passages or even preach about them, when confronted with LGBTIQ people. They ignore these inclusive parts of the scriptures and only talk about the ones that fit their worldview. Reading the Quran and actually understanding it are two different things. The text that dominates their preaching is the story of Sodom and Gomorrah. Yet when you read about these two cities, is there not more to it than just homosexuality?

God tells us that his work is to guide us, but the day of judgement is his. At the end of the day, I will get the sum of my actions – the good and the bad. The Quran tells us that there are two angels, one seated on the right shoulder writing down our good deeds and on the left shoulder, writing down our bad deeds, until the last day. On the basis of their records, we shall be judged by God. Thus, when it comes to LGBTIQ issues I believe that one has to make a fundamental decision: do you want to spread hatred, or tolerance? My mission is to promote and protect rights. I am not promoting homosexuality, as some accuse me of, but rather protecting the human rights of people who are part of our community. What they do in their private room is not my concern; rather my focus is to ensure that their human rights are not violated, nor should they be discriminated against. I do not go beyond human rights and non-discrimination. If they engage in same-sex sexuality that is about their lives and only their God will be their judge. Since I have decided to do this advocacy work, my focus became single-minded, and I will keep working until all community members will feel safe in society. I will not rest until this goal is realized.

6. This is not explicitly stated in the Quran, but in the Hadith (Book 16, Hadith 72).

7. Surah Al-An'am 6:57.

Story 20

SHEIKH ABDALLAH: 'LGBTIQ PEOPLE HAVE GIFTS WHICH WE NEED FOR THE *UMMA* TO GROW'

Sheikh Abdallah is an Islamic teacher in the coastal region of Kenya. As a religious leader, he has engaged in interfaith work and in advocacy for children, women and also sexual and gender minorities. As he narrates in this story, the latter has been the most challenging and it resulted in him losing his position some years ago. Despite these difficulties, he remains convinced that LGBTIQ people are part of God's creation and make a valuable contribution to the umma, the Muslim community. He is motivated by his sense of calling from God and by the example of the Prophet Muhammad.[1]

I am a Kenyan Muslim born in Mombasa County. I was educated in formal and informal Muslim institutions. Today, I am a husband of three wives and a father of eleven children. I thank God for my family. As a religious leader, I am working tirelessly to promote harmony and unity within the community. I used to work as an insurance salesperson. But my fellow Muslim believers challenged me, saying that such a career was forbidden for devout Muslims. They said it was *riba* and therefore forbidden under Islamic law.[2] Yet when I would ask why

---

1. This story is based on an interview with Sheikh Abdallah (pseudonym) on 20 December 2022 in Mombasa, Kenya.
2. *Riba* is an Arabic word meaning 'excess' or 'increase', and it refers to exploitative financial practices that are considered *haram* (forbidden) in Islam.

it is *riba*, no one could answer me. So, in 1998 I decided to quit my job and start attending madrasa, so that I could learn about Islam and know what *riba* is. That is how my journey to being a religious leader started. After four years in class, I left the madrasa as a trained Islamic teacher. Going back to work with the insurance company was out of question. Instead, I started preaching Islam. I was given posts in Islamic centres across the country, first in the coastal region, then in Nairobi, later in Nakuru County and then back to the coast. When we talk of an Islamic centre, this includes the mosque as the house of prayer but also other auxiliary services such as madrasa for Islamic children to learn about their religion.

The first advocacy work that I picked up as a sheikh was advancing children's rights. I had come to observe that many of us religious leaders were using corporal punishments when training them in madrasas. As a result, some of the kids ended up running away from madrasas, so this approach to instilling discipline was not helping. I held workshops for other preachers to explore how we are going to instil discipline in our centres without corporal punishments. I thank God this is now working well. At the time I became a religious leader in the coastal region, we also had the challenge of interreligious rivalry. The coastal region in Kenya is largely dominated by Muslims but also has a significant Christian population. The rivalry between them had deteriorated to such an extent that a Muslim teacher could not teach a Christian pupil in school and a Muslim pupil could not be trained by a Christian teacher. It also happened that churches were put on fire and burned down. I began to bring together Muslim and Christian religious leaders and we created an interfaith organization with the objective of building peace and harmony between Muslims and Christians. I used to tell them that we are brothers and sisters as we are all descendants of Abraham, and Abraham is the father of our faiths. So, if Abraham is the father, why should we kids fight? It did help and the problem got somehow solved – not completely solved but things calmed down at least.

After we had addressed that challenge, I came to realize that there was yet another one. I became aware of gender and sexual minorities who were facing a lot of stigma and suffering. They were being denied services, persecuted in the streets and even thrown out of their own houses. Which is painful when you realize that they are part of our community and actually are someone's son or daughter. I therefore brought together some of my friends to brainstorm and see how we could address the issues they were facing. Fortunately, we received help from PEMA Kenya and we partnered with them so that we could reach out to religious leaders within our region.[3] We began holding forums with religious leaders of both Muslim and Christian backgrounds. It has taken us time, but as of now in Mombasa and the coastal region at large, the temperatures are moderate. At least a gay person can now stand in front of people and identify himself without anybody pointing fingers.

In Mombasa County, I observed that we have many people who identify as sexual and gender minorities, although they are hidden. These people are very much oppressed behind the curtains, yet there were other people who are benefiting from their suffering. Now my biggest question was and still is: if God is the creator, the fashioner and designer and it is God who designed this person the way he or she is, then who am I to judge that person? For example, if someone feels that she is female in a male body, biologically male but psychologically female, am I supposed to change that person? How can I even do that? Who am I to tell them who they should be like? And why should we oppress that person? So, after observing that many people are suffering for those reasons, I asked, why do we not stop judging people? Why do we not leave them alone? After all, God said that he will open the hearts of whomever he wants to guide, but he will tighten the chest of one whom he has led astray. So, we can leave it to God.

Given this understanding, I accompany those who need my support because they are human beings who are creatures of God just like everybody else. It gives me great motivation when I meet them and hear their stories. One of the things I ask my fellow religious leaders and members of my community to reflect on is: Beyond their sexual orientation or gender identity, what contribution are LGBTIQ people making to our society? Because I have come to discover that among them, there are people who bring lots of development in the community. They are doctors, they are artists, they are nurses, they are counsellors. We need these people. Why should we isolate them and discriminate against them? Even though they identify as LGBTIQ they are people like us with their professions just like everybody else. They make their contributions to the people, supporting the growth of the entire society, the *umma*.[4] Imagine you have your child who is sick and here is a lesbian, who is a doctor, ready to treat your kid, are you going to let your

3. PEMA Kenya is a Mombasa-based organization advancing the rights of gender and sexual minorities.

4. *Umma* is an Arabic word referring to the whole Muslim world or the community of believers that unites all Muslims.

child die because there is no heterosexual doctor nearby? They could be the best cook in the village, and when I want to throw a party, why not hire them to organize that party? She may be a lesbian, but a very good hairdresser, so when I want my wife beatified why would I not get her service? I started telling people in my community, 'Let us forget about what the LGBTIQ people do in the privacy of their homes, and let us instead see the value they bring to society.' In fact, if sex is the problem, everyone has sex regardless of whether they are gay or heterosexual. The Prophet (peace be upon him) tells us that when you expose your neighbours' shame, be prepared to be exposed yourself, too. Meaning that we all have our issues. Let us fight our own issues first, not our friends' issues. Why should we be looking at what someone else is doing and forgetting about what I do? Let us see what value this person has and how we can combine these values with our own, so that together we develop our community. I created a Swahili slogan saying, 'achana na ushoga, angalia shoga', which loosely translates as 'stop focusing on homosexuality, instead focus [on the value] of the homosexual person'. The homosexual will always remain a human being. Why do we not just focus on the human being instead? Accepting and working with them does not mean that I become of their sexuality. It is not infectious. They will remain homosexual, and I will remain heterosexual. But they are people who have their gifts, and we need them for the *umma* to grow.

Unfortunately, due to this work, I have been branded many names. Of all the social justice issues I have worked on, this one has been the most challenging to an extent of me losing my position at the Islamic centre in 2019. Since then, I have been without any stable source of livelihood, with the burden of three wives and the kids who need to eat, learn and have shelter and yet there is no income. But the provider is God. Of course, this work will come with its own hardships, and this is actually contained in the Quran. In one chapter Allah said, 'So, surely with hardship comes ease.'[5] After all these challenges, one day one time, there will come a time to overcome. And why am I living experiencing these challenges, just because I want to serve human beings? God created the first human being to take responsibility for everything in the world, be they animals or other human beings. We have been given that responsibility. Thus, we are meant to love each other, be merciful with each other and at peace. How do you live in peace, when a fellow human in your community is being discriminated and denigrated?

5. Surah Ash Sharh 94:5.

I have been accused of offending a particular part of the scriptures, yet this accusation is based on misinterpretation of scripture. So, it becomes your obligation to make them understand that verse. Unfortunately, this takes time and during that process of making them understand, that person has already been offended for nothing. Many people say, the story of Sodom and Gomorrah condemns these people. Yet we must ask, in Sodom and Gomorrah, was homosexuality the only sin being committed? There were a lot of sins that were being done during that time: killing, murder and praying to idols. Yet we do not talk about these other sins. The Quran mentions so many different sins. We have to look at how the scriptures are used to harm people. That is what we should condemn. For example, many males within our religion do offend their wives just because a man is the head of the family and has the obligation to command of the woman. If he says, my wife let us go right, we must go right; but sometimes, this wife may be having a point which is so beneficial for the family, yet the man will not listen. Another example, and this happens quite often, is with divorce. You see, Muslims are allowed to divorce. But in Islamic law, divorce has its conditions, it is supposed to happen responsibly. Yet sometimes it happens, that a man wants to divorce one of his wives, so he can marry another one, because the maximum allowed is four wives. This is so bad, and yet that person comes asking you to officiate the marriage – and you have no choice but to officiate because if he has decided to divorce one of his wives to marry another one, there is nothing you can do. These are some of the occasions that I feel so low as a religious leader. I know that scriptures are being used to harm people, in this case women.

I see this work as a calling. I trained as a salesman but there was something that developed in me and that led me to believe that the people of God need to be educated on matters pertaining to religion and sharia. So, this is calling – it may not make us rich, but you feel so much happier when you serve the community and serve God's creatures, knowing that tomorrow God will reward you. I remember that God said that the world has been fashioned in green colours to trigger us as human beings, but we are not going to stay here forever and ever. The best and everlasting life will come after death. In addition, there is the story about the Prophet (peace be upon him) when he was passing away, he asked one of his wives, Aisha, how much they had left in store. Aisha said that they had nothing but four dirhams. The Prophet then ordered Aisha to give those four dirhams to charity, after which he closed his eyes and died. Why should I work hard to accumulate wealth, when I cannot take it with me? When we leave the world, we leave it with nothing. What will help me, instead, is if I advocate for other people so that they live a good life and will pray for me. If I would leave a million shilling, my family will fight over it and bring me fire in my death. So, I better spend most of my time here on earth struggling for what will be more beneficial for me in the life hereafter. When you have a calling, it may not sustain you in the here and now, but you will get something out of it tomorrow or in the near future. That is why it is so painful when someone says that I advocate for gay people because I get paid for it well. What am I getting? Nothing.

The first human being was created to take responsibility of the world. Therefore, it is my pleasure to see myself working running up and down taking that responsibility especially for the minorities. I like the image of a human person who holds and lifts the globe with their two hands. It reminds me that God has given us the world to look after, carrying it with all its burdens. I cannot go to every part of the world, but here I am, and I know that whatever I am speaking about and doing today will contribute something good. My words and actions will help the world to become a place of peace, where all people can live in harmony.

Story 21

YOUTH LEADER ABDUL: 'WE HAVE TO STAND WITH THEM BECAUSE OF THAT BROTHER- AND SISTERHOOD'

Abdul is a youth leader at a mosque in Kampala, Uganda. He also is a trained nurse and got involved with the LGBTIQ community through his work at a clinic providing HIV treatment, care and prevention commodities. Knowing that LGBTIQ people are often being discriminated against in the Muslim community, he believes that being LGBTIQ does not stop one from being a good Muslim. In this story, he reflects on his understanding of Islam and his interpretation of the Quran, narrating how his faith motivates him to recognize the humanity of LGBTIQ people and see them as brothers and sisters.[1]

I was brought up as a Muslim and my father was a Muslim leader in the local community. I am now a leader at a mosque in the northwestern part of Kampala myself. I can say that I am quite knowledgeable about Islam. Recently I was elected as the education leader in the mosque. I have been a youth leader for over twenty years. I started to contribute to the mosque as secretary general, and now I am part of the education team. I like helping out. This is part of our religion because as Muslims we are promised that there will be a re-payment for doing good work once we die. I do this work because I know that God will pay me back after death. It is for this reason that I started volunteering as a youth leader since a young age. I am also very committed in political activities. It is well known in my community that I am involved with the opposition movement.

1. This story is based on an interview with Abdul (pseudonym) on 19 January 2023 in Kampala, Uganda.

It gives me great pleasure and high satisfaction to be involved in the decision-making process at the mosque, even if I am still young. Whenever the mosque leadership wants to take major decisions over anything, they consult me. And if the community is interested in asking anything from the leaders, instead of asking others, they reach out to ask me. It makes me feel valued as a youth leader. Amongst Muslims, we normally have marked differences of opinion between the elders, who are not well educated, and the younger generation, that is more trained in theology and Islamic studies. I try to build bridges between these divides. There was a time when there was no communication across generations at all. There had been a leadership struggle and the elders did not know how to resolve the issue. So, they reached out to me to talk at the mosque to talk to the protagonists and we settled all the issues. Another time some elders planned to sell off the land around the mosque. People did not know how to deal with this issue, so I wrote an article in the newspaper about it and with the support of the community we were able to stop it. We were able to prevent the sale. To this day, that is one of my happiest moments as a leader. I should add that even though I have had such successes, there are also times when I have failed. I recall a time when we wanted to do fundraising for construction work on the mosque. I was one of the persons taking the lead on the project, but on the day of the biggest fundraising activity nobody turned up. We failed. It was not only embarrassing but also sad because we could not realize the project we had in mind.

My interaction with the LGBTIQ community started through my job. I am trained as a nurse and I work in a community health clinic. As such, I am frequently invited to attend programmes of an organization concerned with sexual and reproductive health. Three-quarters of their membership are LGBTIQ people. When I first attended their training, I did not like it for religious reasons, or what I thought was the right religious teaching. Imagine, it was the first time I met people who identified as lesbian, gay and so on! But when I started to investigate more, I was particularly struck by the verse in the Quran that says that you cannot say you are fearing God when you have not been tested.[2] So, with that verse in mind I decided to go ahead. I started to treat patients referred to us by this organization. They were referred to my clinic and with time we got to know each other; they would come for safe sex

---

2. Surah Al-'Ankabut 29:2: 'Do the people reckon that they will be left to say "We believe", and will not be tried?'

commodities, and I would give them. With time we started to socialize even beyond the clinic, they considered me part of their community because they were inviting me to non-health-related events.

I recognize the humanity of LGBTIQ individuals coming from two different perspectives. First, as a medic, I am supposed to treat all people the same, no matter what they do or what their convictions are. Second, as a religious leader, I still treat LGBTIQ as human beings since I am educated. I may not agree with their lifestyle or choices, but the Quran says that you cannot make everybody do what you want.[3] So, it means that if I tell you to do what God wants, but you choose not to do it, that is no reason for me to fight you; instead, I should respect your views. Therefore, when you come to me as a person, I will welcome you. But there are many Muslim leaders who are not educated this way. They are only now beginning to go to school, those are the ones who have problems with LGBTIQ people, because of the lack of education. In addition, the Quran says that when you help somebody to heal a disease, you have healed the whole nation.[4] So, when we take care of one person, we have taken care of humanity. Thus, we cannot exclude certain groups. For instance, even though as a Muslim I do not drink, when I see someone who is drunk and needs my help, I will help him. Taking alcohol is their decision but treating them is my duty. Likewise, with LGBTIQ persons, people may talk about how they are dressed, and people may even run away when they see a gay person attending the mosque, but I will go out and hug that person.

When they ask at the mosque why I am working with this community, I respond by telling them that the Prophet (peace be upon him) teaches us not to run away from someone who is in the wrong; instead, you should stay with them so that you can explain what is good and right and then let them make their own decisions. At the mosque, because I am well respected, nobody says anything negative about me working with the LGBTIQ community. This could be because they see me as a medic, so they do not speak – or at least not directly to me – about their views regarding my work with the LGBTIQ community. In this work, my favourite Quranic verse is the one I mentioned earlier, which says that when you help one person you have helped the whole universe.

3. Surah Al-Qasas 28:56: 'Thou guidest not whom thou likest, but God guides whom He wills, and knows very well those that are guided.'

4. Surah Al-Maidah 5:32: 'Who gives life to a soul, shall be as if he had given life to mankind altogether.'

This helps me to do work with everybody in society. There is no reason for not spending time and helping the LGBTIQ community. After all, God says, 'I knew you when I was creating in your mother's womb, so never boast around that you are righteous.'[5] We therefore cannot say that we know who is wrong and who is right before God. And for that reason, I cannot say that this one or that one should not come close to me because I am righteous. I normally follow this Surah.

The religious leaders who hate LGBTIQ people do so because they do not know Islam well enough. If you learn and know Islam, it will be clear that you are not supposed to hate anybody. The moment one understands Islam, you become free; you cannot hate anybody. Moreover, Islam teaches us that if someone is a non-believer, be with him, feed him and let them know about God. You only need *hekima*,[6] you should use knowledge. The same applies to LGBTIQ people; some of them are actually our Muslim brothers and sisters, they are part of our community. We have to stand with them because of that brotherhood and sisterhood. The story of Sodom and Gomorrah is often used to discriminate against LGBTIQ people. However, does this story direct me to punish them? No, it is God who will be the judge. When you look at that story, God did not tell people to punish those who did evil. It is God who did the punishing. I am not called to actively intervene and punish anyone; I leave that to God.

I can also give another illustration, not related to LGBTIQ people, to better explain this point. One day, I was passing by a street preacher in Kampala. He was talking about Jesus, saying that Muslims and other non-believers should give their life to him. But when he saw me, he stopped his preaching and asked for 1,000 shillings, saying he was hungry and needed some money to buy food. Initially I declined to give him money. But then I decided to call someone who knows Islam better than me. I told him of this Christian preacher who was speaking bad about Islam, and I asked whether I should help him. The sheikh I consulted told me that I should go back and give him the money. Even if what he was preaching was wrong, we are not supposed to let anyone die of hunger. He gave me an example from the Hadith that says that if a pig is hungry, you are not supposed to kill it; instead, you should give the animal food and water. That was an important moment, as I learned

5. Surah Ayah an-Najm 53:32: 'Very well He knows you, when He produced you from the earth, and when you were yet unborn in your mothers' wombs'.
6. An Arabic word for wisdom.

that if someone is doing something that I think is wrong, I do not need to intervene. All I am supposed to do is to tell them what I believe the Quran says and leave it to them to make their own decision.

There is need to sensitize religious leaders about LGBTIQ people. In Islam, if you have sex with another man, you have done something wrong; when you practise adultery, you have also done something wrong; when you borrow money with interest, you have also done something wrong; but in all these cases, you still remain a Muslim. Only when you practise witchcraft, you stop belonging to the Muslim community, because if you associate God with other powers, you are no longer a Muslim. However, in Uganda we are killing LGBTIQ people. Yet we have family members who have charms for good luck or practise final rites for the dead. While the latter is what excludes you from being a Muslim! There are many who have done much worse things than being gay. Yet, we see LGBTIQ as the worst sinners, and we leave alone those who practise *shiriki*.[7] For me, before considering sexual minorities, it is more important to make everyone understand that they should not associate Allah with anything. Even in mosques you find people who look at LGBTIQ people as being very bad, but at the same time they may have some small gods in their pockets; while this should exclude you from being a Muslim.

When you look at Quranic rules in Islam, we are not allowed to kill anyone. There are only two exceptions to that rule, where stoning to death is allowed. One, someone who has killed someone else. Yet in that case, the prescribed process has to be followed; the Islamic leaders must sit down and be satisfied that all the laid down conditions have been met surrounding the said murder. Second, someone who has been caught committing adultery. Still, to kill that person, there are conditions to be met: it requires two witnesses of forty years of age and above who have independently witnessed the act need. Meeting these conditions is very difficult because the witnesses must be of a certain age, must have independently come to the site of the act and found the person in the very act of committing adultery. So, in both cases, it is actually very hard, almost impossible, to sentence death penalty in Islamic law. So, when people say we have to kill LGBTIQ people, we should simply remember that we are not allowed to kill them. The Quran also never told us not to associate with LGBTIQ persons. When a gay person comes to the mosque, you see imams and sheikhs chasing them away.

7. Swahili word for witchcraft.

These gestures come out of ignorance of the real Islam. LGBTIQ people are human and in fact we should befriend them.

When the Prophet (peace be upon him) came, he taught Islam for twenty-three years. Islam has got five pillars; one pillar was taught by the Prophet for thirteen years and the other four pillars were taught for the remaining ten years. Which then of these pillars would you say is most important? The first pillar is to belief in the Oneness of God and not to associate God with any other god; the second is praying daily, five set times; the third is *zakat* or almsgiving; the fourth pillar is fasting especially during Ramadan; and lastly the fifth is pilgrimage to Mecca at least once in a lifetime. A gay person has not necessarily disrespected any of these pillars, in fact he can be a good Muslim. When you understand Islam, you know that a person may be a gay and can still lead us during prayers. Yet, many Muslims in Uganda do actually offend the first pillar, which is the most important one. They may perform the last funeral rites for their dead, meaning that they associate Allah with other gods; or they contribute funds for such final rites for other Muslims; or they carry an occult charm for wealth in their pockets, sometimes even when coming to the mosque. Each of these practices disqualify you from being a Muslim. Yet these people are the loudest when fighting LGBTIQ people or fighting those who drink alcohol. While they themselves have disrespected the Oneness of God, by associating God with something else. If you cannot obey the first pillar, you cannot do the other four. To understand and faithfully follow the other four pillars of Islam, one must first observe the first pillar, and that is why I say that people who are so much opposed to LGBTIQ people do not understand Islam.

To those religious people who are homophobic, I would like to tell them that the Quran tells us not to discriminate against anyone. It does not tell us to force anybody to be righteous. The best thing is to be friend with those people and explain to them what you believe is right, and what the Quran teaches and then leave them to make their own decisions. There is a verse in the Quran in which Allah says, 'You may hate something, and it is good for you; and perhaps you love something, and it is bad for you.'[8] Meaning that we don't always know what is right for ourselves and for others, only Allah knows. We only have to pray for wisdom and for the ability to choose the right thing. It may be that we hate these gay people, but in reality, they may be good before Allah and

8. Surah Al-Baqarah 2:216.

we do not know. Giving them their rights is mandatory. Should we deny them their money or services because of their sexuality? We should accept and understand them. It does not mean that by helping them we are also doing what they are doing, because we all make our own decisions and make choices in life. As Islamic leaders, we are counsellors. We guide our people, but we do not decide for them. Whatever their choices are, you can only explain what you know to be right and wrong; it will be up to that person to take their own decisions. God never said that we should not be close to, or associated with LGBTIQ.

My hope is that in a few years Uganda will be a free society. We used to hear about LGBTIQ issues and run away, but things are slowly changing. They were not even talking about themselves openly but now they do. In a few years we may even have same-sex marriage in Uganda. I hope that in helping somebody you will be rewarded. It does not matter who but if it is a human being that you have helped, you will be rewarded for it. I even help non-Muslims. Why? Because they are human beings and God is watching and he will reward me for it. That is why we have to help LGBTIQ people, as they are our fellow human beings and our brothers and sisters.

Story 22

BISHOP JOSEPH: 'WE WILL COME TO ACCEPT OUR LGBTIQ CHILDREN AS A BLESSING'

Bishop Joseph has been ministering for over twenty-five years at a Pentecostal church in the Kisumu region, western Kenya. After participating in a training about sexual orientation and gender identity, he decided to become an ally of the LGBTIQ community and welcome them to his church. Comparing LGBTIQ people today to people living with leprosy in biblical times, twin babies in traditional Luo culture and people living with HIV and AIDS not so long ago, he is optimistic that societal stigma can be overcome through knowledge and understanding. In this story, he expresses the firmly belief that one day LGBTIQ people will be recognized as a blessing from God.[1]

My journey to become a religious leader springs from my family background because I was brought up in a Christian family. My father was a pastor. So, throughout my youth, secondary school and college, I was in the church. When my dad's time was over, I had to take over from him. In our church there are three ways of becoming a church leader: you can be chosen by the Holy Spirit, people can see your gifts and elect you, or you volunteer yourself. With me, I was chosen by the people after my father passed away. Our church places a big emphasis on the Holy Spirit. We believe in the prominent manifestation of the gifts of the Holy Spirit such as speaking in tongues and prophesying. In our worship, we play drums and cymbals, and we dance, just like Psalm 150 tells us, but we do it in an organized way.

1. This story is based on an interview with Bishop Joseph (pseudonym) on 16 March 2023 in Kisumu, Kenya.

My ministry as an LGBTIQ inclusive religious leader began with an invitation to a religious leaders meeting by Nyarwek.[2] The training was about gender and sexual orientation, and about the experiences of stigma and discrimination that LGBTIQ people face in society. At first, the trainers did not mention that it was about LGBTIQ issues. We started by going through Bible verses that talk about love, compassion and things like that. Then we looked at the challenges that we face in this world and particularly in Kenya such as climate change and corruption. From there they drove us to look at other challenges that we could not immediately think about, asking, 'What issues are not included in this list?' That is when the question of LGBTIQ came up. I cannot remember how it came up exactly, but I think it came in response to a question of how some people in our communities suffer silently through discrimination. During that training, participants started realizing that there was something that we were not aware of and yet it was a real problem. We learned that people are being chased away from their homes by landlords, disowned by parents, removed from schools and in some cases even forced to seek asylum abroad. I was touched by those conversations and at that moment, I decided to become an ally. I am not LGBTIQ myself, but I care for them; so, I am an ally. After this five-day training workshop, I started to become deeply involved. We then later held a meeting with LGBTIQ people of faith, and I was impressed by how many of them believe in God so strongly.

My favourite story in the Bible is in 2 Kings chapter 7. This story encourages me in my work with people who are discriminated. It talks about four men suffering from leprosy, which was a very infectious disease at the time. They were Israelites and had been thrown out of their houses because of leprosy. And it happened that they were hungry, and they were wondering what to do, 'If we stay here, we will die, and if we go to the city, we will also die.' So, they decided to go the camp of the enemy, the Arameans, hoping that they would spare them and help them survive. Yet when they got there, they discovered that the camp has been abandoned, so the four men entered the tents and ate and drank, took valuables and hid them away. Then they went back to tell the Israelites about how the camp of the enemy had been abandoned; that way, these men with leprosy become important messengers. The

2. Nyarwek is a network of LGBTIQ organizations in western Kenya, which has its offices in Kisumu. For several years, they have been running programmes with religious leaders.

reason why I am telling you this story is that people who are excluded
and discriminated against, such as the LGBTIQ in our society, at times
they may be the ones who rescue the world. They can bring something
good, because people who are discriminated against have the blessings
from God. After all, according to Genesis, when God had created
everything in the world, he looked around and he saw what everything
he had created was very good.[3] Not just good, but very good. Clearly,
that includes everyone and everything, including LGBTIQ people. God
confirmed that it was very good. No creature came from anywhere else;
everything was created by God. This story encourages me, that whatever
war we are fighting, there is somebody who can make miracles and
it can be the person you least expect to. If God includes people with
leprosy in his plans, then we should certainly include LGBTIQ people
in ours.

I think religious leaders who are against LGBTIQ inclusion lack
knowledge. I am speaking about the knowledge that we are having
through training, meeting LGBTIQ people and learn from their
experiences. Unfortunately, the majority of religious leaders do not have
this knowledge. They can only cite the clobber passages from Leviticus,
or the story of Sodom and Gomorrah. Yet, they do not realize that these
texts are not about LGBTIQ people. The story of Sodom and Gomorrah
is about people who want to have sex with visitors. God destroyed these
two cities as a result, but we cannot say it is about homosexuality. What
is most important is that the Bible talks about love, all throughout. It
says, love your neighbour as you love yourself.

Having been a historian, I was teaching to my students about
evolution, which has been a contentious topic in the church. So is our
understanding of LGBTIQ issues. We now know that this is how these
people are born, and no one forces himself or herself into it or even
chooses it. This is the kind of knowledge that we did not have in the
past. No one can just wake up in the morning and say, today I am a
lesbian or I am a gay. Why would anyone want to do that, given the
hardship that comes with it? So, this thing needs to be approached with
very sober minds.

Even the people who are LGBTIQ are our children and our relatives.
We are living with them and we have been living with them. I want to
tell a story that challenges this idea of homosexuality being a Western
issue. In my village, when I was a boy, there was an old man who

3. Gen. 1.31.

everybody knew used to have carnal knowledge with other men. Now I know that he was gay, but at that time there was not much talking about homosexuality, and I do not even know if he was identifying himself as gay. In any case, he did not recruit others into it; it was simply who he was. Currently there is a lot of heat after the Supreme Court ruling, with people claiming that it is a new thing.[4] Yet when I was at secondary school, we knew these things happened. At that time, those who were caught were not sent away, they simply completed school. But these days, if pupils are caught, everyone panics, and they are expelled from school.

There are so many things in the Bible we can preach about, but you see that certain religious leaders pick this small thing, they get fixated, and it becomes the only thing they preach about. We, religious leaders, should be the ones who preach about compassion and love. Yet we are not doing that, we are not loving or opening safe spaces. Jesus said that there are people with planks in their eyes, but instead of removing these planks, they are more worried about the speck in other people's eyes.[5] According to the scriptures, Jesus never allowed the community to stone the adulterous woman, even if the law called for that.[6] He was compassionate and loving, and he made people reflect on themselves, asking them, 'Who of you is without sin?'

The Bible says that God saw that the world was sinning, so he sent his only begotten son so that whoever believes in him will not perish but have everlasting life.[7] Now, by condemning people and excluding them from our communities, we risk denying them the chance of having everlasting life. They should have it and abundantly! Which is why we should include them and welcome them. That is why the Bible says, 'do not judge and you will not be judged',[8] and 'love your neighbour as you love yourself'.[9] Our churches should be safe and hospitable places for those ones persecuted in society. We can compare today's persecution of LGBTIQ people to the stigma that people with HIV used to face. It is

4. On 24 February 2023, the Supreme Court of Kenya ruled that the National Gay and Lesbian Human Rights Commission must be allowed to officially register as a non-governmental organization.

5. Matt. 7.3–5.

6. Jo. 8.1–11.

7. Jo. 3.16.

8. Luk. 6.37.

9. Mar. 12.31.

very sad that a religious leader can stand in church and say that people with HIV are harlots and that they should not even be in church. You do not know how that person contracted the disease; it may not be because they were harlots or unfaithful. Even if it was that way, they may be sinners but we still need to offer them a safe space. We do not need to castigate them.

I would be lying if I told you that my church supports LGBTIQ people. Because of this lack of knowledge, many people are against it. After having been taught by Nyarwek and other organizations, I started to hold conversations in our church about reading the Bible in an affirming way. I talked about the work I am doing with LGBTIQ people openly. Some responded by saying, these teachings should have come earlier as there are people suffering in our villages because of the homophobic preaching from the pulpit of their church. Once, a man phoned me to tell me about his sister who was so depressed and was taking drugs because she was forced into getting married while she was a lesbian. He wanted to know from me how he could support her. However, other people in my church resisted me talking about these issues, so I have to navigate it carefully.

I have spent many years not being aware of LGBTIQ members in my church. I did not give them space and did not hear them. Now I have learned that those people are here in our midst, and we should do service to them, make them feel part of our religious community. Change is happening, slowly. In the past, in our region there was a custom among the Luo people that when someone gave birth to twins, the babies would be thrown away because they were believed to be a curse.[10] Yet, nowadays people see twins as a blessing. So even with LGBTIQ people, I believe this hot wind of hatred will die one day. I am sure, just like we have come to recognize twins as a blessing, we shall accept our LGBTIQ children in the future.

10. The Luo are the main ethnic group in western Kenya.

Story 23

PROFESSOR VASHTI: 'MY GRANDMOTHER
TAUGHT ME THAT FAITH AND ACTIVISM GO
HAND IN HAND'

Vashti is a Kenyan theologian who has written about same-sex sexuality from a progressive point of view. She is a source of pastoral support and offers counselling to members of the LGBTIQ community while also advising religious leaders on becoming accepting and inclusive towards LGBTIQ people in their communities. In this story, Prof. Vashti narrates her journey and reflects on the intersections of questions of gender and sexuality in her religious upbringing and theological development. Although Vashti has written and spoken about LGBTIQ issues in public, given the current tense climate in Kenya, she has requested for this story to be anonymized.[1]

Originally, I did not want to become a theologian, I wanted to become a lawyer. This is because I grew up in a village where I saw a lot of gender-based violence, even though I could not have used that language at the time. For instance, I saw women being battered for not preparing the right food. My grandmother, who raised me, would open up her home for these women. They would be sitting at my grandmother's house, crying while narrating the reasons why they had been beaten. And when I realized that it was not their fault that they were being beaten, I became very inquisitive and asked my grandmother, 'Why can't they run away from their marital homes?' My grandmother would say, 'It is not that easy, we shall however provide a place for her to sleep and then tomorrow she can go back.' That used to bother me. In my own

---

1. This story is based on an interview with Professor Vasthi (pseudonym) on 24 February 2023 in Limuru, Kenya.

family, I had an aunt whose husband was very violent. When she was beaten up, she would come to my grandmother's house and after a week or so her husband would come, and speak to my grandfather outside, then they would make a meal for him and he would go back, and two days later my aunt would be asked to return to her home. I was asked to help carry her luggage as her home was two kilometres away from her mother's house. Within a few months, it would happen again, and the cycle of abuse would be repeated. I hated it and asked my grandmother, 'Why do you allow her to go back? The husband does not even apologize', because for me to apologize is to change and he was not changing. And my grandmother would use euphemisms like, 'Men do not apologize publicly, men apologize under the blanket.' Yet, to me it made no sense at all. So, as I grew up, I kept on getting really angry and feeling that somebody should speak for them. I realized I could only speak for them if I would undertake law. Because I felt that a lawyer can get men to be arrested and held accountable for the violence they are perpetrating. This made me grow up with a social activist mind, although I did not have a place to practise it. I always wondered why some marriages were a painful space for women, as it is them who I saw being violated. Thank goodness, I never saw violence in my own family, I never saw my father shout at my mother. Yet it was prevalent in my surroundings, and that is how I developed the urge of becoming a lawyer.

I was brought up in a Quaker home. My grandmother was a Quaker, and although she had not received a high education, she had been trained to be a preacher. She held the Quaker ethos of peace, simplicity, equity, and integrity very high, and I saw these values reflected in her. I realized that this is why she opened her home to violated women. She had also been assigned the role of visiting women prisoners in our town. Each Sunday, when she would come home from the prison, she shared with us some of the stories of the women prisoners and how she had encouraged them and affirmed them as children of God even when the laws of the land had condemned them for the mistakes that they had done. My grandmother observed that for some women the crimes they had committed were out of fending for the children, while some it was about defending themselves in violent situations. For her as a Quaker, the belief that there is that of God in everyone meant that you cannot discriminate or marginalize anyone. She felt that responsibility of showing them that God loves them. I learnt faith and social activism from my grandmother. You can see why I became sensitive and wanting to stand for those who are marginalized.

When I grew up, it was common for girls in our community to go for female circumcision.[2] Yet my grandmother did not think it was useful and she protected the girls in her home from it. But it was one thing to protect us from undergoing the rite, but another thing to live as a minority in a community for not undergoing the rite. My grandmother gave us skills to survive as minorities both in school and in the community. The rite of circumcision was about identity and gaining a social standing in the community. If you did not have it, you were taunted and lacked social friends. You were treated as different, and you did not belong. It was difficult to go to the stream and fetch water with other girls as you were treated with contempt. My grandmother gave us the language to talk back at our tormentors. One of those was to claim the fact that we were human without the rite of circumcision. Grandma taught us to stand up straight and claim our space in the society because we belonged. She taught us to turn the negative language into positive. When they called us immature, we responded by saying that we were mature and that no one should deny us our humanity. In those days, if you were not initiated you would have to get water last, but she told me to just walk in and fetch water from the river. She gave me the social skills to survive. Do not run away, she would say, you are a whole human being! So, I grew up in a setting where I was given skills to argue and challenge, but there was also a wider society which did not allow me to argue.

My granny served the church with great dedication. I loved the way she read and spoke about Bible stories. I think back of this sometimes today, and although I may not agree with her interpretation now, at that time I could not argue with her and was just impressed. When finishing school, I did not get the grades to do law, which was very disappointing. I ended up going into teaching. The skills my grandmother had given me helped me to navigate a very strong cultural and religious dominated patriarchal space. Thanks to her, I was able to find my way and survive. I did suffer violence, because of questioning male authority. In the culture of the time, women were not supposed to talk back to men. But she had taught me to talk back, so I got a few slaps.

When I finished my training, I went into teaching. However, I did not like teaching school children, I wanted to teach people I can argue with. That is how I found my way into theology, which was a big

2. Several ethnic groups in Kenya, such as the Kikuyu, traditionally practise female circumcision.

disappointment to my parents, particularly my father. Because theology then was understood as preaching, and he wondered how as a woman I could preach and who would hear me. I would refer to grandma who was preaching, but they would rebut saying, 'Grandmother is grandmother, but you are a young woman who is wasting her brain.' Yet, my grandmother came to my aid and said, 'Let her go and study theology.' However, she also warned me that theological schools are 'places of jackets'. Jackets and suits were her euphemism for men and patriarchal nature that characterized religious leadership. She was right. In the college with about hundred students, only seven were women, and we were not heard or even seen. As women were tried to stay together and protect each other. The men were very critical, asking why the church was allowing women to join in the study of theology. Because at the time, no church allowed women into positions of leadership. It was like we were pilots in that space. The teaching there also was very patriarchal, mostly given by white men. Thus, we struggled with issues of race, we struggled with clericalism, and those who were single also with marital status. I did realize that even in sacred spaces, in between these holy walls, there was discrimination and sexism. As female students, we shared with each other about the men who were bullies or predators and whom we should better avoid. That made me realize that indeed it was a place of jackets. When I would go home, I would share with my grandmother; se supported me through the three years, she was my confidant theologian.

When I finished my degree, I did not get a job, so I went back to teaching at high school. After a year I was invited to teaching in a Bible school. The diocese had just been created and at that time it did not have many theologically trained clergy. Lots of them were evangelists who had just been made clergy, but the bishop wanted to improve theological standards. When I came for the interview the first time, his board said they could not hire a single woman and one who did not profess the evangelical language of faith. But the bishop told the board that if they could not find someone with similar qualifications, then they would have to hire me. So, six months after the interview I was called and hired. When I turned up, some of the student clergy said they would not be taught by a child. As a woman who was unmarried, I was seen as a child. A few students stayed in, but older men walked out. I also was an outsider by not being of the same ethnic background. Me wearing earrings and all that was also seen as problematic. People could not understand how I was a theologian – I did not look Christian enough in their eyes. Moreover, other staff were ordained, but I was not. So, they would have staff meetings and exclude me. One or two of them did not agree with women leadership. There was the thinking that the bishop had hired me so that he could smuggle women ordination in his diocese. The other thing that happened was that I was not given a house. It was said, if I lived on my own, what testimony would that give? Who would I entertain in that space? This was again an example of controlling women's bodies. I was put to live in the house of a local priest, who was also my student. He did not agree with my teaching but because he had this huge vicarage, I was to stay there so that I could be monitored.

After some time, I had an opportunity to enrol for a master's degree. It was not easy to navigate the space to get the paperwork signed for a scholarship to study. But I finally did and went abroad to Ireland. The students were both clergy and laity from different countries. In my class I was the only woman from Africa, but I met with Roman Catholic sisters who were theologically very strong. My roommate identified herself as a feminist and was strong on issues of equity and equality in society. She would challenge those who used exclusive or discriminatory language. My lecturers were also very empowering in their theological presentation. And I met with women theologians. In short, I found a space that was like that of my grandmother, both affirming and encouraging. For me it was a space of real growth and increasing questioning. I had Africans studying with me, and they would warn me against becoming too Westernized. They were telling me, do not follow these women too much, they may destroy you because if you go back home, you may have become too liberalized and not be able to find a husband.

After my master's I came home and went back to teaching at a Bible school offering diplomas. With a master's degree I had courage to speak about issues of injustice as I saw them. I began advocating for women to be included in the school. Two women were accepted to the training but there was no accommodation for them. They were pushed to stay at my house, which was the smallest house on the site. That was because of the view that if you are single, you do not need your own space. In any case, these two girls, they had opened the way as no one would push the agenda of excluding women from college after that. However, it was one thing to study theology, but it was quite another to get ordained! So, I had to push for women's ordination by presenting the motion in the diocesan synod. This was not well received as most delegates including my male students resisted it. But it had entered into the discussions and in the next synod meeting the discussion took pace;

it was agreed that a commission was to be formed to get the views of the people. The members appointed to the commission were all against women's ordination, but I was pushed in as the secretary. It looked like it had been planned for it to fail. Yet I started doing questionnaires with groups of church members across the diocese, and it became quite clear that they did not mind the gender of their minister. So, I could now prove it with these questionnaires and the notes that people were supportive of women's ordination. The following year when we brought in the report, a prominent member of the synod commented that the woman secretary of this commission had done a lot of work. He moved the motion and the motion sailed. I had of course undertaken some advocacy with women who were married and respected, and they spoke out in support. Unfortunately, my old bishop with whom I started this journey died in 1990 and ordination of women in that diocese only took place in 2000.

This first bishop was very much into issues of social justice, and he understood that I was struggling with patriarchy and gender discrimination. He also was keen on bringing women to the centre, which explains why he hired me and respected the work I was doing. So, he understood, and he pushed for two things: first, for young people to be included in the ministry as he was himself at that time young; and second, for women to be welcomed into our school. It was great to have a bishop I could rely on in pushing the boundaries. I also fought for women to be ordained in ministry, even though I have never been ordained myself. It was a joy to be debating with people like the former speaker of the Kenyan parliament, who also was a member of the synod. He would say, our culture does not allow it, the Bible and the tradition do not allow it. But I would say, the Bible does not allow many things and yet you still do them. After the bishop died, I continued to teach but I wanted to do further studies. I still faced the same patriarchy and gendered discrimination in accessing scholarships. You had to go through an interview process in Nairobi, and I would not hear back after the interview – not because I had failed the interview but because I did not check all the boxes, such as marriage. Finally, by providence I was able to secure a grant to do my PhD in Scotland. Initially I wanted to study systematic theology with a focus on African theology, yet in the end I chose to do Quaker studies and research on women and culture. Quakers are one of the first post-reformation religious organizations that allowed women to participate in meetings, something even the Church of England had not. In Kenyan churches, too, women were still left out. My grandmother was special but even she said that church was a place of jackets. So, for my PhD I looked at Quaker ideals of women's inclusion.

At that time, personally I got more and more engaged in the Anglican Church, where debates about women's ordination, and later about same-sex relationships, became so prominent. I attended the 1998 Lambeth conference as a student. There was joy in being engaged at the conference, I enjoyed the debates, but I was shocked at the racism, sexism and homophobia. The polarization in the LGBTIQ debate was largely between the Global North and the Global South. Yet here I was, coming from the Global South but not wanting to be identified with it theologically because I did not agree with the discrimination and exclusion of other human beings. Yet, in the pro-LGBT camp, which was largely Western, I also struggled with the racism and sometimes sexism. So, I was caught in between these race, gender and sexuality issues. But I had made up my mind that I would not go into the African cocoon nor go into the white cocoon. Because I realized that the debate brought to light the hidden issues from both camps, and as a woman I suffered in both camps. I chose to oscillate between the two spaces knowing that in both I was an outsider and could not belong. It is an interesting space to be in because you are not at home in either space, but you identify with some aspects of each of the spaces.

When I came home with a PhD, I was everything that my context struggled with. Neither my academic qualification nor my theological positions were welcomed. Being lay, single and unmarried made a trinity of unacceptability. The diocese that I had served before argued that they did not have a job for a highly qualified woman. They did not say the same when ordained men came back from studies. I was asked why I came back, friends thought I was a fool to return to Africa. It was the structural adjustment period, so nobody was hiring due to the tough economic situation. I was living with friends at their home, but I was happy to be back home and wanted to build a career here. In the end, I got a lecturer position at a theological college here in Kenya. One of the most important moments in my life has been entering that space and being there to debate and argue for gender equity and equality. Obtaining a PhD gave me status, which I did not have through marriage or by coming from a family with a big name. So, getting a PhD and later a professorship were achievements that have opened many doors. I am able to speak out and advocate for the marginalized. I am invited to participate in spaces, for instance I have been invited to speak at the Lambeth conference. If the powers that be were asked to nominate someone to speak, many would not consider me as I do not tick all their boxes of who is a full human being. I still find myself in situations where I am forced to explain myself and justify my being as I have not fulfilled all the cultural and church expectations. So, when I speak about justice issues for all in society, I get labels. Speaking about gender and power is the most trying because it leads to debates that are not healthy.

This can cause you a lot of anxiety, and I have struggled with anxiety and burn out because of having to speak for and side with those whom society has tried to marginalize and discriminate. You struggle with patriarchal systems reflected in different cultural systems such as clericalism and leadership in the different institutions that one serves. The issues around sexuality have been the most difficult because it is perceived as LGBTIQ and nothing else. Several years ago, I contributed a chapter to a book about homosexuality in the global church, focusing on the Kenyan context. It was used against me in various forums. Some of the people who were critical of me had not even read the article! I was constantly reminded that the church had a position on this matter, and I should not go against it. Yet I chose not to hold the dominant narrative which justified marginalization and discrimination.

Growing up I was exposed to different sexualities even though I would not have used that language. Maybe at the time the language and understanding were different. The custom of woman-to-woman marriage which was not a lesbian relationship was common.[3] This custom was to support women who were childless to have children. A woman would marry another woman who would have children that were referred to as hers. These were things that my grandmother helped me to understand when she sent me to these homes who were neighbours. It made me realize that there are different things going on in society and that people are not boxed. I grew up with that in mind. My grandmother had a way of explaining things and I could ask her anything.

When I look back, growing up in strong Quaker home and being taught by my grandmother, the Quaker ideals of peace, simplicity, equity, and the belief that there is that of God in everyone had an impact on my outlook of people in the community. Social inclusion was a strong component of my grandmothers' teachings. While studying theology, I could hear people saying nasty things about people of a same-sex orientation, and reflecting on it I realized that they were saying the same nasty things about women, about single mothers

---

3. E.g. see Njambi and O'Brien (2000).

and about you not being circumcised. Later, when I got to study my master's degree, is when I began to know individuals who would say, 'This is who I am.' I remember a class where a lecturer said something nasty about gay people, and then one of the students stood up and said, 'If this is how you are going to talk about other human beings then I rather leave this place.' So, at master's level I not only studied theology and social justice but got engaged with actual people who are being discriminated. Knowing people who identified themselves as queer gave me the courage to support and speak about them positively. For me sexuality or LGBTIQ people have never been an 'issue' – it is about people with lived realities! As one who knows how it feels to be discriminated on the basis of gender, race or marital status, I feel solidarity with them. I remember at the Lambeth conference in 1998, I was standing there with three women, we were all single. One Kenyan bishop passed by, paused and said to the three of us, '*Nyinyi Watoto* (you children) who have refused to marry, you're hoping that the Communion will pass this motion for same-sex couples so that you to marry each other?' I became numb, I was so angry. Such comments encouraged and empowered me to become and remain an ally of LGBTIQ communities.

The reasoning that being queer is un-African and un-Christian continues to be a basis of denying the queer community dignity. Speaking about un-African is like saying Africans are a unique species in the world, which of course is not the case. Africans may have unique ways that are different from other cultures, but being purely heterosexual is not among their unique characteristics. Scholarship has also traced and documented the existence of gender and sexual nonconforming practices in Africa, including Kenya and Uganda, before the advent of European missionaries and colonialists. The last precolonial Kabaka (king) Mwanga of the Buganda Kingdom had sexual relations with his male subjects as well as female subjects. In the story of the Ugandan martyrs, ten have been increasingly portrayed as having died due to their refusal to engage in the Kabaka's sexual advances. In these interpretations, the notion that the Kabaka, a Ganda man, had homosexual desires, is side-lined through emphasis on the righteous Christian martyrs who refused him after their conversion.[4] Based on

---

4. A key text in the historiography of the Ugandan martyrs is Faupel (1962); for the way in which the story of the martyrs shapes contemporary discourses about sexuality in East Africa, see Rao (2015).

this historical evidence, I chose to refuse this narrative of queerness as un-African.

I also refuse the narrative about it being un-Christian and a sin. As a woman I know that there is a theological tradition that seems to say that women have sinned more than men because of the interpretation of Genesis 3. Likewise, the church today seems to say that non-heterosexual people are the worst sinners. Yet, three theological aspects give me the impetus to think differently: creation, incarnation and the gift of the Holy Spirit. With regard to creation, usually the Genesis creation stories are quoted to say that God created humankind as male and female, 'it's Adam and Eve, not Adam and Steve'. However, there are other texts. The psalmist in Psalm 139 speaks about creation in an intimate and personal way, it is about God who knits us in our mother's womb, and who knows how our being is formed. If that is true, did God not also create LGBTIQ people? Such texts give us a basis to claim and affirm that each of us has been beautifully and wonderfully made.[5] Moreover, the story of the incarnation – of God becoming human in Jesus Christ – makes me believe that Jesus came to live and show God's love among us, *all* of us. Remember, Jesus' ministry begins with a Nazarene Manifesto which is about freedom for the oppressed.[6] Jesus went against the grain of gender, patriarchy and even the politics of his day. The message of Jesus is about liberation of the oppressed, the blind and the marginalized. Thus, in society today, where we are so good at excluding people of different sexual orientation, I have to ask, what would Jesus do? As a woman, I believe that Jesus has delivered me, liberated me, and has empowered me to be at the centre where I would never have been because of my sex. Mercy Oduyoye has reminded us that theology is not what is in books, but what we struggle with in our lives.[7] My struggle in living a Christian life is to oppose systems that oppress and marginalize people at all fronts. That is the theology that I want to espouse, and it means that I cannot go and exclude others. I believe in the formulation of the church as a community where people are not defined by their age, gender, class, race or tribe or sexual orientation. I believe in the church as a community where *all* are called and receive gifts from the Holy Spirit, and I want to practise that. So

5. Ps. 139.14.

6. Luk. 4.18.

7. Mercy Amba Oduyoye is a leading African feminist theologian, originating from Ghana.

theologically, for me it is the creation, it is the incarnation and it is the foundation of the church through the Spirit that makes me challenge the dominant narratives.

In the Bible there are characters who, according to today's standards, would be nowhere. For instance, women such as Tamar, Rahab, Bathsheba – yet they are included in the genealogy of Jesus. In the gospels, look at the women who go to the tomb early in the morning, who wanted to embalm the body – they were not women who had social standing, and yet they are the ones who discover and then tell everybody that Christ is risen! One of the many biblical characters I like is Miriam, the sister to Moses – she never got married but she put her life on the line and took care of her brother who later became the leader, and she was there to support him. She was in the community, she was selfless and even challenged her brother when needed. She lived in a community where marriage was important but we never read that she was married or had children, yet she was important for the story of the Jewish people's liberation to take shape. I also identify with the prophets in the Bible, who challenged the dominant systems of exploitation in their day – whether they were political, religious or economic. In the prophets I see grains of liberation. There are characters and parts of the scriptures where I see that liberative motif. Scripture may be sexist and patriarchal, but within it there are potions that are also liberative. If only the church would read these alternative texts! Women and men who are called for social justice, these stories lift me up.

I know that the lived realities of people have a context, and their story is their story; I want to hear and believe their stories. I do not want to believe a story that is dominant. That is a single story and as the author Chimamanda Adichie says, a single story comes with power; a single story comes with dominance and with exclusion.[8] So, I constantly look out for the other stories, that are being downplayed and made invisible. When I do community work, I try to bring out those stories that we are not used to hearing. That has been my journey. It is a lonely journey because you have a minority view that is seen as immoral. There are people who may be allies of LGBT people, but they would not want to be known. Yet, although I may not be on the road with placards, I use other ways of supporting the queer community. As a theologian I begin from a position that God is a God of justice. And, that we do not have God in our pockets. There are many things about God that I will never

8. Adichie (2009).

fully comprehend. But one thing I know: our beliefs about God should not be a weapon of mass destruction but rather bring wholeness and be affirming. After all, I believe in Jesus who says, 'I came so that you may have life and have it abundantly.'⁹ So whom am I to say that life in abundance is mine and not for others? It is sad that many in the church know this theology, but do not practise it. I have chosen to be faithful to what I know to be true.

9. Jo. 10.10.

Story 24

BISHOP SENYONJO: 'GOD IS STILL CREATING, AND HE CONTINUES TO REVEAL THINGS'

Bishop Christopher Senyonjo is a clergyman who served as bishop of the Church of Uganda (the Anglican Church). Following his retirement in 1998, he became involved in ministry among LGBTIQ people. Shortly after, his church barred him from performing services, and several years later they revoked all his remaining privileges as bishop. As co-founder of several faith-based LGBTIQ advocacy initiatives in Uganda, Bishop Christopher is one of the most outspoken religious leaders in the country supporting sexual and gender minorities. In this story, he reflects on his journey into and motivation for this ministry and on his understanding of human sexuality.[1]

As a young man, I never thought I would be joining church ministry. When I was still in school, I thought that I was going to become a medical doctor. Yet, the beginning of my call into ministry happened when my first wife died, only seventy days into our marriage. I was a teacher at that time, and some people came to my school to tell that my wife has been bitten by a snake. So, I returned home about three miles from the school, and we took her to the hospital; but her condition got worse. When she passed away, a verse from the Bible came to me. This verse says, 'No temptation has overtaken you except what is common to mankind. And God is faithful; he will not let you be tempted beyond what you can bear. But when you are tempted, he will also provide a way out so that you can endure it.'[2] In other words, for every temptation or

---

1. This story is based on an interview with Bishop Christopher Senyonjo on 20 January 2023 in Kampala, Uganda.
2. 1 Cor. 10.13.

trial in life, God will show you a way of handling it so that you may be able to endure it. That meant that I was not supposed to die with her, but instead somehow, I had to live.

Shortly after, on 9 August 1959, I accepted the Lord as my personal saviour. I started getting interested in religious affairs and felt that God wanted me to serve in the church. By the end of 1960 I had an interview and was accepted into Buwalasi Theological College, where I started in 1961. We were among the first cohort to do a diploma in theology in East Africa. Three years later I graduated, and I was ordained deacon on 15 December 1963. So that is my story of being called into church ministry. It is a wonderful story because I did not say I wanted to become a bishop – which is not something I ever sought – but I just accepted the call to serve the church. Soon after my ordination, on 28 December, I also got remarried, to my wonderful dear wife, Mary, with whom I have shared fifty-eight years of marriage until she sadly died, on 5 September 2021. We started our life together and she too accepted the Lord as her Lord and Saviour. We created a wonderful family together. She joined me to the United States in 1964, where I went to study for a masters at Union Theological Seminary in New York. When we came back in Uganda in 1967, we worked in ministry together, and she herself studied and was made a deacon and later a priest.

It has not been easy since she left. But the good thing is that on the day she passed on, I was by her bedside. It was on a Sunday, and I looked at her condition and knew she was passing away. That morning I read a verse from the Gospel of John which says that all who received Christ have been granted the status of children of God.[3] Those who accepted Jesus' name and accepted him, he gave them power or admitted them to being children of God. So, I comforted Mary, saying: you have received Jesus, so you have been admitted as a child of God.

My journey into the ministry towards LGBTIQ people began around the time that I retired in 1998. Throughout my ministry as a bishop, I have always had a concern about people who are marginalized in society. I started counselling a number of young people that came to me with problems commonly regarded as unacceptable. Some in the church told me that I should condemn these people. Yet, I responded by saying that Christ was not in the habit of sending people away; these ones are also welcome. My fellow bishops said, no these ones should be converted from their wicked ways. After my retirement, I became

3. Jo. 1.12.

active in counselling in Kampala. It was mostly marriage counselling. But one day, a priest came to me. He was a youth worker and he told me about a group of young people thought to be gay, they had issues with their sexuality. At that time – it was around the year 2000 – I had been studying about human sexuality and I knew that sexuality is varied. So, I invited these young people to see me, and they told me how they were rejected by society. I asked them, is there anybody influencing you to be gay, or is it part of how you feel? They told me that no one had influenced them. They believed that this is who they were. But they also wondered why God had created them that way, given the suffering they were going through in society. I told them not to run away from who they were because of what people told them. That they should accept themselves. Nobody should influence you to be what you are not. We should not force anybody to be what they are not. It is wrong to force somebody to be something they are not.

Honestly, there is a lot of misunderstanding about human sexuality. Even in today's newspaper there is an article that says that there is a lot of homosexuality in Ugandan schools, and parliament has even started to investigate it. People misunderstand and say that this is being promoted and taught in schools – but sexuality is not taught. They even say that people are being recruited into homosexuality, which is ridiculous. Even my fellow bishops in the Church of Uganda say that we may cut off links with Lambeth[4] because of this issue of homosexuality. We need to overcome these misunderstandings and be able to discuss these issues openly. Sometimes when I talk to people, they say that LGBTIQ persons are not genuine, they go into it for money or whatever, or they are harming our children. But my question is, what money are you talking about, because most LGBTIQ persons I know are not wealthy? And what is the harm that they are doing? If there is any harm, then let us address the harm. Of course, we are not supporting any harm – even among heterosexuals there are things that could be harmful because we are all sinners. And my question to LGBTIQ persons is, is this who you really are? Because some may have been forced by different circumstances, but most of them are genuinely LGBTIQ; it is who they are.

In my own studies, I have found out that human sexuality is there for four main purposes: one is reproduction – and reproduction is

---

4. The Lambeth Conference is a decennial assembly of bishops of the worldwide Anglican Communion convened by the archbishop of Canterbury. It has become deeply divided on issues of sexuality.

important for the human race to continue. Unfortunately, some people think that it is the only purpose. That is why, if they see you are not reproducing, they will at best only tolerate you, because they think you have not done what you were supposed to do with that sexuality. The second purpose is companionship. God said, it is not good for a human being to be alone. In fact, it is very interesting when God was saying it was not good for Adam to be alone and He made him a helper. It shows that reproduction was never the primary goal. In theology there are two groups – one which says, 'Be fruitful and increase in number; fill the earth,'[5] and another one saying, 'It is not good for the man to be alone. I will make a helper suitable for him.'[6] Third, sexuality is also meant for pleasure. Many people do not like to think about this. This is one area people are afraid of, yet it is God who created these senses. For me when I speak, I am free because this is the reality. If you can have all these, in your marriage then that is wonderful. Lastly, there is the issue of identity – to accept who you really are, so you are not pretending. If we lead our lives not out of pretence, but on the basis of who we are, then we will be more creative – not necessarily reproductive, but creative nevertheless. You become more creative when you accept yourself and are not ashamed of yourself. God blesses you because that is how God created us.

These four purposes should guide the church's conversation with LGBTIQ persons. To begin, the church needs to learn love! Love them as you love yourself. Do you like sex? If so, why then would you want to deny it others? The question then is, what is the purpose of sex? As for reproduction: would you like to have that for yourself? Then why deny it others? And if there is a problem, then we shall use modern scientific means to address that problem! The other purpose is companionship. Would you like companionship yourself? What kind of person would you like to have companionship with? Now here a homosexual will say someone different from yours. But that is the companion, you cannot force me and say you should have this companion instead of this one. The Bible says, a companion fit for you – that is what it says. So, a homosexual will have a companion fit for him or her. Would you like to have a companion who is not fit for you? No, of course not. Then why do you want that for someone else? Then there is pleasure. Would you like to be forced to derive your pleasure in a way that does not suit you?

5. Gen. 1.28.
6. Gen. 2.18.

No, of course not. Then why do you want that for the other person? Finally, there is identity. We all want to be ourselves, to be authentic. So, why should we ask LGBTIQ persons to pretend being something that they are not? Let them be the way they are! Or otherwise, instead of them being creative, they will lose their creativity. So, starting the conversation from this principle of love – love others as we love ourselves – is key. God allowed me to be a supporter when I am not LGBTIQ myself, because it helps me to understand the command to love the other person as you love yourself!

God is glorious and powerful – he created human beings with love, in his image. We have love but have also developed other aspects of our being while neglecting to develop this aspect of love in us. We have neglected to explore the ways in which we can grow the love that God shared with us. This is the revelation that I have had. So, for me the question is, what can I leave for the young people? God does not want us to destroy ourselves because he said in one of the prayers for us, 'Thy kingdom come, thy will be done on earth'. He would like to see heaven here as we prepare for eternity. But we cannot have that heaven here without love. In our society we kill each other, but God would like us to enjoy our life on earth as a taste of the eternity to come. Without love we have lost an essential ingredient of living the best life that God desires for us. My joy would be full if we could learn to love in this way, as a taste of the eternal life. But instead, we put our focus on creating nuclear bombs.

We should love each other in the diversity that God created us with. So, we should seek to live-in-love in society. By this I am not saying that we welcome evil for the sake of evil, but I am saying, do not take difference and diversity to be evil but learn to love the other person as you love yourself. So, we should love one another as we love ourselves, and this is key. We do not allow people to do things that are harmful. But also, you have the burden to convince us that this is harmful, not to force us just because you hold a different view from us. Differences should not be an opportunity to advance hate but rather an invitation to seeking understanding.

I believe that God is still creating. Some people read that God rested on the seventh day and think that this means that he stopped creating – they take this text literally. Yet, God is still creating. Also, our Lord said, 'I have much more to say to you, more than you can now bear.'[7] It means

7. Jo. 16.12.

that God continues to reveal things that we did not know before. Even at my age, God is still revealing. As a society, today we continue to see things we never saw before. We are learning about the universe. Some people don't like evolution, but God has many ways of creating, why would you exempt God from using evolution in the process of creation? God continues to create. Even the Lord says, 'My Father is always at his work to this very day.'[8] People may not have known about gender and sexuality the way we do now. We have discovered that there are people who are like that, we are discovering it now. There are many things we did not know and now we are discovering. So, when you discover, then face the reality and know how to deal with it positively.

Back to my own experience. As my ministry unfolded, gradually it became known that I was counselling LGBTIQ persons and was supporting them. It became quite toxic. Even when walking along the streets of Kampala, people were pointing at me saying 'that man …'. I remember one day someone confronted me publicly, and I told him, 'My friend, this is what I know is right, and I have not done anything wrong.' People were so against me! But I went on with my counselling. We set up an organization called St. Paul's Reconciliation and Equality Centre, because I believe that we need to be reconciled. We are different but we are not enemies of each other. Yet, my church started saying that I had become involved in another church. I was accused of having left the Anglican Church, and they said, 'You are no longer a member of our church.' I refused and told them I still attended my church and am part of my congregation. But to no avail. They said I am no longer a member of the Church of Uganda. Also, when you are retired, you are supposed to receive a little pension. They said they were not going to give me any pension any longer. Sometimes I wonder, is this right? Pension is not a privilege; it is a right. I have served up to retirement age and I have not done anything wrong. But they were annoyed that I was counselling LGBTIQ people, and then claimed that I have left the church. I did not want to go to court, but one day I hope to speak to my bishop and tell him that this is not right – not just because it is about me, but it is wrong to do this to anybody. This is a kind of oppression; if we are entrenching oppression in our church, how can we help others who are oppressed in the society? They seem to enjoy that I am suffering. But when God gives you a mission, you are ready to suffer for it. Do not expect things to be just smooth. Things can be hard but when they are hard with the Lord

8. Jo. 5.17.

on your side, then you are happy. This is because you are working not just for your selfish ends, but you are serving God. I still love my church and have no hate for anybody. Differences are there but without love whatever we do is useless.

I am very happy doing this work. Happiness is a deep thing in the heart. I am happy because God in a wonderful way has given me many friends. I have people that I love, and they love me back, not only here in Uganda but across the world. I have many friends, which shows that my work has made a contribution to people's lives. The service I give is of so much joy to me and I cannot say that I could have done otherwise. This is the grace of God, and I am grateful for it. It has cost me quite a lot, but I do not regret doing this work. Instead, it gives me great joy and fulfilment beyond measure doing what God wants me to do. And it gives me hope to see young people who are taking over this work!

CONCLUSION

The personal stories of change and transformation presented in this volume tend to be silenced within dominant narratives in and about contemporary East Africa, where leading conservative religious and political figures dominate public discourses, espousing discriminatory views of, and attitudes against, LGBTIQ people. Counternarratives supporting the dignity and rights of LGBTIQ communities are under constant threat of legal prosecution and social persecution in spaces that, as discussed in the Introduction to this book, are increasingly anti-queer. In Uganda, public pronunciations and commentaries in support of, or that normalize the life of, sexually non-conforming citizens are not allowed (see, for example, the analysis of LGBTIQ representations in media by Bompani and Terreni Brown 2015). The new Anti-homosexuality Act 2023 signed into law by President Museveni on the 29th of May seeks to punish anyone defending LGBTIQ rights with twenty years of imprisonment under the broad and blurred accusation of 'promoting homosexuality' (as mentioned in the Introduction to this collection). When MP Fox Odoi-Oywelowo, one of only two MPs opposing the passing of the new AHB 2023 (the other one was Paul Kwizera Bucyana, both from the ruling party), made his pronunciation in the Ugandan parliament, he was loudly booed and ferociously attacked in social media. Opposing dominant discourses does not come without a price. In an interview, he said, 'There were people who called me to tell me that they will stone me. There were those who called me to tell me that they will hang my children' (Neiman 2023). In neighbouring Kenya, queer-friendly spaces that were until very recently somewhat tolerated (Ombagi 2019) have come under attack by the increasingly aggressive moralization campaign of Christian and Muslim leaders, supported by President William Ruto and his wife Rachel Ruto, as well as Deputy President Rigathi Gachagua and his wife Dorcas Rigathi, who is herself an evangelical pastor. LGBTIQ organizations, in the aftermath of the Kenyan Supreme Court's decision to allow the National Gay and Lesbian Human Rights Commission (NGLHRC) to officially register overturning the unconstitutional stance of banning organizations on the basis of sexual orientation, became targets of social and verbal aggression with activists fearing for their lives (Woensdregt and van Stapele 2023) and several leaving cities to seek refuge in other towns where their sexual orientation or gender identity is less salient. Similar developments are reported from other countries in the region, such as Tanzania (Awami 2023). Currently, and increasingly, social, religious and political publics in East Africa do not allow for the surfacing of stories regarding LGBTIQ lives and rights; there is a danger in telling counterstories, a price to be paid, as clearly demonstrated by the experiences of several religious leaders in this collection.

The religious leaders participating in this book project were fully aware of the dominant narratives that exist about them or around the people they take care of, as they experience the impact of those discourses in their everyday lives, at multiple levels. Their stories express their preoccupations and fears about working in opposition to these powerful narratives, yet at the same time reflect their commitment and courage to do exactly that. Some leaders defined their work in support of LGBTIQ rights in this hostile environment as a necessary martyrdom for positive change, as, for example, Bishop James (Story 8) elaborated:

> We must dare to go where others have not dared to go. You know, we have martyrs in Uganda. Many Christians have come to respect and celebrate the Ugandan martyrs. Today, some of us are martyrs by doing this work. It gives me hope and courage that yes, the ground may not be conducive, but we stand our ground and will not run away from this country where we started our work. This is Africa and as Africans we must stand our ground and do the work and prove to the world that being LGBTIQ is not foreign or evil but Godly. It is how God who has designed us with different colours yet as one people.

The reference here to the story of the Ugandan martyrs, who were pages in the royal court of the Kingdom of Buganda and were executed after their conversion to Christianity, towards the end of the nineteenth century, is significant. This story, which is foundational to the history of Christianity in Uganda, and which plays a complex role in the politics of homosexuality in the country (Rao 2015), serves as an archive of memory and meaning in which Bishop James, as a gay religious leader, inscribes himself. The narrative suggestion is that LGBTIQ Christian advocates are continuing the history of Christianity in Uganda in the present day, rewriting it in a way that renders Christian faith and same-sex relationships as compatible. Yet, obviously, this advocacy comes at a personal cost.

Like Bishop James, several allies, too, articulated the costs they had to pay and fears they had to endure in their work for and testimony in support of LGBTIQ people in their own countries. As Sheikh Abdallah (Story 20) narrated, his pastoral care and open support towards LGBTIQ people cost him his job. Several leaders told stories of physical and verbal attacks towards them and their pastoral work. Many allies feared judgement and even the accusation of supporting the queer community for economic gain or because 'they have been corrupted' and becoming themselves members of LGBTIQ communities. Indeed, one of the dominant narratives is exactly the depiction of homosexuality as a 'choice' or 'lifestyle' and not a sexual identity or orientation. Reflecting on this, Pastor Neema (Story 10) said:

> Currently there are few openly LGBTIQ affirming religious leaders in Kenya. However, there are many more who are hiding because they do not want to lose their jobs, or because their families or children judge them harshly. I know a few bishops who are my friends, and they are inclusive, but they cannot state that publicly. Even many women pastors, who have struggled with patriarchy in the church themselves, they do not have that courage to come out and say, 'I am LGBTIQ inclusive.' Many are hiding because if they are known, they may lose their jobs or authority and they may be rejected by fellow pastors. They also fear the baseless accusation that they became LGBTIQ allies because they have been given money.

With the signing of the Anti-homosexuality Act in May 2023 in Uganda and growing anti-LGBTIQ feeling in the sociopolitical and religious Kenyan and Tanzanian publics, these fears and costs will only rise for those who challenge dominant discourses. However, in the stories recounted in this book, the religious leaders were able to deconstruct their meanings, highlight the contradictions that exist within them and give testimony to the emotional, physical and spiritual impacts those dominant narratives have on LGBTIQ individuals and allies. Religious leaders in this collection rejected and challenged the many aspects of these narratives they refute (McEntarfer and McVee 2014), making the process of storytelling an important tool for resilience- and resistance-building strategies among LGBTIQ communities and allies in East Africa. With their actions and words, they are shaping a new narrative while simultaneously resisting the dominant discourse that has threatened them and queer communities. It is through countering the norm that challenging dominant narratives becomes a political act (Mishler and Squire 2020, 5) and those counternarratives become powerful forms of resistance.

As the stories presented in this volume show, the lived experiences and testimonies of the religious leaders are entangled within bigger contexts as – beyond the personal – they address different spaces, including political, social, economic, religious and theological fields. In this way, those narrating voices function as agents of social change and social justice for the right of queer individuals to exist, and flourish, in their religious communities, in religious texts, in society, in political spaces and through the law (Murray 2000). The stories themselves are narrative accounts of personal change, from becoming a religious leader within a LGBTIQ community in order to cater to the members of the community's spiritual needs, as articulated by Pastor Deron in Kampala, to the journey of becoming LGBTIQ allies having previously served as agents of discrimination, as narrated by Evangelist Josephine from western Kenya. Yet, the stories also reveal the radical implications of the narrated transformations, not only for the storytellers' own lives but also for the lives of those surrounding and touching them.

These stories of change follow a model component (Mishler and Squire 2020, 8) that, similar to feminist storytelling in African theological spaces, starts from a position of vulnerability and moves to something powerful and dialogical (Nadar 2012, 274). Firstly, narrators present the challenge they faced; secondly, they introduce the choice they made in response to that challenge, a choice that transformed their course of action; thirdly, they reflect on the outcomes that are the results of that choice, and through this teleological – and often also theological – process they offer possible future scenarios of change, as well as hope. While those stories were typically unique and deeply personal, it is nonetheless possible to identify emerging themes that link them together in a collective effort for change.

Emerging themes

Most of the religious leaders' stories offer dialectic representations of *pain* and *joy*. Suffering, and the realization of it, is often described as the catalyst that moved them, as leaders in their communities, to an act of personal transformation. Leaders who identified as LGBTIQ themselves articulated the need to move from a position of suffering in their previous religious community because they were discriminated against by the pastor or churchgoers, or because they were constantly exposed to interpretations of religious texts that not only did not represent them but also attacked their own existence. As Pastor Caroline (Story 1) from the Cosmopolitan Affirming Church in Nairobi said:

> When I joined the Catholic Church, it was like the Old Testament passage of Sodom and Gomorrah was at the centre of every single preaching. They were speaking about how homosexuals are bad people, cursed people who will bring curses to the land, as if every bad thing that happens is because of them. So, I thought, I do not want to hear these things constantly.

The mirroring experience of suffering and discrimination that two female religious leaders, Pastor Neema (Story 10) and Professor Vashti (Story 23), had in the patriarchal church was the catalyst for them becoming LGBTIQ allies and fighting against gender and sexual discrimination within religious spaces. 'As a woman I know that there is a theological tradition that seems to say that women have sinned more than men because of the interpretation of Genesis 3. Likewise, the church today seems to say that non-heterosexual people are the worst sinners', said Prof. Vashti. Or the realization of suffering had moved some religious leaders from a position of anti-queer feelings and rejection to an inclusive and supportive one. For example, Pastor Laura (Story 15) narrates that after participating in a training workshop run by PEMA Kenya, she came to realize that the suffering inflicted on LGBTIQ individuals in her community was unjust and unnecessary:

> I remember during the training there was this one person, I could not tell if it was a girl or a boy. She told us of how she always had to be careful of where she rents a place to stay. For example, she cannot live in a place where people share bathrooms, because it has happened that housemates attempted to break the bathroom when she was taking a shower, so they could see how she looks like when naked. Her story really touched me. Being a mother myself, I realized that she is somebody's child. Her story really touched me, and I said to myself: 'People should not discriminate against them.'

For some leaders, the suffering was caused by their theological positioning, as, for example, Pastor Trevor (Story 3), a self-identified gay man, who worked in and belonged to a Pentecostal church where non-normative sexuality was not accepted. In his story of transformation that brought him to live a life of celibacy, he narrates the tumultuous personal path he travelled to carve a place for himself in his religious community:

> In my mind being gay meant to be promiscuous. I felt I did not belong as I did not want to be gay and at the same time I did not feel fully accepted as a Christian. That was a bad place to be in psychologically, because I felt that I did not want to be a Christian, but I did not want to be gay either. Yet I could not stop being a Christian or being gay. I despaired of life, and I was asking myself: 'How can I live in this way? There is no place for me on earth.'

But alongside suffering and the highlighting of pressing and existential challenges, in these stories, *joy* emerges as a recurrent theme. As the Anglican priest Rev. Jalendo (Story 2) mentioned, 'Being a religious leader who is openly gay and is promoting the cause of LGBTIQ inclusion has been a difficult and painful journey, but also a beautiful and engaging one.' Religious leaders mentioned the joy of witnessing LGBTIQ individuals reconciling with religion following discrimination within previous religious communities, the joy of being at peace with scriptures, the joy of helping and fighting for a just world as allies and the joy of feeling accepted in God's presence.

The feeling of joy comes often associated with the idea of *hope* for a better *future*, which also emerges as a recurrent theme. While attempting to change the world surrounding them, these religious leaders are working, with hope, to shape new imaginaries of a new future for their country. This 'queer world-making' (Otis and Dunn 2021) is a process that occurs through the everyday expressions of LGBTIQ identifying people and allies while they push boundaries or claim non-conforming sexual and gender identities in places where these are silenced or encouraged to be invisible (Duon 2012). While narrating their stories, they are already making visible different possibilities that challenge the dominant narrative. As Mama Annette (Story 4) said:

> I think a lot about the future because as Christians we believe in change. I know that right now we are enduring a lot of problems, problems that I would not wish to my worst enemy. Nobody should

be put in the situation of being hunted by those challenges. Working for a better future is what motivates us. As a believer I know that in five or ten years from now we will see the foundation for the next generation. I do not want the next generation to face the same challenges that I am facing right now. The generation that will come after us shall not suffer the same way we are suffering – enough has to be enough.

Scriptures are a central point of reflection in the great majority of these stories. Not surprisingly, given the demographic, most of the religious leaders take time to consider the holy texts in their narratives and the way they have been used as tools to persecute and discriminate sexual minorities in their countries. This theme is often associated with the issue of *authority*, as many narrators highlighted the powerful role played by religious leaders in the region, with their voice having a telling impact on a very large component of the population. Pastor Caroline (Story 1) expressed it thus:

> Many people believe so much in the words of a pastor, so if a pastor says that your child needs to be prayed for, then everybody will believe that the child needs to be prayed for. This is because they believe the pastor speaks to God every day and God gives him the message to pass on to us. So, when it comes to someone being gay or lesbian, a pastor may say that this person is an abomination and needs deliverance from an evil spirit, and people will then seek exactly that.

The story of Sodom and Gomorrah in Genesis 19 and the laws in Leviticus 18 and 20 that appear to condemn same-sex behaviour, in particular, are addressed by several leaders who reference the specific literal interpretation offered in public and religious sites by the great majority of religious authorities without considering the context and the full meaning of those Old Testament texts. In many narratives, there is a clear intention to reclaim sacred texts as sources of liberation, rather than oppression, continuing and extending a trajectory of what Musa W. Dube (2003) has called 'other ways of reading' the Bible in Africa. Such readings go against the grain of popular yet colonialist, patriarchal and heteronormative interpretations and are important, in the words of Stella Nyanzi (2022, 74), for queer communities 'to achieve epistemic justice'. As Bishop James (Story 8) and Pastor Neema (Story 10) said, respectively:

What inspires religious leaders who are opposed to LGBTIQ inclusion is the story of Sodom and Gomorrah and the way they interpret it. They call LGBTIQ people an abomination, saying they are the reason why an entire race was wiped out. However, when you read Ezekiel 16:49, you find out that it is not true. The sin of Sodom and Gomorrah was not about sexuality was about their hateful behaviour towards strangers. It had nothing to do with sexuality but with injustice towards strangers and a failure of hospitality. (Bishop James)

I thank God that I am a trained theologian because 98% of pastors in Kenya have not been theologically trained and their reading of the scriptures is literal. What I mean is, if you read the Bible in a literal way, you easily make mistakes. But when you do exegesis, you are able to get the key meaning of the text. A good example is when the Bible says that women should not speak in church. It is very important to understand the history of that text, its background, what the mood was at the time of writing, and why Paul was saying that in that context. (Pastor Neema)

The lack of *training* and *education*, as expressed in Pastor Neema's quote but also highlighted in other stories, is frequently pinpointed as a problem among the religious leadership in the region. Literal and fundamentalist readings of the Bible and of the Quran are indicated as a problem that comes with the lack of training into proper exegesis and historical and cultural understandings. A narrator also highlighted a generational gap between most of the religious leadership – usually older and not well educated – and the emerging but still not established younger generation of religious leaders with better theological training, 'Amongst Muslims, we normally have marked differences of opinion between the elders, who are not well educated, and the younger generation, that is more trained in theology and Islamic studies', said Abdul a young Muslim leader (Story 21). The possibility of training was not only about the exegesis of sacred texts; it was also highlighted as a positive tool for creating points of contact with and knowledge about LGBTIQ people and their rights by several allies in their personal stories. It catalysed significant transformations from obliviousness or antipathy towards LGBTIQ people and their rights towards new roles as allies and supporters. Some allies in this collection clearly depicted this deep transformational shift that occurred since exposure to narratives and experiences that countered the dominant narrative to which they were habitually exposed. As Pastor Neema (Story 10) narrates:

Thus, in addition to doing good theology, there is a need to build the capacity of pastors on LGBTQ issues. I recall a training we held at a university. Before the training, many pastors were looking at LGBTIQ community members as animals. But after the training the pastors were able to understand they were wrong. By the time the training was coming to an end, all those pastors had become allies, me being one of them. They were able to sit together with LGBTIQ people, eat together and share stories with each other. We need to come together as a community, with the religious leaders, eat together, sing together, share together. Only that way, we can begin to question all the assumptions and stereotypes, such as about inhuman nature, the association of homosexuals with rapists etc. Only through such personal encounters, pastors will be able to understand that they are wrong.

These encounters touched some of the participants and encouraged them to reconsider their 'conservative' and exclusionary *theological* positions (with theology being a clear theme for reflection in the book), shifting towards affirming theologies. Yet not all of them went through such a process of change. Some allies continued to subscribe to aspects of the dominant discourse that homosexuality remains a choice and fundamentally a sin. While clearly embracing and recognizing the humanity and rights of LGBTIQ people, those leaders did not dissociate themselves from 'conservative' theological stances. As Evangelist Vincent (Story 11) said:

> I treat LGBTIQ individuals as full human beings with rights and a sound mind. They have a soul like I do, and a heart like I do. They have red blood like everyone, but the only difference is their choice. You have your choice, they have their choice, and each of us makes choices out of their own consciousness. … What matters to me is sharing Christ.

Across the spectrum of radical activism, those interpretations may not seem as very subversive, but in contexts like Uganda and Kenya, these are indeed already significant steps of change and openness that in some ways begin to challenge the single narrative of non-acceptance, discrimination and criminalization (van Klinken, Bompani and Parsitau 2023). Thus, the following quotation from Sheikh Dawoud (Story 19) illustrates how some religious leaders are careful not to be seen as 'promoting' homosexuality, yet nevertheless seek to acknowledge the fundamental humanity LGBTIQ people share with anyone else:

The moment I learned that these are our brothers and sisters, and they are fellow human beings, I started to recognize our shared humanity. And if they are human, who am I to judge them? ... My approach to this work should not be seen as if I am promoting LGBTIQ people; what I am trying to do is to emphasize that they are human beings, and we should not subject them to judgments or deny them their rights.

In those interpretations, there is an attempt from the narrators to reposition the act of same-sex 'sinning' within popular Muslim and Christian interpretations, as they make the point that homosexuality is, incorrectly, treated as a different kind and greater sin in comparison to other sins. In fact, several narrators made the point that all other sins are condoned and forgiven in many religious traditions, leaving only God to be the final judge; with regard to homosexuality, the ultimate judgement (and punishment) is pretty much a human affair. Abdul, a Muslim youth leader (Story 21), elaborated in this way:

There is need to sensitize religious leaders about LGBTQ people. In Islam, if you have sex with another man, you have done something wrong; when you practice adultery, you have also done something wrong; when you borrow money with interest, you have also done something wrong; but in all these cases, you still remain a Muslim. Only when you practice witchcraft, you stop belonging to the Muslim community, because if you associate God with other powers, you are no longer a Muslim. However, in Uganda we are killing LGBTQ people. Yet we have family members who have charms for good luck or practice final rites for the dead. While the latter is what excludes you from being a Muslim! There are many who have done much worse things than being gay. Yet, we see LGBTQ as the worst sinners.

One of the narrators powerfully reflected on his own theological position as a self-identified gay man and religious leader within his church, a conservative Pentecostal one, where he did not find space for inclusive and accepting positions regarding 'the sin' of homosexuality. While still embracing the orthodoxy of his church, he then sought a way to reconcile, not without difficulties, with his sexual identity. This was a very individual and personal process of change within the same church and the same theological space, a reminder that change is not a linear process and may occur in many different and sometimes inchoate ways. The same experience of faith evolved in our narrators (Fowler

1981, 92), with reflections on *faith* being a central theme in these stories of change. While narrating their experience of change and the different ways they were experiencing their own self, others and the world and their purpose in life, their faith also transformed, materially and spiritually. 'We need to tell our stories of change, as a testimony of how God has enlightened us', said Evangelist Josephine (Story 14).

In opposition to the hate and persecution perceived and experienced in different publics, *love* emerges as the final theme in the narratives of this collection. From hateful and discriminatory interpretations of the sacred texts to harmful and aggressive actions perpetuated against LGBTIQ individuals, there is a shift towards readings of the Bible and the Quran in ways that include, respect, acknowledge and cherish the existence of LGBTIQ minorities, and towards religious leaders who stand strong beside those communities. Rediscovering the sacred texts as spaces of love for those communities, frequently pointing towards alternative interpretative readings, is a recurrent thread in many stories. Love for the self and for the others is presented as something once lost but then regained, as Pastor Deron put it, 'The Lord is using me and other pastors to teach LGBTIQ people to love again and to bring back faith into the life of people' (Story 7). But also as a tool to disrupt dominant narratives of hate, as Bishop James stated:

> You remember that our Lord Jesus said, 'A new command I give you: Love one another. As I have loved you, so you must love one another. By this everyone will know that you are my disciples, if you love one another.' ... So, this is the greatest weapon LGBTIQ people need to use: love. I see love as the only weapon we need to use.

Lastly, these religious leaders manifest a real and genuine *desire* to minister LGBTIQ people and are committed to creating and maintaining religious spaces where queer experiences can be validated. They demonstrate that even in the context of nearly unanimous voices of hate and exclusion, there are religious leaders and faith communities that are inclusive and welcoming. The voices of these religious leaders give hope to many LGBTIQ people who would like to make spiritual and theological contributions to their faith communities as well as to their countries – these voices may, for now, be 'black swan' rare, but their presence gives reason for hope and optimism about the future.

These recurrent themes transcend the individual experience of the religious leaders presented in this volume, already powerful individually, while building a body of experiences that acts as a counter to dominant narratives. Through the authority and significance of their own experiences of personal change, the voices of these religious leaders indicate a possible collective transformation where religion may cease to be associated and entrenched with queerphobia in East Africa. Spaces for counternarratives, the 'right to narrate', should be guaranteed in healthy societies (Bhabha 2014). As the curators of this volume, we had the privilege to listen to those stories first hand and had the honour to collect and prepare them for publication. Hopefully this offers a small contribution to the 'right to narrate' and to the building of queer African archives (Macharia 2015). Now that these stories are published and out in the world, we hope they will continue to generate new narratives and new possibilities.

REFERENCES

Achebe, Chinua. 2000. 'Today, a Balance of Stories', in *Home and Exile*, 73–106. Oxford: Oxford University Press.

Adichie, Chimamanda Ngozi. 2009. 'The Danger of a Single Story', *TEDGlobal*. Available online: www.ted.com/talks/chimamanda_ngozi_adichie_the_d anger_of_a_single_story/no-comments (accessed 19 April 2023).

Akam, Simon. 2010. 'Outcry as Ugandan Paper Names "Top Homosexuals"', *The Independent*, 22 October. Available online: www.independent.co.uk/ news/world/africa/outcry-as-ugandan-paper-names-top-homosexuals-2113348.html (accessed 13 May 2023).

Amanpour, Christiane. 2018. 'President: Gay Rights "of No Importance" in Kenya', *CNN*, 20 April. Available online: https://edition.cnn.com/videos/ world/2018/04/20/kenya-uhuru-kenyatta-gay-rights-intv-amanpour-intl. cnn (accessed 27 April 2023).

Amory, Deborah P. 1998. '*Mashoga, Mabasha*, and *Magai*: "Homosexuality" on the East African Coast', in Stephen O. Murray and Will Roscoe (eds), *Boy-Wives and Female Husbands: Studies of African Homosexualities*, 67–87. New York: Palgrave.

Anderson, Allan H. 2001. *African Reformation: African Initiated Christianity in the 20th Century*. Trenton, NJ: Africa World Press.

Awami, Sammy. 2023. 'Viewpoint: East Africa's Battle over Culture and Homosexuality', *BBC News*, 12 April. Available online: www.bbc.co.uk/ news/world-africa-65239117 (accessed 4 June 2023).

Awondo, Patrick. 2016. 'Religious Leadership and the Re-politicisation of Gender and Sexuality in Cameroon', *Journal of Theology for Southern Africa*, 155, 105–20.

Azuah, Unoma. 2016. *Blessed Body: The Secret Lives of Lesbian, Gay, Bisexual and Transgender Nigerians*. Jackson, TN: CookingPot.

Barasa, George (producer). 2016. 'Same Love (Remix)', *YouTube*, 15 February. Available online: www.youtube.com/watch?v=8EataOQvPII (accessed 28 April 2023).

Bhabha, Homi. 2014. 'The Right to Narrate', *Harvard Design Magazine*, 38. Available online: www.harvarddesignmagazine.org/issues/38/the-right-to-narrate (accessed 5 June 2023).

Bompani, Barbara. 2013. 'Homophobic Bill a Festive Gift for Uganda's Pentecostal Churches', *The Conversation*, 24 December. Available online: https://theconversation.com/homophobic-bill-a-festive-gift-for-ugandas-pentecostal-churches-21694 (accessed 13 May 2023).

Bompani, Barbara. 2016. 'For God and for My Country: Pentecostal-Charismatic Churches and the Framing of a New Political Discourse in Uganda', in Adriaan van Klinken and Ezra Chitando (eds), *Public Religion and the Politics of Homosexuality in Africa*, 19–34. London: Routledge.

Bompani, Barbara, and Stephanie Terreni Brown. 2015. 'A "Religious Revolution"? Print Media, Sexuality and Religious Discourse in Uganda', *Journal of Eastern African Studies*, 9:1, 110–26.

Bompani, Barbara, and Caroline Valois. 2016. 'Sexualizing Politics: The Anti-Homosexuality Bill, Party-Politics and the New Political Dispensation in Uganda', *Critical African Studies*, 8:2, 1–19.

Bompani, Barbara, and Caroline Valois (eds). 2017. *Christian Citizens and the Moral Regeneration of the African State*. London: Routledge.

Burchardt, Marian. 2013. 'Equals before the Law? Public Religion and Queer Activism in the Age of Judicial Politics in South Africa', *Journal of Religion in Africa*, 43:3, 237–60.

Byamugisha, Gideon. 2009. 'Bringing Change Is Not Easy: The Anti-SSDDIM and Pro-SAVE HIV & AIDS Imperative' (video). Harare: WCC/EHAIA/Christian Aid.

Byarugaba, Clare, and Maria E. Burnett. 2023. 'Uganda's Horrific Anti-LGBTIQ+ Bill Returns: The Stakes Are Higher than Ever', Centre for Strategies and International Studies, 3 May. Available online: www.csis.org/analysis/ugandas-horrific-anti-lgbtiq-bill-returns-stakes-are-higher-ever (accessed 14 May 2023).

Camminga, B. 2020. 'Encamped within a Camp: Transgender Refugees and Kakuma Refugee Camp (Kenya)', in Jesper Bjarneses and Simon Turner (eds), *Invisibility in African Displacement: From Structural Marginalization to Strategies of Avoidance*, 36–52. London: Zed.

Chitando, Ezra, and Tapiwa P. Mapuranga. 2016. 'Unlikely Allies? Lesbian, Gay, Bisexual, Transgender and Intersex (LGBTI) Activists and Church Leaders in Africa', in Ezra Chitando and Adriaan van Klinken (eds), *Christianity and Controversies over Homosexuality in Contemporary Africa*, 171–83. London: Routledge.

Chitando, Ezra, and Adriaan van Klinken (eds). 2016. *Christianity and Controversies over Homosexuality in Contemporary Africa*. London: Routledge.

Citizen TV Kenya. 2023. 'President Ruto Says Homosexuality Is Unacceptable', *YouTube*, 2 March. Available online: www.youtube.com/watch?v=NISr61sa5Go (accessed 28 April 2023).

Currier, Ashley, and Joella M. Cruz. 2013. 'Civil Society and Sexual Struggles in Africa', in Ebenezer Obadare (ed.), *The Handbook of Civil Society in Africa*, 337–60. New York: Springer.

Decker, Corrie. 2021. 'Sexuality in Colonial Africa: Current Trends and New Directions', in Chelsea Schields and Dagmar Herzog (eds), *The Routledge Companion to Sexuality and Colonialism*, 42–54. London: Routledge.

Dreier, Sarah, James Long and Stephen Winkler. 2020. 'African, Religious, and Tolerant? How Religious Diversity Shapes Attitudes toward Sexual Minorities in Africa', *Politics and Religion*, 13:2, 273–303.

Dube, Musa W. (ed.). 2003. *Other Ways of Reading: African Women and the Bible*. Atlanta, GA: Society of Biblical Literature.

Duong, Kevin. 2012. 'What Does Queer Theory Teach Us about Intersectionality?', *Politics and Gender*, 8:3, 370–86.

EAVA. n.d. 'Documenting and Combating Religious Homophobia'. Available online: https://eavisualarts.org/program/documenting-and-combat ing-religious-homophobia/ (accessed 30 July 2022, webpage no longer available).

Ekine, Sokari, and Hakima Abbas (eds). 2013. *The Queer African Reader*. Dakar: Pambazuka Press.

Epprecht, Marc. 2009. 'Sexuality, Africa, History', *American Historical Review*, 114:5, 1258–72.

Epprecht, Marc. 2013. *Sexuality and Social Justice in Africa: Rethinking Homophobia and Forging Resistance*. London: Zed.

Faupel, John F. 1962. *African Holocaust: The Story of the Uganda Martyrs*. London: Geoffrey Chapman.

Finerty, Courtney E. 2013. 'Being Gay in Kenya: The Implications of Kenya's New Constitution for Its Anti-sodomy Laws', *Cornell International Law Journal*, 45:2, 431–60.

Fisher, Jonathan. 2014. 'When It Pays to Be a "Fragile State": Uganda's Use and Abuse of a Dubious Concept', *Third World Quarterly*, 35:2, 316–32.

Fowler James W. 1981. *Stages of Faith*. San Francisco: Harper and Row.

Freire, Paulo. 2018. *Pedagogy of the Oppressed* (50th anniversary ed.). London: Bloomsbury.

Gichuru, Evans, Bernadette Kombo, Noni Mumba, Salla Sariola, Eduard J. Sanders and Elise M. van der Elst. 2018. 'Engaging Religious Leaders to Support HIV Prevention and Care for Gays, Bisexual Men, and Other Men Who Have Sex with Men in Coastal Kenya', *Critical Public Health*, 28:3, 94–305.

Gutierrez, Gustavo. 1973. *A Theology of Liberation: History, Politics, and Salvation*. Maryknoll, NY: Orbis.

Hansen, Hans. 2020. *Narrative Change: How Changing the Story Can Transform Society, Business, and Ourselves*. New York: Columbia University Press.

Hellweg, Joseph. 2015. 'Same-Gender Desire, Religion, and Homophobia: Challenges, Complexities, and Progress for LGBTIQ Liberation in Africa', *Journal of the American Academy of Religion*, 83:4, 887–96.

Hill, Wesley. 2010. *Washed and Waiting: Reflections on Christian Faithfulness and Homosexuality*. Grand Rapids, MI: Zondervan.

Hoad, Neville. 2007. *African Intimacies: Race, Homosexuality, and Globalization*. Minneapolis: University of Minnesota Press.

Howard, Brian. 2020. 'Religion in Africa: Tolerance and Trust in Leaders Are High, but Many Would Allow Regulation of Religious Speech', *Afrobarometer Dispatch*, 339. Available online: www.afrobarometer.org/wp-content/uploads/migrated/files/publications/Policy%20papers/ab_r7_dispatchno339_pap12_religion_in_africa.pdf (accessed 5 May 2023).

Human Rights Watch. 2015. *The Issue Is Violence: Attacks on LGBT People on Kenya's Coast*. New York: Human Rights Watch. Available online: www.hrw.org/sites/default/files/report_pdf/kenya0915_4upr.pdf (accessed 8 June 2023).

Hyvärinen, Matti. 2010. 'Revisiting the Narrative Turns', *Life Writing*, 7:1, 69–82.

INERELA+. n.d. 'About Us'. Available online: https://inerela.org/about/ (accessed 8 June 2023).

Jackson, Michael. 2013. *The Politics of Storytelling: Variations on a Theme by Hannah* Arendt. Copenhagen: Museaum Tusculanum Press.

Jjuuko, Adrian. 2013. 'The Incremental Approach: Uganda's Struggle for the Decriminalisation of Homosexuality', in Corinne Lennox and Matthew Waites (eds), *Human Rights, Sexual Orientation and Gender Identity in the Commonwealth: Struggles for Decriminalisation and Change*, 381–408. London: Institute of Commonwealth Studies.

Kahiu, Wanuri (director). 2018. *Rafiki*. Nairobi: Big World/Film Movement.

Kaluma, George Peter. 2023. The Family Protection Bill Proposed to the National Assembly of the Republic of Kenya. Available online: https://eu.docs.wps.com/l/sIH-m9aGmAbL5w6EG?sa=00&st=0t (accessed 27 April 2023).

Kaoma, Kapya J. 2017. *Christianity, Globalization, and Protective Homophobia: Democratic Contestation of Sexuality in Sub-Saharan Africa*. New York: Palgrave Macmillan.

Kenya Human Rights Commission. 2011. *The Outlawed amongst Us: A Study of the LGBTI Community's Search for Equality and Non-discrimination in Kenya*. Nairobi: KHRC. Available online: www.khrc.or.ke/mobile-publications/equality-and-anti-discrimination/70-the-outlawed-amongst-us/file.html (accessed 8 June 2023).

Kenyatta, Jomo. 1965. *Facing Mount Kenya*. New York: Vintage.

Le Roux, Elisabet Neil Kramm, Nigel Scott, Maggie Sandilands, Lizle Loots, Jill Olivier, Diana Arango and Veena O'Sullivan. 2016. 'Getting Dirty: Working with Faith Leaders to Prevent and Respond to Gender-Based Violence', *Review of Faith & International Affairs*, 14:3, 22–35.

Lewin, Ellen. 2018. *Filled with the Spirit: Sexuality, Gender, and Radical Inclusivity in a Black Pentecostal Church Coalition*. Chicago: University of Chicago Press.

Macharia, Keguro. 2013. 'Queer Kenya in Law and Policy', in Sokari Ekine and Hakima Abbas (eds), *The Queer African Reader*, 273–89. Dakar: Pambazuka Press.

Macharia, Keguro. 2015. 'Archive and Method in Queer African Studies', *Agenda*, 29:1, 140–6.

Magesa, Laurenti. 2004. *Anatomy of Inculturation: Transforming the Church in Africa*. Maryknoll, NY: Orbis.

Makena, Mumbi. 2022. 'What Lies behind Kenyan President-Elect William Ruto's Homophobia', Open Democracy, 2 September. Available online: www.opendemocracy.net/en/5050/william-ruto-kenya-presid ent-elect-homophobia-transphobia-evangelism-colonialism/ (accessed 28 April 2023).

Mangone, Emiliana. 2022. *Narratives and Social Change: Social Reality in Contemporary Society*. Dordrecht: Springer.

Matebeni, Zethu. 2021. 'The State of LGBT Rights in Africa', in Olajumoke Yacob-Haliso and Toyin Falola (eds), *The Palgrave Handbook of African Women's Studies*, 465–78. New York: Palgrave Macmillan.

Mbetbo, Ntetmen J. 2013. 'Internalised Conflicts in the Practice of Religion among *Kwandengue* Living with HIV in Douala, Cameroun', *Culture, Health and Sexuality*, 15:1, 76–87.

Mbote, David K., Esther Mombo, Zablon B. Mutongu, Chris Alaro, Anthony Mkutu and Theo G. M. Sandfort. 2021. 'Religious Fundamentalism and Attitudes towards Sexual and Gender Minorities and Other Marginalized Groups among Religious Leaders in Kenya', *Pastoral Psychology*, 70, 167–78.

Mbote, David K., Esther Mombo, Zablon B. Mutongu, Anthony Mkutu, Adam Ciarleglio and Theo G. M. Sandfort. 2022. 'Facing Our Fears: The Impact of a 4-Day Training Intervention to Reduce Negative Perspectives on Sexual and Gender Minorities among Religious Leaders in Kenya', *Journal of Sex Research*, 59:5, 587–98.

Mbote, David K., Theo G. M. Sandfort, Esther Waweru and Andrew Zapfel. 2018. 'Kenyan Religious Leaders' Views on Same-Sex Sexuality and Gender Nonconformity: Religious Freedom versus Constitutional Rights', *Journal of Sex Research*, 55:4&5, 630–41.

McEntarfer, Heather K., and Mary B. McVee. 2014. '"What Are You, Gay?" Positioning in Monologues Written and Performed by Members of a Gay-Straight Alliance', *Linguistics and Education*, 25, 78–89.

Mishler, Elliot, and Corinne Squire. 2020. 'The Personal Is Political: The Social Justice Functions of Stories', in Corinne Squire (ed.), *Stories Changing Lives: Narratives and Paths toward Social Change*, 1–18. Oxford: Oxford University Press.

Mombo, Esther. 2006. 'Kenya Reflections', in Terry Brown (ed.), *Other Voices, Other Worlds: The Global Church Speaks Out on Homosexuality*, 142–53. London: Darton, Longman and Todd.

Murimi, Peter (director). 2020. *I Am Samuel*. Nairobi: We Are Not the Machine.

Murray, Michael. 2000. 'Levels of Narrative Analysis in Health Psychology', *Journal of Health Psychology*, 5:3, 337–47.

Murunga, Godwin R. 2014. 'Elite Compromises and the Content of the 2010 Constitution', in Godwin R. Murunga, Duncan Okello and Anders Sjogren (eds), *Kenya: The Struggle for a New Constitutional Order*, 144–62. London: Zed.

Mwachiro, Kevin. 2013. *Invisible: Stories from Kenya's Queer Community*. Nairobi: Goethe Institute.

Mwaura, Philomena Njeri. 2004. 'African Instituted Churches in East Africa', *Studies in World Christianity*, 10:2, 160–84.

Mwikya, Kenne. 2013. 'The Media, the Tabloid and the Ugandan Homophobia Spectacle', in Sokari Ekine and Hakima Abbas (eds), *The Queer African Reader*, 141–54. Dakar: Pambazuka Press.

Nadar, Sarojini. 2012. 'Feminist Theologies in Africa', in Elias K. Bongmba (ed.), *The Wiley-Blackwell Companion to African Religions*, 269–78. Malden, MA: Wiley-Blackwell.

NBC News. 2015. 'Kenya's William Ruto Says There's "No Room" for Gays in His Nation', 4 May. Available online: www.nbcnews.com/news/world/ken yas-william-ruto-says-theres-no-room-gays-his-nation-n353161 (accessed 27 April 2023).

Ndjio, Basile. 2013. 'Sexuality and Nationalist Ideologies in Post-colonial Cameroon', in Saskia Wieringa and Horacio Sivori (eds), *The Sexual History of the Global South: Sexual Politics in Africa, Asia, and Latin America*, 120–43. London: Zed.

Ndzovu, Hassan J. 2016. Un-natural, Un-African and Un-Islamic: The Three Pronged Onslaught Undermining Homosexual Freedom in Kenya', in Adriaan van Klinken and Ezra Chitando (eds), *Public Religion and the Politics of Homosexuality in Africa*, 78–91. London: Routledge.

Neiman, Sophie. 2023. '"Born Out of Hatred": New Uganda Bill Terrifies LGBTQ Community', *Al-Jazeera*, 31 March. Available online: www. aljazeera.com/features/2023/3/31/born-out-of-hatred-uganda-bill-terrif ies-lgbtq-community (accessed 10 May 2023).

The Nest. 2015. *Stories of Our Lives: Queer Narratives from Kenya*. Nairobi: The Nest Collective.

Njambi, Wairimũ Ngarũiya, and William E. O'Brien. 2000. 'Revisiting "Woman-Woman Marriage": Notes on Gĩkũyũ Women', *NWSA Journal*, 12:1, 1–23.

Nouwen, Henri J. M. 1972. *The Wounded Healer: Ministry in Contemporary Society*. London: Darton, Longman and Todd.

Nyanzi, Stella. 2014. 'Queer Pride and Protest: A Reading of the Bodies at Uganda's First Gay Beach Pride', *Signs: Journal of Women in Culture and Society*, 40:1, 36–40.

Nyanzi, Stella. 2022. 'Balancing an Unequal Partnership for Studying Ugandan Queer Refugees' Appropriation of Bible Stories', *African Journal of Gender and Religion*, 28:2, 69–78.

Nyanzi, Stella, and Andrew Karamangi. 2015. 'The Social-political Dynamics of the Anti-homosexuality Legislation in Uganda', *Agenda*, 29:1, 24–38.

Nyarwek. 2017. *Safe Spaces: A Training Manual on Religious Inclusion for Christians at the Periphery*. Kisumu: Nyarwek. Available online: https://ser ene.leeds.ac.uk/wp-content/uploads/sites/105/2020/03/NYARWEK-Religi ous-leaders-training-manual-booklet-1.pdf (accessed 5 May 2023).

Nyeck, S. N., and Marc Epprecht (eds). 2013. *Sexual Diversity in Africa: Politics, Theory, Citizenship*. Montreal: McGill-Queen's University Press.

Nyoni, Zanele. 2020. 'The Struggle for Equality: LGBT Rights Activism in Sub-Saharan Africa', *Human Rights Law Review*, 20:3, 582–601.

Obinyan, Aiwan (director). 2020. *Kenyan, Christian, Queer*. London: AiAi Studios. Available online: www.youtube.com/watch?v=bsU6QR0lfzs (accessed 28 April 2023).

Oliver, Marcia. 2013. 'Transnational Sex Politics, Conservative Christianity, and Anti-gay Activism in Uganda', *Studies in Social Justice*, 7:1, 83–105.

Ombagi, Eddie. 2019. 'Nairobi Is a Shot of Whisky: Queer, (Ob)scenes in the City', *Journal of African Cultural Studies*, 31:1, 106–19.

Østebø, Marit Tolo, and Terje Østebø. 2014. 'Are Religious Leaders a Magic Bullet for Social/Societal Change? A Critical Look at Anti-FGM Interventions in Ethiopia', *Africa Today*, 60:3, 83–101.

Otis, Hailey N., and Thomas R. Dunn. 2021. 'Queer Worldmaking', in *Oxford Research Encyclopedia of Communication*. Available online: https://doi. org/10.1093/acrefore/9780190228613.013.1235 (accessed 8 June 2023).

Parsitau, Damaris S. 2021. 'Law, Religion, and the Politicization of Sexual Citizenship in Kenya', *Journal of Law and Religion*, 36:1, 105–29.

PEMA Kenya. 2018. *Facing Our Fears: A Training Manual on Stigma Reduction, Tolerance, and Brotherly/sisterly Acceptance in Diversity*. Mombasa: PEMA Kenya. Available online: https://serene.leeds.ac.uk/ wp-content/uploads/sites/105/2022/02/FACING-OUR-FEARS-MANUAL. pdf (accessed 5 May 2023).

Pettigrew, Thomas F., and Linda R. Tropp. 2000. 'Does Intergroup Contact Reduce Prejudice: Recent Meta-analytic Findings', in Stuart Oskamp (ed.), *Reducing Prejudice and Discrimination*, 93–114. Mahwah, NJ: Lawrence Erlbaum.

Pew Research. 2022. 'Religious Composition by Country, 2010–2050'. Available online: www.pewresearch.org/religion/interactives/religious-composition-by-country-2010-2050/ (accessed 5 May 2023).

Rao, Rahul. 2015. 'Re-membering Mwanga: Same-Sex Intimacy, Memory and Belonging in Postcolonial Uganda', *Journal of Eastern African Studies*, 9:1, 1–19.

Rao, Rahul. 2020. *Out of Time: The Queer Politics of Postcoloniality*. Oxford: Oxford University Press.

Reid, Alvin. 1998. *Introduction to Evangelism*. Nashville, TN: Broadman and Holman.

Robertson, Megan. 2021. 'Queer Studies and Religion in Southern Africa: The Production of Queer Christian Subjects', *Religion Compass*, 15:1, e12385.

Rodriguez, S. M. 2018. *The Economies of Queer Inclusion: Transnational Organizing for LGBTI Rights in Uganda*. Lanham, MD: Lexington.

Sadgrove, Joanna, Robert Vanderbeck, Johan Andersson, Gill Valentine and Kevin Ward. 2012. 'Morality Plays and Money Matters: Towards a Situated Understanding of the Politics of Homosexuality in Uganda', *Journal of Modern African Studies*, 50:1, 103–29.

Sandfort, Theo, Fabienne Simenel, Kevin Mwachiro and Vasu Reddy (eds). 2015. *Boldly Queer: African Perspectives on Same-Sex Sexuality and Gender Diversity*. The Hague: Hivos.

Senyonjo, Christopher. 2016. *In Defense of All God's Children: The Life and Ministry of Bishop Christopher Senyonjo*. New York: Morehouse.

Stone-Mediatore, Shari. 2003. *Reading across Borders: Storytelling and Knowledges of Resistance*. New York: Palgrave Macmillan.

Tabengwa, Monica, and Matthew Waites. 2020. 'Africa and the Contestation of Sexual and Gender Diversity: Imperial and Contemporary Regulation', in Michael J. Bosia, Sandra M. McEvoy and Momin Rahman (eds), *The Oxford Handbook of Global LGBT and Sexual Diversity Politics*, 201–17. Oxford: Oxford University Press.

Tamale, Sylvia. 2003. 'Out of the Closet: Unveiling Sexuality Discourses in Uganda', *Feminist Africa*, 2, 42–9.

Thoreson, Ryan R. 2014. 'Troubling the Waters of a "Wave of Homophobia": Political Economies of Anti-queer Animus in Sub-Saharan Africa', *Sexualities*, 17:1&2, 23–42.

Titeka, Kristof. 2023. 'Unpacking the Geopolitics of Uganda's Anti-gay Bill', African Argument, 10 March. Available online: https://africanarguments.org/2023/03/unpacking-the-geopolitics-of-uganda-anti-gay-bill/ (accessed 14 May 2023).

Tomalin, Emma. 2013. *Religions and Development*. London: Routledge.

UCAA. n.d. 'About Us'. Available online: https://ucaaug.org (accessed 6 May 2023).

UNDP. 2015. *Guidelines on Engaging with Faith-Based Organizations and Religious Leaders*. Geneva: UNDP. Available online: www.undp.org/publications/undp-guidelines-engaging-faith-based-organizations-and-religious-leaders (accessed 5 May 2023).

Vaggione, Juan Marco. 2005. 'Reactive Politicization and Religious Dissidence: The Political Mutations of the Religious', *Social Theory and Practice*, 31:2, 233–55.

van Klinken, Adriaan. 2017. 'Culture Wars, Race, and Sexuality: A Nascent Pan-African LGBT-Affirming Christian Movement and the Future of Christianity', *Journal of Africana Religions*, 5:2, 217–38.

van Klinken, Adriaan. 2019. *Kenyan, Christian, Queer: Religion, LGBT Activism, and Arts of Resistance in Africa*. University Park, PA: Penn State University Press.

van Klinken, Adriaan. 2020a. 'Changing the Narrative of Sexuality in African Christianity: Bishop Christopher Senyonjo's LGBT Advocacy', *Theology and Sexuality*, 26:1, 1–6.

van Klinken, Adriaan. 2020b. 'The Future of Christianity and LGBT Rights in Africa: A Conversation with Rev. Dr Bishop Christopher Senyonjo', *Theology and Sexuality*, 26:1, 7–11.

van Klinken, Adriaan, Barbara Bompani and Damaris Parsitau. 2023. 'Religious Leaders as Agents of LGBTIQ Inclusion in East Africa', *African Affairs*, 122:487, 299–312.

van Klinken, Adriaan, and Ezra Chitando (eds). 2016. *Public Religion and the Politics of Homosexuality in Africa*. London: Routledge.

van Klinken, Adriaan, and Ezra Chitando. 2021. *Reimagining Christianity and Sexual Diversity in Africa*. London: Hurst.

van Klinken, Adriaan, Johanna Stiebert, Sebyala Brian and Fredrick Hudson. 2021. *Sacred Queer Stories: Ugandan LGBTQ+ Refugee Lives and the Bible*. Suffolk: James Currey.

Vanderbeck, Robert, Joanna Sadgrove, Gill Valentine, Johan Andersson and Kevin Ward. 2015. 'The Transnational Debate over Homosexuality in the Anglican Communion', in Stanley D. Brunn (ed.), *The Changing World Religion Map: Sacred Places, Identities, Practices and Politics*, 3283–301. London: Springer.

Wainaina, Binyavanga. 2014. 'I Am a Homosexual, Mum', *The Guardian*, 21 January. Available online: www.theguardian.com/commentisfree/2014/jan/21/i-am-a-homosexual-mum-binyavanga-wainaina-memoir (accessed 29 April 2023).

Ward, Kevin. 2015. 'The Role of the Anglican and Catholic Churches in Uganda in Public Discourse on Homosexuality and Ethics', *Journal of Eastern African Studies*, 9:1, 127–44.

Ward, Kevin, and Emma Wild-Wood (eds). 2013. *The East African Revival: History and Legacies*. Farnham: Ashgate.

Wepukulu, Kathondi Soita. 2023. 'Christian Fundamentalism Lies behind Harsh New Anti-LGBTIQ Bill in Uganda', Open Democracy, 23 March. Available online: www.opendemocracy.net/en/5050/uganda-anti-homose xuality-bill-church-us-england-odoi-oywelowo/ (accessed 14 May 2023).

West, Gerald, Charlene van der Walt and Kapya J. Kaoma. 2016. 'When Faith Does Violence: Reimagining Engagement between Churches and LGBTI Groups on Homophobia in Africa', *HTS Theological Studies*, 72:1, a3511.

WHO. 2021. *World Health Organization Strategy for Engaging Religious Leaders, Faith-Based Organizations and Faith Communities in Health Emergencies*. Geneva: World Health Organization. Available online: www.who.int/publications/i/item/9789240037205 (accessed 5 May 2023).

Woensdregt, Lise, and Naomi van Stapele. 2023. 'Queerphobia in Kenya: A Supreme Court Ruling on Gay Rights Triggers a New Wave of Anger against the LGBTIQ+ Community', *The Conversation*, 2 May. Available online: https://theconversation.com/queerphobia-in-kenya-a-supr eme-court-ruling-on-gay-rights-triggers-a-new-wave-of-anger-agai nst-the-lgbtiq-community-204575 (accessed 5 May 2023).

Wyrod, Robert. 2016. *AIDS and Masculinity in the African City. Privilege, Inequality and Modern Manhood*. Berkeley: University of California Press.

INDEX

Abdul (youth leader) 169–75, 169 n.1
abomination 32, 41, 83, 209, 210
Abraham 164
Achebe, Chinua 2
activism
  advocacy and 8, 13
  queer 39
  radical 211
  social 184
Adam 161, 192, 198
Adichie, Chimamanda Ngozi 2,
  193
Affinity 142–3
Africa Inland Church (AIC) 27, 27 n.2
African theology 106 n.2, 188
AHB. *See* Anti-homosexuality Bill (AHB)
AIDS. *See* HIV-AIDS
Aisha 167
Almighty God 161
Amos 74
ANERELA+ 14
Anglican Church 7, 9, 11, 15, 27, 85 n.10,
  142, 144–6, 189, 200
Anglican Communion 9, 144, 144 n.4–5,
  145 n.6, 197 n.4
Anglican(ism)
  priests 14
  sister churches 9
Anti-homosexuality Act 10, 205
Anti-homosexuality Bill (AHB) 1,
  9–12, 28 n.3
anti-LGBTIQ 2, 9, 11–13, 205
anti-queer 11, 23
  animus 2–3
  feelings and rejection 207
  rhetoric and attacks 9
Apollo 98
Aquila 98
Arameans 178
authority 35, 102, 205, 209, 214
  influence and 16

male 185
power and 119–21
Awondo, Patrick 13
Azuah, Unoma
  *Blessed Body: The Secret Lives
  of Lesbian, Gay, Bisexual and
  Transgender Nigerians* 3

Bahati, David 9
bakoras 159
baptism 35–6, 112
Barasa, George
  Same Love (Remix) 8
Bible 19, 37, 46, 47–8, 54, 58, 65–6, 83, 92–
  5, 118–20, 132, 138–9, 147, 150, 154,
  158, 178–81, 185–8, 193, 195, 198
  in Africa 209
  college 113
  command to love one another 74
  evangelism 107
  gay 28
  homosexual tendencies in 38
  on human creation 68
  Jephthah 115
  Jo. 8.1–11 33 n.10
  Job in 61
  against LGBTIQ people 30, 47
  Lydia 98
  Mary Magdalene 109
  Naomi 138
  Queen Esther 131, 131 n.3
  queer Christians 52–3
  queer theology and 35, 38, 40, 58
  queer women 33
  reading in literal way 98–9, 101, 210
  science and 116
  sexual and gender diversity in 18
  St Paul 41
  study coordinator 90
  tradition 38
  trainings 90

Bill of Rights 6
Bishop James 79–85, 85 n.10, 204–5, 209
Bishop Joseph 177–81, 177 n.1
Bishop Roger 135–9, 135 n.1
blasphemy 91
Blessed Body: The Secret Lives of Lesbian, Gay, Bisexual and Transgender Nigerians (Azuah) 3
boda boda 74, 74 n.4
body 109, 120, 142, 151, 165, 213
    gender identity 60
    leadership 80
    as one 94
    sexuality and 42
Bonnke, Reinhard 136, 136 n.2
Book of Esther 131–2, 131 n.3
British Royal Navy 142
Bucyana, Paul Kwizera 203
Buganda Kingdom 85 n.10, 153 n.4, 191
Buwalasi Theological College 196
Byamugisha, Gideon 14

Catholic Church 28, 85 n.10, 105, 109, 153 n.4, 154, 155, 207
Catholic(ism) 24, 28–9
    calendar 150
    evangelist 105
    priest 39 n.5, 80, 149
    sisters 187
chaplaincy 67, 142, 144, 146
chaplains 144
Children Act 2022 6
Chitando, Ezra 14
Christianity 47, 89–90, 153
    evangelical 63 n.2
    faith and 41
    history in Uganda 205
    inclusive form of 64 n.4, 81 n.3
    queer 53
    reconvertion/conversion 89–90, 153 n.4, 204
    in Uganda 85 n.10, 205
Christians 37, 48, 54, 58, 85, 118
    faith 45, 63
    faithfulness 46
    gay 49
    Kenyan 32 n.9
    LGBTIQ 21, 47

peace and harmony between Muslims and 164
    queer 52–4
    shouting against homosexual 118
Christian Union (CU) 43, 43 n.2, 89–90, 89 n.2
    leadership 44
    membership 44
Church of Uganda 9, 15, 197, 200
circumcision/circumcised 185, 191
clericalism 186, 190
colonial(ism) 4–6, 9, 112
coming out 102, 121
Communion 42, 91
    Anglican 9, 144, 144 n.4–5, 145 n.6, 197 n.4
    Holy 35, 112
compassion 20, 33, 50, 94, 114, 178, 180
conservative 1, 3, 7, 11, 13, 20, 36, 38, 40–1, 211–12
Cosmopolitan Affirming Church (CAC) 27, 29, 31–3, 35, 42, 42 n.9
creation of God 65, 89, 92, 100, 102, 113, 114, 131–2, 154, 163
crucifixion 58, 109. *See also* Jesus Christ
culture
    African 18, 150, 153 n.5
    intolerance 3, 17
    patriarchal 65
    Quaker studies and research on 188
    of social and political homophobia 18
    of the time 185

Dar es Salaam 106
David (and Jonathan) 29, 47, 66, 83, 138, 147
decision-making 17, 170
dehumanization 2
Democratic Governance Facility (DGF) 10
demonic 1, 103, 110, 130, 132, 152
diocese 186–9
discrimination 39, 54, 101, 103, 130
    get equal treatment without 160
    individual and collective experiences of 101
    marginalization and 91, 190
    patriarchy and gender 188
    stigmatization and 17, 19–20, 178

suffering and 207
    against transgender women 72
    violence and 158
diversity (of sexuality and gender) 1–14,
        16, 18–21, 23–4
    difference and 199
    LGBTIQ community 47
    love and 199
    sexual and gender 68
Do-No-Harm 157
Dube, Musa W. 209

East Africa 3, 21–2
    sexual and gender diversity politics
        in 4–12
East African Revival Movement
        35, 35 n.1
East Africa Visual Artists (EAVA) 20–1
Elohistic tradition 100, 100 n.8
Episcopal Church 9, 45
Epprecht, Marc 13
error 41, 144 n.4
Eucharist 42
euphemisms 184, 186
evangelical(ism) 8
    becoming born-again 43 n.3
    Christianity 63 n. 2
    Christian Union (CU) 43 n.2, 89 n.2
    church in Kenya 27 n.2
    language of faith 186
    pastor 204
    saved by Christ 40 n.7
    standing in the gap 64 n.3
evangelism 107, 107 n.5, 108
exegesis 98–9, 98 n.2, 103, 145, 210
Exodus 29, 30
Ezekiel 83, 210

faith
    based coalition 15
    based organizations 15
    Christianity and 41, 42, 45, 63, 83,
        153 n.5
    communities 3, 14, 16, 19, 64, 158, 213
    in decision-making 17
    expression of 40, 41
    gatherings 67
    hope and perseverance 68
    inclusive 16

of queer Christians 53
    related homophobia 20
    religion and 37
    sexual ethics 50
    sexuality and 41, 46
family(ies) 11, 31, 37, 59, 63, 119
    African 154
    Catholic 135
    Christian/Christ 27, 80, 177
    counselling 143
    disgrace 61
    The Family Protection Bill 7
    heteronormative 5
    heterosexually reproductive 5
    homes 53
The Family Protection Bill 7
Faupel 191 n.4
The Fellowship of Affirming Ministries
        (TFAM) 15, 29 n.5, 64, 64 n.4, 67
        n.8, 81 n.3
female circumcision 185 n.2
forgiveness 32, 33, 77, 83, 114
Franciscan 149–50
Francis of Assisi 151
Freire, Paulo 150
Friends Church of Quakers 111
fundamentalist/ism 13, 14, 154, 210

Gachagua, Rigathi 203
gender and sexual minorities (GSM) 1
gender-conforming 73 n.3
gender discrimination 188. *See also*
        discrimination
gender identity 52, 54, 60, 116
    biological sex 73
    dress in conformity 74
    sexuality and 57, 96, 160
    sexual orientation and 114, 116, 126,
        131, 165, 204, 208
Genesis 92, 100–1, 179, 192, 207
'getting saved' 63 n. 2
Gikuyu 6
Global Anglican Future Conference
        (GAFCON) 144–5, 144 n.4
Global North 11, 189
Global South 189
God 27–33, 42, 54, 68, 115, 161, 168, 199
    creation 65, 89, 92, 100, 102, 113, 114,
        131–2, 154, 163

existence 105
fearing nation 8
glory of 66
love 38, 41–2, 49, 51–5, 59–60,
    67–8, 75–6, 80, 94, 101–2, 115, 147,
    199, 201
    principles 67
    as a punitive deity 106
Gomorrah 28, 49, 83, 99, 120, 138, 167,
    172, 179, 209, 210
Gospel of John 196
Gospel of Luke 147
Gospel of Matthew 118

Hadith 161 n.6, 172
Haman 131 n.3, 132
happiness 73, 94, 201
haram (forbidden) 163 n.2
hekima 172
Hellweg, Joseph 13
heresy 41
heterosexual/heterosexuality 47–8,
    60, 68, 132, 142, 147, 154, 166,
    191–2, 197
    couples 143
    hegemonic identity 6
    marriage 5
    mentality of 60
    national 5
    protection of reproductive family
    5
Hill, Wesley
    *Washed and Waiting: Reflections
    on Christian Faithfulness and
    Homosexuality* 45
HIV-AIDS 8–10, 14, 16, 19, 53, 139,
    157–8, 181
Holy Communion 35, 112
Holy Spirit 32, 105, 112, 177, 192
homophobes 75
homophobia 13, 67, 99, 111–16, 189
    document faith-related 20
    political and religious 16
    social and political 18
homophobic 65, 82, 174
    church 40
    hatred and preaching 68
    pastors 76, 147
    preachers 68, 181

homosexuality/homosexual 6, 7, 41, 47, 52,
    66, 68, 92, 99, 102, 114, 115, 126, 131,
    138, 143–4, 145, 151–4, 167, 179, 180
    aggravated 9
    attempted 9
    Christian faithfulness and 45
    Christian tradition against 38
    dangers of 126
    gang rape 49
    gender nonconformity 14
    opposition to 147
    promotion of 10, 11, 161
    same-sex marriage and 7
    'the sin' of 212
    in Uganda 85 n.10, 197
    'unacceptable' in Kenya 7
human rights
    activists 12
    homosexuality 6
    LGBTIQ rights 10
    organizations 9–11
    political conflicts over 4
    protection of 19
    sexual health and 14, 20

I Am Samuel (Murimi) 8
inculturation 153, 153 n.5
INERELA+ 14
intersex 1, 5, 113, 137, 137 n.6
    activists 6
    child 131
    rights of 6–7 n.2
    transgender and 5
*Invisible: Stories from Kenya's Queer
    Community* (Mwachiro) 3, 8
Islam 4, 12, 14, 16, 19, 24, 89, 163 n.2,
    164, 169, 172–4, 212
Islamic law 163, 167, 173

Jackson, Michael 23
    The Politics of Storytelling 22
Jephthah 115
Jeremiah 100, 120
Jesus Christ 38, 43 n.3, 48, 65, 68, 90, 93,
    110, 138, 146, 147, 180, 192
Jonathan. *See* David (and Jonathan)
Joseph 83
Josephine (Catholic evangelist) 123–7,
    123 n.1, 213

judgement 84, 91, 92, 101, 107, 136, 138, 160, 161, 212

Kadaga, Rebecca 10
Kahiu, Wanuri
    Rafiki 8
Kaluma, Peter 7
Kamba (also known as Akamba) 141–2, 142 n.2
Katoloni Prayer Mountain 32 n.9
Kenya 5–8, 23, 28
    Kisumu 15, 111 n.1, 123 n.1, 124 n.2, 135, 135 n.1, 136 n.5, 138–9, 158–9
    Migori 158–9
    Mombasa 6, 15, 16, 89 n.1, 90–1, 91 n.5, 105 n.1, 108, 108 n.6, 111 n.1, 117 n.1–2, 123 n.1, 124 n.2, 129 n.1, 130 n.2, 135, 135 n.1, 136 n.5, 138–9, 143, 157 n.1, 158–9, 158 n.3, 159–60, 163, 165, 165 n.3, 177 n.1, 178 n.2
Kenya Christian Professional Forum 7
Kenya Human Rights Commission 5
Kenyan, Christian, Queer (Obinyan) 8
Kenya National Gay and Lesbian Human Rights Commission 240
Kenyan Peace and Justice movement 149
Kenyatta, Jomo 5–6
Kenyatta, Uhuru 6
kesha 91, 91 n.4
key populations 136–7, 136 n.4
Kibagendi, Kwamboka 137 n.6
Kikuyu 185 n.2
Kill the Gays Bill 9
Kimindu, Michael 141–8, 141 n.1
Kiswahili 151

Lambeth Conference 9, 145 n.6, 189, 191, 197 n.4
lesbian, gay, bisexual, transgender, intersex and queer (LGBTIQ)
    abomination 83
    advocacy 146
    affirming church 29, 35
    anti politics 2
    churches 76
    Communion to 42
    communities 10, 44, 47, 52, 54, 69, 71–2, 76, 77, 82, 84, 102, 106, 108,

115, 126, 130, 159, 170, 171, 172, 203, 205–6
    homelessness 54
    inclusion of 39, 48, 74, 84, 141, 148, 157
    inclusive 64, 80–1, 113, 178
    jokes about 49
    lives and rights 204
    not seeking sympathy or justification from religious leaders 68
    opposed by ministers and bishops 75
    organizations 8–10, 204
    people 30, 32
    queer theology and pastoral work for 40
    rights of 1, 5, 8, 28, 81, 85, 133, 203
Leviticus 47, 74, 94, 179, 209
LGBTIQ+ 81
liberation theology 38 n.3, 105–6, 105 n.2
life stories 3, 4
    social change and 21–4
love 15, 20, 48, 213
    embrace and 39
    God 38, 41–2, 49, 51–5, 59–60, 67–8, 75–6, 80, 94, 101–2, 115, 147, 199, 201
    preaching 117–21
    sacrificial 47
Luo 181, 181 n.10

Macharia, Keguro 3, 5
madrasas 164
Mama Annette 51–5, 58, 208
Mapuranga, Tapiwa 14
Marangi, Ettore 149–55, 149 n.1
marginalization 2, 17, 190
marriage 28, 198
    counselling in 197
    family counselling and 143
    family forms and 154
    heterosexual 5, 7, 60
    as painful space for women 184
    polygamous 153
    proposal 27
    same-sex 7, 175
    woman-to-woman 190
martyrs 79–85
    Christian 191

in Namugongo, Kampala 85 n.10,
    153 n.4
of Uganda 85, 191, 191 n.4, 204
Mary
    Magdalene 109–10
    Virgin 150, 153–4
Matebeni, Zethu 12
Mbote, David Kuria 23
Mbugua, Audrey 6
Methodist Church 43
Metropolitan Community Churches
    146 n.7
Minority Women in Action 28
Miriam 193
missionary(ies) 4, 32 n.9, 191
Moabites 138
modern(ity) 6, 13, 145, 198
Mombo, Esther 15
Mordecai 132
Moses 193
Muhammad (the Prophet) 163
Mukajanga, Patrick Leuben 15
Murimi, Peter
    I Am Samuel 8
Museveni, Janet 11
Museveni, Yoweri 9–11
Muslims 16, 19, 24, 89, 118, 157–9,
    163–5, 167, 169, 171–5, 210, 212
    minority 11
    umma 165 n.4
Mwachiro, Kevin
    *Invisible: Stories from Kenya's Queer
    Community* 3, 8
Mwanga of the Buganda Kingdom
    191

Nadar, Sarojini 22
Namugongo, Kampala
    martyrs in 85 n.10, 153 n.4
National Gay and Lesbian Human Rights
    Commission 114 n.5, 126 n.3,
    180 n.4
National Gay and Lesbian Human Rights
    Commission (NGLHRC) 204
National NGO Council 6–7
New Testament 45, 99
non-discrimination 8, 160–1
Nouwen, Henri J. M. 39 n.5
Nyanzi, Stella 209

Nyarwek 15, 19, 124, 124 n.2, 125, 136
    n.5, 178, 178 n.2, 181
Nyinyi Watoto (you children) 191
Nyoni, Zanele 8

Obinyan, Aiwan
    Kenyan, Christian, Queer 8
Odede, Calliston 7
Odoi-Oywelowo, Fox 203
Oduyoye, Mercy Amba 192, 192 n.7
Old Testament 28, 99, 209

Pastor Aggie 57–62
Pastor Caroline 27–33, 42 n.9, 67
    n.8, 209
Pastor Deron 71–7, 71 n.1, 206
Pastor Dorcas 117–21, 117 n.1
Pastor Laura 129–33, 129 n.1, 207
Pastor Neema 97–103, 97 n.1, 205,
    209, 210
Pastor Ria 63–9
Pastor Silvana 89–96, 89 n.1
Pastor Stephen 111–16
Pastor Trevor 43–50, 43 n.1, 208
patriarchal culture 65
patriarchy 108, 188, 192, 205
Paul, St 41, 131
    Reconciliation and Equality Centre 15,
        80, 80 n.2, 200
    training 131
    United Theological College 142
    University in Kenya 15
    Voice Centre 15
Paul, the Apostle 84, 98, 139
PEMA Kenya 15, 91–2, 91 n.4, 108, 108
    n.6, 117, 117 n.2, 119, 130–1, 130
    n.2, 158, 158 n.3, 160, 164, 165
    n.3, 207
Penal Code in 2003 5
Pentecostal-Charismatic churches 64 n.5
Pentecostal Christian 8, 11
Pentecostal church 7, 43, 79, 89, 117, 129,
    135, 177, 208
Pentecostal(ism) 7–8, 10–11, 24, 32 n.9
Peter 110
pharisees 40, 48
The Politics of Storytelling (Jackson) 22
Pope Francis 155
Priscilla 98

procreation 147–8
promoting homosexuality 203
Prophet
in the Bible 166–7, 171, 174
Muhammad (*see* Muhammad (the
Prophet))
Protestant(ism) 24
churches 35 n.1, 154–5
Psalm 139 192
public fundraising 112
public religion 12

Quaker 111, 113, 184, 188–90
Queen Esther 131–2, 131 n.3
queer
activism 39
affirmation to 39
African archives 3
Christians 52–4
community 193
Cristianity 53
theology 35, 38, 40, 58
transgender and 57
women 33
world-making 208
Quran 18–19, 158, 161, 161 n.6, 166,
171, 210

Rafiki (Kahiu) 8
Ramadan 174
Rev. Bonnke 136
Rev. Jalendo 35–42, 208
Rev. Kimindu 158
riba 163–4, 163 n.2
Rigathi, Dorcas 203
riswa 114, 114 n.4
Robinson, Gene 144, 144 n.5
Roho churches 111
Roho people 112, 112 n.3
Rolling Stone 9
Roman Catholic 187
Ruth 66, 138
Ruto, Rachel 7, 203
Ruto, William 6, 8, 11, 203

Sacred Queer Stories (van Klinken) 3
salvation 64, 83, 135
Same Love (Remix) (Barasa) 8
same-sex 43–50

intercourse as unconstitutional 6
marriage 7, 175
orientation 148, 190
partnership 144 n.5
relationships 7, 9, 13, 189
relations in Kenya 5
sexuality 142, 161
sinning 212
Sapit, Jackson Ole 7
'saved by Christ' 40 n.7
scriptures 209
Senyonjo, Christopher 15, 80 n.2, 195–
201, 195 n.1
sexual and gender minorities (SGM) 117,
119, 121
sexual health 14, 19
sexual identity 107
sexuality 8, 40 n.7, 65
body and 42
faith and 41, 46
gender identity and 57, 96, 160
same-sex 142, 161
Sexuality and Religion Network in East
Africa (SERENE) 23–4
Sexuality Minorities Uganda (SMUG)
9–10, 15
sexual orientation 81, 85, 108, 114, 116,
126, 131, 160, 165, 178, 204
Sheikh Abdallah 163–8, 163 n.1, 205
Sheikh Dawoud 157–61, 157 n.1
shelter 71, 71 n.1
shiriki 173
simba 36
sin 33, 37, 43 n.3, 83, 99, 108, 109, 110,
114, 151, 154, 167, 180, 210, 212
social change 206
life stories and 21–4
religious leaders as agents of 12–21
Sodom 28, 49, 83, 99, 120, 138, 167, 172,
179, 209, 210
Soon, Tae 32 n.9
spiritual growth 61
'standing in the gap' 64 n.3
St Francis of Assisi 150
stigma 19–20, 164
discrimination and 17, 19
Stories of Our Lives (The Nest) 3, 8
storytelling 3, 21–3
suffering 206–7

Suluhu, Samia 11
Surah Al-'Ankabut 29:2 170 n.2
Surah Al-Baqarah 2:216 174 n.8
Surah Al-Maidah 5:32 171 n.4
Surah Al-Qasas 28:56 171 n.3
Surah Ayah an-Najm 53:32 172 n.5
swahili 173 n.7
systematic theology 188

Tabengwa, Monica 4
Tamale, Sylvia 8
tax collector 49
TFAM Global, Rwanda 29 n.5, 64, 64
    n.4, 81 n.3
The Nest
    Stories of Our Lives 3, 8
theology/theologian 14, 38, 112, 186, 192
    African women 22
    narrative 22
    queer 35, 38, 40, 58
    womanist 33
Titeka, Kristof 11
Tolton, Joseph 29 n.5, 81, 81 n.3
transgender
    activist 6, 107
    Christians 52
    community 72
    intersex and 5
    queer and 57
    women 51–4, 58, 71–3
Transgender Education and
    Advocacy 240
trans pastor 51–5
trans people 57, 71–2
tribalism 141 n.1
Tutu, Desmond 136–7

ugali 126
Uganda 8–12, 23, 24, 28
    anti-gay bill in 7
    Anti-homosexuality Bill 28 n.3
    Christianity in 85 n.10, 205
    homosexuality in 85 n.10
    martyrs in 85, 191 n.4, 204
    supporting minority groups 81
    transgender women 71

Ugandan Penal Code Act 9
umma 165–6, 165 n.4
un-Christian 12, 191–2
Union Theological Seminary,
    New York 196
United Nations Development
    Programme 16, 17
Universal Coalition of Affirming
    Africans (UCAA) 81

van Klinken, Adriaan
    Sacred Queer Stories 3
Vasthi (Professor) 183–94, 183 n.1, 207
Vincent (Catholic evangelist) 105–
    10, 211
violence
    discrimination and 158
    gender-based 16, 151, 158, 183
    and harassment against LGBTIQ
        people 5, 11
    for maintaining social values 14
    against minorities 68

Wainaina, Binyavanga 8
Waites, Matthew 4
*Washed and Waiting: Reflections
    on Christian Faithfulness and
    Homosexuality* (Hill) 45
Wawa Aba Institute 33, 66–7, 67 n.8
WhatsApp 102
women 5–6, 20
    advocacy group 28
    African 22
    lesbian, bisexual and queer 33
    marginalized 27
    transgender 51–4, 58, 71–3
    unmarried 28

Yahwistic tradition 100
Young Catholic Students movement
    123
Youngren, Peter 136 n.3

Zacchaeus 94, 94 n.10
zakat (almsgiving) 174
zealot 49